Risk Assessment in Psychiatry:
A Guide for Lawyers

Risk Assessment in Psychiatry: A Guide for Lawyers

B Mahendra

Published by Family Law
A publishing imprint of Jordan Publishing Limited
21 St Thomas Street
Bristol BS1 6JS

© Jordan Publishing Ltd 2008

British Library Cataloguing-in-Publication Data

A catalogue record for this book is available from the British Library.

ISBN 978 1 84661 109 4

Typeset by Letterpart Ltd, Reigate, Surrey

Printed in Great Britain by Antony Rowe Limited, Chippenham, Wiltshire

CONTENTS

Introduction   xi
Glossary   xv
Table of Cases   xxiii
Table of Statutes   xxv

Part I
The Psychiatric Disorders

Chapter 1
The nature and scope of psychiatric disorder   3
Introduction   3
The provenance of psychiatric disorders   3
Illness and disorder   3
Abnormality and pathology   4
Origins of mental disorders   4
Diagnosis   5
Treatment   6
Mental illness and behaviour   7

Chapter 2
Organic mental disorders   9
Introduction   9
The dementias   10
Dementia – clinical features   11
Dementia – the causes   12
Dementia – the management   12
Dementia – the risks   13
The confusional states   13
The confusional states – causation   14
The confusional states – management   14
The confusional states – risks   14
Head injury   15
Head injury – post-concussional state   15
Head injury – risks   17
Summary   17

Chapter 3
The psychotic disorders   **19**
Introduction   19
Schizophrenia   19
Schizophrenia – clinical features   19
Schizophrenia – causation – genetics   21
Schizophrenia – causation – the environment   22
Schizophrenia – treatment   24
Schizophrenia – prognosis   25
Schizophrenia – the risks   26
Other paranoid disorders   26
Other paranoid disorders – the risks   27
Summary   27

Chapter 4
Disorders of mood   **29**
Introduction   29
Depressive illness – clinical features   29
Mania – clinical features   31
Bipolar disorder   32
Bipolar disorder – causation   32
Bipolar disorder – treatment   33
Bipolar disorder – prognosis   36
Bipolar disorder – risks   36
Summary   37

Chapter 5
The neuroses   **39**
Introduction   39
Minor depressive illness   39
Anxiety states   40
Generalised anxiety states   41
Panic states   41
Phobic disorders   42
Anxiety states – causation   42
Anxiety states – treatment   43
Anxiety states – prognosis   44
Anxiety states – risks   45
Obsessive-compulsive disorder   45
Stress reactions   46
Hysteria   48
Somatoform disorders   49
Summary   50

Chapter 6
Disorders of dependence and appetite   **53**
Introduction   53
Alcohol   53

Alcohol – the effects   54
Alcohol – the risk factors   55
Alcohol – treatment   56
Alcohol – the prognosis   58
Illicit drugs   59
Cannabis   59
The opiate drugs   60
Amphetamines   62
Cocaine   62
Some other illicit drugs   62
Illicit drugs – treatment   63
Pathological gambling   65
Substance misuse – the risks   65
Disorders of appetite   66
Eating disorders – causation   67
Eating disorders – treatment   68
Summary   68

Chapter 7
Disorders of personality and psychopathy   **71**
Introduction   71
Personality disorders – general features   71
Personality disorders – classification   73
Psychopathy   75
Personality disorders – causation   76
Personality disorders – management   79
Personality disorders – prognosis   80
Personality disorders – the risks   81
Summary   81

Chapter 8
Learning disabilities and developmental disorders   **83**
Learning disabilities   83
Learning disabilities – causation   84
Learning disabilities – management   85
Learning disabilities – prognosis   86
Learning disabilities – the risks   86
Other developmental disorders – childhood autism   86
Asperger's syndrome   88
Summary   90

Chapter 9
Special situations and unusual disorders   **93**
Introduction   93
Post-partum psychiatric disorders   93
Post-partum depressive illness   94
Post-partum or puerperal psychosis   94
Cultural influences   96

Morbid jealousy   99
Erotomania   100
Munchausen's syndrome   101
Summary   102

Part II
Risk Assessment in Psychiatry

Chapter 10
Risk assessment of violence   **107**
Introduction   107
Suicidal behaviour   107
Deliberate self-harm (DSH)   111
Aggression turned outwards   112
Violence associated with mental disorder   112
Violence unassociated with mental disorder   116
Some conclusions from forensic psychiatry   119
Sexual violence   122
Summary   123

Chapter 11
Risk assessment in family and child law practice   **125**
Introduction   125
Domestic violence   125
Domestic violence directly involving children   129
Domestic violence involving children indirectly   130
Parental alienation   131
Domestic sexual violence   133
Sexual violence against children   134
Summary   137

Chapter 12
Risk assessment in employment   **139**
Psychiatric aspects of employment   139
Introduction   139
Secondary disability   140
Secondary disability associated with litigation   143
Work-related psychiatric injury   144
Disability discrimination   146
Summary   148

Chapter 13
Risk assessment in post-traumatic states   **149**
Introduction   149
Interactions causing post-traumatic injury   149
Pre-existing and concurrent psychiatric disorder   151
Exaggerated responses to post-traumatic injury   152

Secondary disability following trauma 153
Malingering 154
Summary 155

Chapter 14
Risk assessment of changing mental states **157**
Introduction 157
Capacity 157
Capacity in civil cases 159
Testamentary capacity 163
Witness competence 165
Suggestible defendant 166
Changing diagnosis 166
Summary 167

Chapter 15
Risk assessment of nuisance behaviour **169**
Introduction 169
Antisocial behaviour 169
Neighbour disputes 171
Parental disputes 172
Stalking nuisance 174
Vexatious litigants 175
Summary 177

Appendix 1
Practice Direction:
Experts in Family Proceedings Relating to Children **179**

Appendix 2
Disability Discrimination Act 1995, Pt 1 **197**

Appendix 3
Hatton v Sutherland; Barber v Somerset County Council; Jones v
Sandwell Metropolitan Borough Council; Bishop v Baker
Refractories Ltd **[2002] EWCA Civ 76** **201**

Appendix 4
Mental Capacity Act 2005, Pt 1 **231**

Appendix 5
Select Bibiography **269**

Index **271**

INTRODUCTION

Risk is part of the human, indeed all animal, condition. All living entails risk. As we are constantly reminded, most human beings die in their beds but risk is associated with the activities they engage in before that inevitable end. As such, it is not surprising that human endeavour in its diverse forms has attracted risk assessment. We read, for example, of the risks attending climate and environmental change. Insurers earn their corn assessing risk. The financial markets, on which virtually all rely for their livelihood or security, are subject to constant evaluations of risk. Every mundane activity is subject to risk and needs assessment by formal procedures or informally. As we also know, the methods of risk evaluation are imperfect. The finest financial and mathematical minds in the United States were concentrated on 'super cats' – chances of the earth-shaking catastrophes that could assail them in such forms as another earthquake in Los Angeles – and on evaluating these probabilities when, instead, what struck them was the terrorist outrage in New York in September 2001. The assessment of national and personal security risk is now a growth industry. The fallibility of measures undertaken to mitigate risk identified on assessment or learned through experience is further illustrated, even as these words are being written, by the colossal loss of money by a speculating trader in one of the leading banks of France who appears to have managed to evade the systems of risk mitigation controls put in place by financial institutions in the wake of the Leeson/Barings Bank contretemps of over a decade ago. However, imperfect as the methods of risk assessment might be, the probability of some untoward incident occurring has still got to be evaluated in many circumstances.

Risk assessment in any situation involves, in essence, the asking of the following questions:

(1) What harmful outcome is potentially present in this situation?
(2) What is the probability of this outcome coming about?
(3) What risks are probable in this situation in the short, medium and long-term?
(4) What are the factors that could increase or decrease the risk that is probable?
(5) What measures are available whose employment could mitigate the risks that are probable?

This book deals with the risks that are associated with and attendant upon psychiatric disorders. It is commonly believed that risk assessment in psychiatry is mostly if not wholly concerned with the calculations involved in predicting the risk of violence in all its manifold manifestations. This is often the preoccupation of the criminal and family and child law. But a few moments of contemplation will reveal that risk associated with psychiatric conditions could apply in many other situations. Psychiatric disorders, in common with all medical conditions, carry also the risk of occurrence and recurrence of pathology. This has enormous significance going well beyond the situations of potential violence that usually require to be evaluated. Employment, for example, requires adequate health, both physical and mental, on the part of employees if they are to discharge their duties effectively. An employee afflicted with a disorder may give rise to concern that the persistence or recurrence of illness could compromise the effective execution of his duties. The conditions of the work place may themselves lead to disorder being suffered. In personal injury cases, a tortious act may lead to disorder. The risks involved with the possible recurrence and the complications arising out of that disorder will need to be studied with care if compensation is to be fair and adequate. The progress of genetic studies of medical conditions has meant that the assessment of the incidence of disorders may now be reaching the outer boundaries of rational computation. Insurance premiums may soon come to be calculated on the computation of probable genetic risk of ill health before such risk is assumed.

The limits of psychiatric risk assessment must be properly appreciated. Psychiatry deals with illness and disorder. Human behaviour involved in risk creation and mitigation comprises a myriad aspects beyond the psychiatric. This will become readily apparent throughout the course of this book. A psychiatrist assessing risk needs the skills – and also the realism and humility – to realise that his task involves just one, albeit important, part of the overall assessment of risk in any situation or concerning any individual. It is one of the purposes of this book to demonstrate both the possibilities and the limitations of psychiatric risk assessment. There must be few situations where a psychiatric assessment alone will suffice for any proper evaluation of risk.

This book is divided into two parts. In the first part of the book the general aspects of psychiatric conditions are discussed with special emphasis being placed on the symptoms and behaviour that have a bearing on situations involving risk. These descriptions are based on the accounts of psychiatric conditions given in *Adult Psychiatry in Family and Child Law* (Family Law, 2006) and the opportunity has been taken in the current work to amend, update and clarify the points made in the earlier book. In the second part of the book some common situations involving risk of one kind or another are taken up in relation to those psychiatric features of relevance that have been discussed in the first part of the book.

The purpose of the book is to promote an understanding of the concepts that are involved to a non-specialist audience. No attempt has been made to offer any comprehensive description of the psychiatric conditions involved – a sufficient number of outstanding works exist already for this purpose. The emphasis is, rather, on understanding and the bias is practical, not academic. There are no footnotes and a few references are given in the form of a select bibliography. The audience for this book is anticipated to come from among lawyers in various fields of specialisation and also others who work within the legal system – social workers, probation officers – and also those in the fields of insurance, personnel management or human resources, among others, who are called upon to advise on or deal with risk that is associated with psychiatric disorder. It is hoped that this work will prove to be a source of useful information to these professionals.

B Mahendra
London, Spring 2008
mahen@supanet.com

GLOSSARY

Abnormal – Outside of the norm in a statistical sense. Not necessarily pathological.

Aetiology – Cause(s) of a disorder.

Affect – Mood.

Affective disorder – Mood disorder, especially where mood is pathologically elevated or lowered as in mania or depressive illness.

Agoraphobia – A phobic anxiety disorder in which the patient has a pathological fear of venturing into situations where crowds of people may be met.

Alzheimer's disease – A dementing disorder due to degenerative processes taking place in the brain. Believed to be the commonest cause of both senile and pre-senile dementia.

Anorexia nervosa – An eating disorder, suffered predominantly by females, due to a distortion of body image leading to fear of weight gain.

Anxiety state – A disorder in which there is a pathological and disproportionate sense of fear in the presence of trivial or no stimuli. Usually divided as between generalised anxiety disorders and phobic anxiety disorders.

Asperger's syndrome – A disorder placed within the higher end of autistic spectrum disorders due to a pervasive developmental disorder. It is characterised by mild autistic features involving impaired social functioning and stereotypical repetitive behaviour. There is no impairment of intelligence.

Attention-deficit hyperactivity disorder (ADHD) – A disorder of childhood involving overactivity, distractibility and impulsive behaviour.

Autism – A pervasive developmental disorder of childhood within the severe end of the spectrum of autistic disorders. Intellectual impairment is usual.

Benzodiazepines – A group of drugs used as anxiety reducing (anxiolytic) agents. They are depressants of the central nervous system but a paradoxical effect may cause disinhibition and aggression. Highly addictive.

Bipolar affective disorder – A disorder of mood where episodes of mania and/or depressive illness may occur.

Brain scans – Imaging techniques including computerised tomography (CT) and magnetic resonance imaging (MRI) allowing brain structure to be studied.

Bulimia nervosa – An eating disorder in which patients, usually women, display binge eating and preoccupation with weight which is regulated by vomiting, abuse of diuretics and laxatives and excessive dieting.

Cardiovascular – Relating to arterial blood vessels supplying the heart. Impairment of function may lead to ischaemic heart disease and heart attacks.

Catatonia – A collection of behaviours involving disorders of speech, movement, and posture. May be seen in schizophrenia, depressive illness and neurological states.

Cerebrovascular – Relating to arterial blood vessels supplying the brain. Impairment of function may lead to strokes.

Cognitive behaviour therapy – A form of psychological treatment used in dealing with maladaptive behaviours and abnormal mood states by attempting to change negative thought patterns of the patient.

Compulsion – The motor counterpart of obsessional thinking.

Confusion – A symptom resulting from an impairment in consciousness as may be found in acute organic states such as delirium. To be distinguished from disorientation.

Conversion symptoms – A feature of hysterical states. In avoiding inner conflict there is produced psychological energy which is converted into physical symptoms such as paralysis or blindness. There is primary gain for the patient through relief from anxiety.

Creutzfeldt-Jakob disease – The classical illness (and its more recent variant) are rare causes of pre-senile dementia. A viral cause is suspected.

Delirium – An acute organic disorder involving disturbance of consciousness commonly seen in states of alcohol withdrawal (delirium tremens) and infections, especially in the elderly.

Delusion – A false belief unshakeably held despite evidence to the contrary, and out of keeping with the individual's social and cultural background.

Dementia – An acquired global condition which leads to an impairment in functioning of the intellect, memory, personality and social behaviour. The term is entirely descriptive and the causes may be various, for example, degenerative brain disease, endocrine disease, etc.

Depot injection – A drug, usually an anti-psychotic agent, which is given periodically by intramuscular injection. Obviates the need for daily ingestion of medication and thereby improves compliance.

Depression – A pathological lowering of mood.

Depressive illness – A disorder in which the central feature is a pathologically diminished mood.

Dissociative disorders – Formerly hysterical reactions. A disorder in which the integrity in the relationship between memory, identity, sensory perception and motor control appears lost as a result of unconscious mechanisms. Common manifestations include amnesia, fugue (wandering), stupor and motor disorders. An extreme variant is trance or possession states.

Down's syndrome – A disorder with (usually) severe intellectual impairment which is a common cause of mental handicap or learning disabilities. Due to a chromosomal abnormality.

Electroconvulsive treatment (ECT) – A procedure by which seizures are induced by the passage of electricity through the brain. An effective treatment for severe depressive illness.

Epidemiology – The study of the distribution and possible causes of disorders in a population.

Functional disorder – A disorder in which no obvious adverse change in the structure and function of the brain can be discerned in the present state of knowledge.

General paralysis of the insane (GPI) – A condition due to tertiary (ie untreated or incompletely treated) syphilis. In the past a severe untreatable dementia used to be a feature.

Hallucination – An abnormal perception arising in the absence of an external stimulus (cf illusion). May involve any of the senses, for example, auditory, visual, etc. Could be true or pseudo hallucination. Their significance depends on the entirety of the clinical picture.

Huntington's chorea – A cause of pre-senile dementia characterised by abnormal movements and mental disorder including dementia. It is a genetic condition.

Hypomania – A less severe form of mania.

Hysteria – The older term for conversion/dissociative disorders.

Illusion – A misperception due to misinterpretation of stimuli. Usually normal phenomena occurring in such situations as believing a shadow conceals a person.

Incidence – Number of new cases of a disorder occurring within a defined population over a defined period of time, for example, 12 months (cf prevalence).

Insight – The awareness a patient possesses in regard to a condition he suffers from. There are gradations through full, partial and no insight.

Life events – Potentially stressful events such as bereavement, divorce, a house move, loss of employment, etc, which may have a bearing on the onset of psychiatric disorders, in particular depressive illness.

Mania – A form of affective disorder in which the central feature usually is an elevation of mood, for instance, elation. It is associated with increased energy, overactivity, disinhibited behaviour, pressure of speech and grandiose ideas or delusions.

Maternity blues – Transient mood changes involving depression and anxiety occurring in over half of mothers with a newborn baby.

Mental disorder – A compendious term including mental illness, learning disabilities, personality and psychopathic disorders and addiction and other disorders not amounting to formal illness.

Morbid jealousy – A psychotic disorder presenting in its own right or as a symptom of another psychosis such as schizophrenia or alcohol abuse characterised by a false belief in the infidelity of spouse or partner.

Munchausen syndrome – A disorder involving persistent simulation of illness associated with pathological lying, exaggeration of symptoms and the making of importunate demands on hospitals and medical staff. A variant is the controversial, possibly discredited, disorder by proxy in which a carer involves (usually) a child in the simulation or exaggeration of illness. Best understood as a severe personality disorder.

Negative symptoms (of schizophrenia) – Include lack of motivation, apathy, poverty of speech, social withdrawal, emotional unresponsiveness and self neglect. May respond poorly to standard forms of treatment.

Neuroses – Minor psychiatric disorders in which insight and a sense of reality are preserved and there is a discernible contribution of the personality to the disorder. Neurotic conditions include minor depressive illness, anxiety states, obsessive-compulsive disorder and hysterical reactions (dissociative/conversion disorders).

Obsessive-compulsive disorder – A neurotic disorder in which ideas and thoughts are found that are persistent, intrusive, unwelcome and subject to resistance without success on the part of the patient. The motor counterparts are called compulsions.

Organic – Refers to disorders where there is demonstrable structural or functional (ie pathophysiological) disturbance of brain function.

Orientation – An individual's awareness of time, place and person. Disturbed in the dementias.

Parasuicide – Deliberate self-harm in which the element of intention is absent from the behaviour leading to self-harm. Usually associated with reckless behaviour.

Personality disorder – Involves an abnormal personality whose behaviour is at odds with the norms and standards applying in his culture. The disorder is enduring and is separate from any formal illness which may from time to time come to overlie it. The diagnosis is made at presumed maturity but the onset is invariably in childhood as behaviour disturbance. There are problems usually in the personal, social and occupational spheres. Many categories are described (see text).

Phobic anxiety state – An anxiety disorder which is situation-specific such as claustrophobia or social phobia.

Positive symptoms (of schizophrenia) – These include symptoms such as delusions, hallucinations and speech disorder which are features of acute illness and usually respond to standard treatment.

Post-traumatic stress disorder (PTSD) – A delayed and/or protracted response to a stressful event of an exceptionally threatening nature likely to cause distress. Probably overdiagnosed. Clinical utility suspect as features may be subsumed within depressive illness and anxiety states.

Pre-morbid – Antedating illness, especially in the case of personality before onset of illness.

Prevalence – Total number of cases of a disorder in a defined population at any given time (cf incidence).

Pseudohallucination – A hallucination, usually auditory, arising from within an individual's mind and not relating to the world outside. May be seen in states of grief and is less significant than true hallucinations.

Psychopathology – A study of abnormal mental states either in terms of their description (also called phenomenology) or as mode of causation (psychodynamic psychopathology).

Psychosis – A mental disorder which leads to loss of contact with reality and insight along with the presence of symptoms such as delusions and hallucinations.

Psychosurgery – A specialised and controversial form of brain surgery for modifying behaviour and emotions.

Rehabilitation – Procedures aimed at minimising or preventing secondary social disability due to mental disorder by restoring previous levels of functioning.

Schizoaffective disorder – A disorder in which the symptoms of a schizophrenic illness and an affective illness are both present.

Schizophrenia – A psychotic disorder in which pathological changes occur in thinking, behaviour, perception and, occasionally, mood.

Schizophreniform – Schizophrenia-like. A symptomatic form of schizophrenia akin to true illness. May be seen in cases involving drug abuse.

Selective serotonin reuptake inhibitors (SSRIs) – A group of antidepressant drugs including fluoxetine (Prozac) and paroxetine (Seroxat).

Senile dementia – Dementias occurring at the age of 65 or after. Pre-senile dementias occur before that age.

Somatic symptoms – Usually seen in cases of depressive illness. Involve symptoms such as sleep disturbance and changes in appetite, bowel habits, menstrual regularity and libido.

Somatoform disorders – Disorders in which the patient makes persistent complaint of physical symptoms (for which no obvious cause can be found) and refuses to accept the assurances of his doctors.

Suicidal behaviour – Deliberate self-harming behaviour which involves an element of intent.

Tricyclic antidepressants – Older generation of antidepressant drugs including such agents as amitryptiline and dothiepin. Now out of favour on account of adverse side effects and potential for a lethal outcome on overdose.

TABLE OF CASES

References are to paragraph numbers.

Attorney General v Benton [2004] EWHC 1952 (Admin)   15.6
Attorney General v Chitolie [2002] EWHC 1943 (Admin)   15.6
Attorney General v Perotti [2006] EWHC 1002 (Admin)   15.6

Banks v Goodfellow (1870) LR 5 QB 549, [1861-73] All ER Rep 47, 39 LJQB
    237   14.3, 14.4
Barber v Somerset County Council [2004] UKHL 13, [2004] 1 WLR 1089, [2004] 2
    All ER 385   12.5
Battan Singh v Amirchand (1948) AC 161 (1948) AC 161   14.4
Bird v Luckie (1850) 8 Hare 301   14.4
Bohrmann's estate, Re Caesar v Watmough v Bohrmann (1938) 1 All ER 271   14.4
Boughton v Knight (1873) LR 3 P and D 64 (1861–73) All ER Rep 40   14.4

C, Re [1994] 1 All ER 891   14.3
Clancy v Clancy (2003) WTLR 1097   14.4

Dew v Clark and Clark (1826) 3 Add 79   14.4

Hartman v South Essex Mental Health and Community Care NHS Trust [2005]
    EWCA Civ 6   12.5

Masterman-Lister v Brutton & Co (Nos 1 and 2), Masterman-Lister v Jewell and
    Another [2002] EWCA Civ 1889, [2003] EWCA Civ 70, [2003] 1 WLR 1511,
    [2003] PIQR P310 CA   14.3
MB (an adult: medical treatment), Re [1997] 2 FLR 426, [1997] Fam Law 542,
    CA   14.3
Meah v McCreamer [1985] 1 All ER 367, [1986] 1 All ER 943   7.5, 10.8

Parker v Felgate (1883) 8 PD 171   14.4
Phillips and others v Symes and others [2004] EWHC 1887 (Ch), [2004] All ER (D)
    592 (Jul)   14.4, 14.5

R (AL) v Home Secretary [2005] EWCA Civ 2, [2006] 1 WLR 88, [2005] NLJR
    140   14.7
R v Antor (2004) *The Times*, 4 November   14.6
R v Beatty [2006] EWCA Crim 2349, 92 BMLR 22, [2006] All ER (D) 197 (Oct)   14.7
R v Blackburn (2005) *The Times*, 10 June   14.6
R v Hardie [1984] 3 All ER 848, [1985] 1 WLR 64, CA   10.5
R v Jan [2006] EWCA Crim 2314, [2006] All ER (D) 141 (Oct)   15.2
R v Sed [2004] EWCA Crim 1294, [2004] 1 WLR 3218, [2005] 1 Cr App Rep 55   14.5

Schloendorff v Society of New York Hospital (1914) 105 N.E.92   14.3
Sharp v Adam [2006] EWCA Civ 449, [2006] All ER (D) 277 (Apr)   14.4

Sutherland v Hatton; *sub nom* Jones v Sandwell MBC; Hatton v Sutherland; Barber
    v Sutherland CC; Bishop v Baker Refractories Ltd; Somerset CC v Barber;
    Sandwell MBC v Jones; Baker Refractories Ltd v Bishop [2002] EWCA Civ
    76, [2002] 2 All ER 1, [2002] ICR 613, [2002] PIQR P21, CA   12.5

White v Fell (unreported) 12 November 1987   14.3

TABLE OF STATUTES

References are to paragraph numbers.

Criminal Justice Act 1988	14.5	Human Rights Act 1998	15.2
s 23	14.5		
s 26	14.5	Mental Capacity Act 2005	14.2
Criminal Procedure (Insanity) Act		s 1(2)	14.2
1964	14.7	s 2(1)	14.2
s 5(1)(a)	14.7	s 2(3)	14.2
		Mental Health Act 1983	7.4, 8.1, 10.2,
Disability Discrimination Act			14.7
1995	12.6		
s 1	12.6	Youth Justice and Criminal	
Sch 1, para 2	12.6	Evidence Act 1999	14.5
		s 53	14.5

PART I

THE PSYCHIATRIC DISORDERS

CHAPTER 1

THE NATURE AND SCOPE OF PSYCHIATRIC DISORDER

1.1 INTRODUCTION

The term mental disorder occasionally leads to confusion among the lay public. One may say that it is a collective term used to include formal mental illness and also what amounts not to illness but involves behaviour of such a kind that makes it appropriate for inclusion among the subject matter that is studied within psychiatry, the medical speciality that deals with such disorders. The test of what is a mental disorder is just that, namely, whether or not it is a condition that is deemed fit for study by a psychiatrist. A more detailed study of the background to mental disorders has been undertaken in the general part of *Adult Psychiatry in Family and Child Law*.[1] In this chapter a brief summary of the issues involved is given.

1.2 THE PROVENANCE OF PSYCHIATRIC DISORDERS

A little thought will convince that all mental illness, mental disorder and behaviour must have its ultimate origin in the brain. There is nowhere else, as far as we know, for these behaviours and symptoms to come out of. But, in the present state of knowledge, while we are aware that all mental disorders must originate in the brain, we do not have sufficient information concerning the precise locations in the brain and the mechanisms of function involved therein to establish the study of mental disorders as a branch of the applied neurosciences. That is a task for the future. In the present all we can do is to describe and classify the symptoms and behaviours we can observe.

1.3 ILLNESS AND DISORDER

Formal mental illness includes such conditions as schizophrenia, depressive illness and bipolar affective disorder. The mental disorders have included among them conditions such as the personality disorders and the behaviours due to the misuse of alcohol and illicit drugs among others. The broad test to be applied is whether there are observable

---

[1]   See B Mahendra *Adult Psychiatry in Family and Child Law* (Family Law, 2006).

symptoms attaching to any condition. If there are, and a systematic study can be made of these symptoms, the condition involved comes to be called a mental illness. If behaviour rather than symptoms is available for study, the condition may, subject to the qualification discussed below, be called a mental disorder.

1.4   ABNORMALITY AND PATHOLOGY

One could ask if there is any matter of reason or logic that determines whether some behaviours are to be deemed to be part of a mental disorder while others are not. While reason and logic cannot, in the present state of knowledge, play any overwhelmingly important part in psychiatric classification, for now the test for inclusion within the ranks of the mental disorders is whether pathology is involved in the behaviour concerned. A delusion, which is classified, broadly speaking, as a false belief held with unshakeable conviction in the face of compelling evidence to the contrary against a background of social and cultural beliefs of the individual concerned, is clearly pathological. But there are other beliefs that are not so clearly demarcated but which may still be odd, eccentric and bizarre. Auditory hallucinations may or may not amount to pathology; the bereaved, the learning disabled and the lonely may be subject to these phenomena. One must, therefore, be able to distinguish between what is normal, abnormal and pathological. The distinction between normal and abnormal may be made by means of statistical measurement. If some measure is common to 95 per cent of the population all those within it may be deemed normal. Where excessive height is concerned, for example, the very tall and the very short may be deemed to be abnormal but only a few rare disease conditions will cause excessive tallness or shortness. Where intelligence is concerned, an IQ measure of 70 is conventionally taken to be the point below which learning disabilities or mental handicap exists. An IQ of 140 or greater is generally taken to indicate genius. The learning disabilities are deemed to be pathological states and constitute one of the mental disorders. There is no pathological cause of genius. The inclusion of a condition such as pathological gambling – said to afflict 300,000 individuals in Britain – among the mental disorders (F 63.0 – ICD-10 Classification of Mental Disorders) may appear to be problematical except for the fact that its subject matter is a form of addictive behaviour which already finds representation among the mental disorders in the form of behaviours due to misuse of alcohol and illicit drugs.

1.5   ORIGINS OF MENTAL DISORDERS

As noted in the Introduction, progress has been made in respect of the greater understanding of the genetic basis of illness and disorder. While these developments have been steady, and knowledge has been accrued and there is much promise, for the present we can only make very general statements about the genetic basis of most psychiatric disorders. Such a basis definitely exists, as can be seen with conditions such as schizophrenia and the bipolar affective disorders, where the closer the relationship between a sufferer and his descendant, the greater the probability of the condition arising in the latter. However, except in rare situations like that obtaining with Huntington's disorder or some metabolic disorders leading to learning disabilities, one cannot generally make any confident prediction of the onset of any disorder in any individual who could be at genetic risk for any given condition. The overwhelming impression that is created at present is that, while genetic vulnerability may exist, it requires interaction with one or more environmental factors before illness or disorder is manifested. This means that environmental factors are given a role to play in the onset of most mental disorders. This is a matter of considerable importance for, in the present state of knowledge, while the chances of intervention to correct a genetic deficiency are next to negligible, there usually exists significant scope for environmental manipulation. One is invariably asked about the genetic prospects for a child about to be placed for adoption, where one or both its parents have suffered a mental disorder such as schizophrenia, when the answer usually given is that a stable and nurturant environment provided for the child could go a long way in mitigating any genetic risk it could have inherited. The influence of the personality of the individual could also be crucial for many psychiatric disorders can be studied in terms of the interaction between personality and the impact upon it of adverse life experiences including trauma. The important role played by both personality and environment in the causation and maintenance of disorder – and recovery from it – will become apparent throughout the course of this book.

1.6   DIAGNOSIS

As will be apparent from the previous description, the study of mental disorders involves descriptions of symptoms or behaviours. These have been placed into clusters which have been named diagnoses. The diagnosis of psychiatric disorders has often been a controversial matter. An outline of how diagnostic classifications arose and evolved and the questions that have been asked of, and remain about, these systems has been given in *Adult Psychiatry in Family and Child Law* (Family Law, 2006). As far as this book is concerned one will do well to appreciate the limitations of the diagnosis arrived at in any given case. A diagnosis is a short-hand method of conveying medical information as between doctors. It has its value in surveys on the epidemiology of disorders. It is obviously useful when research is undertaken, including that which involves the testing of new drugs, as agreed criteria must be satisfied in the selection of subjects for study. But in individual cases, where a particular aspect of a patient's functioning is what is in issue, there are shortcomings in any attempt to extrapolate from diagnosis to behaviour, an issue that must be understood. To say that a patient has suffered from schizophrenia does not, on the basis of the diagnosis alone, answer the question as to whether or not he is fit to undertake parenting or employment or what kind of insurance risk he might be. In order to attempt to answer these questions the patient needs to be studied in the entirety of his functioning and any medical condition he may or have suffered from is only one of the factors to be taken into account. Another way of putting this sentiment is to say that behaviour is more important than diagnosis when some particular function is to be addressed.[2]

1.7   TREATMENT

Broadly speaking, treatment of the psychiatric disorders involves both drug treatment and psychological treatment. Drug treatment is predicated on the belief that the underlying brain dysfunction gives rise, by some mechanisms that are far from fully understood, to disturbances in the chemicals mediating functions in the brain which may be corrected by means of similar or related chemicals that are given to the patient. As the mechanisms of their actions remain largely unknown in the present day much drug treatment is little better than a shot in the dark, based as it is on empirical rather than fundamental evidence. The results, however, from drug treatment are generally satisfactory where the patient and his condition have been carefully chosen. The acute mental illnesses respond best to drug treatment while behaviours are mostly beyond correction by this means. Treatment largely produces symptomatic improvement and the ameliorated clinical state is probably best described as a state of remission rather than a cure. Treatment may need to be continued for several months, occasionally for the rest of the patient's life, and maintenance treatment may also play a prophylactic function. Psychological treatment is primarily aimed at behaviour whose modification may also lead to an improvement in the symptoms. Generally speaking, a combination of drug and psychological treatment furnishes better results than one of these alone. Learning disabilities are a life long affliction and beyond conventional treatment and the same could be said for the personality disorders, although there are those who claim they are able to bring about fundamental change in the personality. Other forms of treatment that may be used as ancillary measures may not be as specific as drug treatment or the psychological treatments are but play an important role in 'getting a patient better', as opposed to attempting to cure him. In this respect supportive treatment plays a very important part. Support is required, for example, in keeping patients suffering from learning disabilities functioning effectively in the community. Supportive therapy is also the cornerstone in the treatment of cases of misuse of alcohol and illicit drugs, there being little by way of specific measures for these conditions. Allied to supportive therapy are all the measures taken for the rehabilitation of the patient. It is not at all uncommon for the

---

[2]   B Mahendra 'Behaviour, not diagnosis, the key: some misconceptions in the psychiatry of family and child law' [Feb 2008] Fam Law 159.

symptoms to be dispersed in a patient without him being able to resume the functioning he had before he fell ill. As will be seen when risks in employment and personal injury are discussed below, inadequate rehabilitation may lead to secondary disability supervening and prolonging the malfunctioning of the patient. In fact, there is increasingly good evidence that what prevents patients suffering from even serious mental illness from resuming the functioning they are capable of, including a return to employment, is a lack of rehabilitation, especially specialised vocational rehabilitation. The processes of litigation – which reward prolonged incapacity – may also play a part in perpetuating disability

1.8 MENTAL ILLNESS AND BEHAVIOUR

The second part of this book deals with a variety of behaviours involving patients who may be suffering from mental disorder or suspected of so doing. It is a popular misconception to believe that the behaviour involving those suffering especially from mental illness is wholly or chiefly due to the condition or the symptoms themselves. Observation will reveal that this is not the case. Even when florid symptoms of illness are present, the behaviour of any patient will be determined, in addition to these symptoms, by a variety of other factors which include his personality and also his personal and social circumstances. Culture is always a heavy influence on behaviour, as much on that of the mentally disordered as on others. Patterns of violence, whether involving suicide or violence directed against others, vary as between different communities even when the symptoms of illness are similar, even identical. Prejudice can be created by the belief that patients with mental illness, as a result of that illness alone, are prone to maladaptive behaviours including violence. That is far from being the case. Only a small minority of patients with mental illness are involved in conduct that may breach the rules and norms of a community. There are some exceptions. The condition of morbid jealousy, for example, may lead to a situation of risk involving a spouse or partner through the fact of the diagnosis itself. But this is a rare instance. As will be seen when situations of risk are considered in Part II of this book, situations of risk involving mentally disordered patients concern primarily the behaviours of individuals. We have already referred to the influence on violent behaviour of factors other than the disorder itself. In family and child practice, the functioning of spouse, partner or parent must be evaluated qua spouse, partner or parent and not merely qua patient. Parenting, in particular, involves many elements beyond the pathological. As will be seen in the chapters on employment and post-traumatic states, recovery from the symptoms of illness does not necessarily equate with a resumption of full functioning. Any disability is capable of being perpetuated by a variety of personal, social and cultural factors. Even those who ought to be deemed unduly suggestible as suspects undergoing interrogation may depend on the circumstances at the time of interview. Mental disorder is an uncommon presence in cases of nuisance behaviour but even when it is present it tends to be heavily affected by other factors that apply in situations involving nuisance behaviours. It cannot be stressed enough that the proper assessment of risk in any situation involves elements that go well beyond the merely psychiatric.

CHAPTER 2

ORGANIC MENTAL DISORDERS

2.1   INTRODUCTION

Convention requires that we describe the subject matter of this chapter as the organic mental disorders, as opposed to the functional mental disorders that will be taken up in the chapters following. This distinction is somewhat illogical. As far as we know, all psychiatric conditions are ultimately traceable to origins in the brain. There is no evidence that there is some parallel medium mediating animal behaviour. All roads therefore lead to the brain, as far as mental phenomena are concerned. Psychiatric disorders should therefore be, strictly speaking, considered brain disorders. The fact that the external environment may influence behaviour should be irrelevant – the brain still needs to intervene before behaviour can be demonstrated. Seeing an object or hearing a sound are cerebral phenomena. However, unassailable logic has to confront, in the present state of knowledge, the inconvenient fact that we do not possess sufficiently precise knowledge of brain function and dysfunction to delineate the origins of most psychiatric conditions in terms of the brain. Thus was born the distinction between organic mental disorders where a cerebral origin can be fairly clearly established, even when the precise details of pathology may be lacking, and the functional mental disorders where brain dysfunction has still, by and large, got to be presumed.

It is customary to classify organic mental disorders as between acute disorders such as confusional states or delirium and chronic conditions such as the dementias. Further, consideration in this category is also given to the psychiatric consequences of head injury and to the psychiatric effects of systemic illness such as endocrine disorders. Even this inclusion carries with it an anomaly. Learning disorders or the cerebral manifestations of alcohol and illicit drug use (the subject matter in the following chapters) are examples of conditions which involve lesions in the brain but, once again by convention, these conditions are studied separately as is done in this book. Further, one must also bear in mind that external or environmental factors, which are given greater prominence in the consideration of functional mental disorders for want of known cerebral pathology for study, are of importance also in the study of mental disorders due to brain dysfunction, for the brain is also affected by external stimuli as one can see when the nature and frequency of epileptic fits, for example, are influenced by common environmental stimuli.

2.2   THE DEMENTIAS

Dementia refers to a condition in which there is an acquired global impairment of brain functions which usually leads to a progressive loss of intellectual and memory powers and a deterioration of the personality and in social behaviour. These are conditions that have come upon the public consciousness fairly rapidly in recent years on account of an ageing population for many of the dementias have an incidence in the population which is related to age. At the age of 65 some five per cent of the population is believed to be affected, the figure rising to 20 per cent when the population reaches the age of 80. There are believed to be some 750,000 individuals suffering from the dementias in the United Kingdom, though the precise figure cannot be reliably established. There may be underdiagnosis in some parts of the country for want of adequate diagnostic services while in others there may be an overestimate by including cases with age-related memory loss which is a normal process and by itself does not amount to dementia. Despite the growing prominence given to this condition, there still tends to be a degree of confusion concerning these conditions. The first element causing confusion is the term 'confusion' itself. It is common to hear even health care professionals referring to a demented patient being 'confused'. This is an inaccurate use of the term. Confusion, as we shall see in the next section of this chapter, is a result of a disturbance in consciousness. A demented patient is not confused, his consciousness is normally clear and unimpaired. What he usually displays is disorientation, that is to say he does not know where he is, what day or place it is, what the date or year are or who his intimates might be. A demented patient may, like anyone else, become confused as well, say, as a result of an infection but the primary underlying feature in dementia is a brain disorder which has global effects on the intellect, memory and personality which, at some stage in the course of the disorder, also comes to include disorientation.

As the definition of dementia given above suggests, it is also an acquired condition. Congenital or childhood brain dysfunctions which lead to impairment in intelligence, memory and character (as personality can be called before maturity has been reached, at least in chronological terms) is more properly referred to as mental handicap or learning disabilities which we shall take up in a later chapter. A patient with learning disabilities may, of course, like anyone else, become demented in later life. As the definition also suggests, the impairment in dementia is global, that is, it refers to a considerable range of the brain's functions being affected, a state of affairs to be distinguished from focal deficits where one part of the brain eg the parietal or frontal lobe is a specific area to be affected. Finally, dementia refers to a clinical description of the phenomena observed. It does not suggest the cause of the brain dysfunction leading to the features of dementia which requires further investigation and analysis for its elucidation where this is possible.

The term 'senile dementia' is to be found in popular usage. In its strict sense the term is doubly descriptive as it refers to a dementia found in the senium. The senium is conventionally defined as being the period after the age of 65 has been reached. The origins of this figure – which, of course, now has enormous social, financial and political significance the world over – are usually attributed to the age at which in 1884 Otto Von Bismarck, then Chancellor of Germany, decreed that citizens became entitled to their state old age pensions. There is no discernible medical significance in this age. Therefore any dementia arising after the age of 65 is a senile dementia, if before that age it is called a pre-senile dementia.

2.3 DEMENTIA – CLINICAL FEATURES

The symptoms of dementia are attributable to the global nature of the brain dysfunction involved. Their course is usually insidious and it is usual for the short-term memory to be first affected, invariably unnoticed at first when it may be put down to the forgetfulness long associated with ageing. The growing impairment of intellectual functioning may also be similarly dismissed at first. Changes in personality may, however, cause early concern. There may be what is called a 'coarsening' of personality. Any individual is usually made up of many elements forming an amalgam of his personality, there being good, bad or indifferent parts to any personality. The whole is usually held together with the glue usually attributable to good manners and the appreciation of the need to conform and behave according to the expectations of a civilised society and adjust to its norms. Dementia has a tendency to cause this glue to dissolve or, perhaps as it may be more aptly described, this coat of civilising varnish to be removed, making more apparent the elements within and the rougher edges to an individual's personality. The result could be the emergence of an exaggerated or parodic picture of the characteristics in the individual's habitual personality. Thus, a person known to be careful with money now begins to acquire a reputation as a miser and a hoarder of objects, mostly valueless except in his eyes. An assertive person who managed nevertheless to keep his need to dominate others within acceptable bounds now turns into an aggressive, even violent, bully. Dementia may also give rise to disinhibited behaviour. Individuals who had been able to keep rogue impulses in check while their personalities were intact and reasonably well adjusted may now cease to conform with the needs and expectations of social and legal norms. Violent behaviour, along with antisocial conduct, sometimes involving sexual matters (including those in relation to young children), are occasionally the result of such aberrant behaviour. The criminal law and family and child law may both express an interest in these circumstances. Mood changes, whether due to the brain dysfunction itself or as a reaction to the realisation of waning powers, are not uncommon. Neurological features such as deficits in speech may also be revealed. Insight is progressively lost as the more common dementias advance at varying speed. The terminal phase of the illness is characterised by a return to a state of infantilisim with loss of speech among other powers, and incontinence supervening.

2.4   DEMENTIA – THE CAUSES

It is believed that there are scores of dementing conditions. The most common cause by far is believed to be a degenerative brain disorder called Alzheimer's disease, suspected to account for 80 per cent or more of all dementias. The diagnosis of this condition is entirely by means of neuropathological analysis, usually undertaken post-mortem. There are no valid laboratory or other tests as yet to aid in the diagnosis and a clinical diagnosis of the condition is little better than an informed guess. Parts of the brain in this disturbance show abnormal structures which are believed to be the result of the pathogenic process rather than being the cause. A clear genetic basis has not as yet been established but it appears that the presence of a first degree relation with the condition leads to a doubling of the risk for a subject developing it. A clear genetic risk may also be observable in cases with pre-senile dementia where the illness runs a notably aggressive course. Various other causative environmental factors have been proposed from time to time but it does not appear that any one of these is a causative factor in the generality of cases. There is also a neurochemical which is believed to be secondary to the structural changes in the brain and which involves acetylcholine metabolism – but other chemicals have also been implicated. Among the other dementias are the group called the vascular dementias which are associated with small strokes and disturbance in the arteries supplying blood to the brain. There are rarer degenerative conditions of the brain such as Huntington's disease, Pick's disease, Creutzfeldt-Jakob disease (in its classical form as well as the more recently emerged variant-CJD), the latter acquired from the meat of cattle infected with bovine spongiform encephalopathy (BSE) and the dementias associated with Parkinson's disease. Huntington's disease involves clear genetic transmission. Other causes of dementia include endocrine disorder (eg thyroid deficiency), head injury, poisoning (eg by heavy metals), excessive alcohol consumption, brain tumours and a variety of infections affecting the brain. Drugs used in the treatment of various conditions may sometimes lead to the clinical presentation of a dementing illness. Their importance lies in the fact that dementias due to some of these conditions or factors may be reversible if prompt steps are taken.

2.5   DEMENTIA – THE MANAGEMENT

This is almost entirely palliative in the present state of knowledge. There was much clamour – by the carers as well as the drug companies – about drug treatment, especially in the earlier stages of dementia due to Alzheimer's disease. It is probably fair to say on the available information that there is no consistent evidence for sustained improvement in the condition in any group of patients whatever the stage of illness they have. This is not surprising as the causes of the dementias appear to be manifold and also because the chemical basis to the condition is in all probability much more complex than is commonly understood. If several chemicals are associated with degenerative dementia, drugs involving just one type of chemical are likely to be limited in their efficacy. It may be that an effective cocktail of drugs is what is needed. Nevertheless, a primary purpose of prompt investigation of a dementia is to establish the presence of a treatable cause such as an underfunctioning thyroid gland, a condition which is treatable by means of a replacement hormone. Prompt treatment of this kind by treating some deficiency appears to lead to the symptoms of dementia being corrected in a minority of cases.

2.6   DEMENTIA – THE RISKS

The risks associated with the dementias will be discussed in greater detail in the appropriate sections of Part II of this book. It will be apparent that in the vast majority of cases of the more common forms of dementia the scope for prediction of individuals who could be at risk is very limited. However, one can attempt more fertile risk assessment of the consequences of dementia. The possible interest the criminal law and family and child law could have in this aspect of the evaluation of risk posed by these patients has already been noted. Another subject of considerable practical importance is in the capacity possessed by these individuals in managing their property and dealing with their affairs. In particular, one notes the issue of testamentary capacity which may be impaired as a result of the presence of cognitive dysfunction in the testator and also that this cognitive state could be subject to rapid change leading to apparent variations in the capacity possessed by the individual.

2.7   THE CONFUSIONAL STATES

As has already been noted, confusional states are characterised by a clouding or an impairment of consciousness. The patient may exhibit drowsiness, a diminished awareness of his surroundings, distractibility and also disorientation. Unlike dementia, where the onset is slow and insidious, confusional states are usually acute in presentation. Their course fluctuates, with a diurnal variation and a worsening at dusk. There may also be associated visual hallucinations (characteristically small animals are perceived although larger creatures including the fabled pink elephants may be seen in *delirium tremens*, the acute confusional state that may follow withdrawal from alcohol). There may also be present persecutory ideas, typically fleeting and in keeping with the distractibility of confused patients. These patients may also show increased motor activity, ranging from anxiety and agitation to aggression and violence. This behaviour may alternate with periods of drowsiness and somnolence.

2.8   THE CONFUSIONAL STATES – CAUSATION

The commonest cause of confusional states is probably infections. Like dementia there is an element of age-related risk with the confusional states and thus the elderly have a greater tendency to become confused. Thus, the demented patient – who, as has been noted, is not normally confused – could become so as a result of some incidental infection. Prescribed drugs also have a well known tendency to induce confusional states, especially in the elderly. The confusional states due to alcohol withdrawal have been noted and a variety of illicit drugs may also lead to this condition following their consumption.

2.9   THE CONFUSIONAL STATES – MANAGEMENT

The rule in treating confusional states is to seek a cause which is invariably present though by no means always found. In its absence, some practitioners may even resort to 'blind' treatment with antibiotics. Review of all medication given and a check being made on other drugs ingested by the patient, especially when young, is a crucial part of the investigation. The results with treatment are usually good except when the patient has some terminal underlying condition.

2.10   THE CONFUSIONAL STATES – RISKS

Some of the risks of developing confusional states have already been noted. An elderly demented patient who is being prescribed medication is clearly at risk of developing a confusional state. Previous episodes of the state, especially in an elderly individual who already also has some sensory impairment (e g blindness or deafness), may be important as these individuals appear to be preferentially at risk. Risks that follow confusional states may involve aggression and violence that these patients may occasionally display. There is also the matter of a confusional state leading to the impairment of capacity on the part of the patient. Capacity is soon regained in the typical case as the condition is usually acute and reversible but one must bear in mind the possibility of a confusional state supervening in a demented patient. The fluctuating course of the condition superimposed on the underlying impairment of memory and intellectual functioning may make an assessment of capacity, including testamentary capacity, unreliable.

2.11 HEAD INJURY

This is a vast subject primarily of neurological and neurosurgical interest. Unlike the dementing illnesses, however, which preferentially afflict an older age group, the psychiatric complications of head injury may affect all age groups. Younger individuals, in particular, on account of their diverse activities, may come to the attention of clinicians as a result of the various consequences of head injury. Head injury being a common phenomenon, its victims not uncommonly interest the psychiatrist on account of the behavioural changes that may follow any insult given to the brain. Head injury may cause obvious brain damage although much psychiatric time is taken up with cases of head injury where there appears to be no obvious brain damage and the blow to the head might seem to have been minor or trivial. This results in the post-concussional state which will be considered later. It may generally be stated that the result of a head injury in psychiatric terms is determined partly by the extent and location of the brain damage (whether provable or not) and the pre-existing personality and the psychiatric state of the patient.

Head injury which actually affects the gross structure of the brain may leave behind specific defects. One such state is the frontal lobe syndrome following injury to that part of the brain. There is often dramatic change in personality and behaviour of patients so affected. These patients may become euphoric or apathetic. Their character can turn gross and they may come to have little regard for social norms and conventions or for the concern of others. They can be irresponsible and cruel and prone to excesses involving all their appetites. Their amoral aggression and violence may lead to involvement with the criminal law and family and child law. They tend to lack foresight, are impulsive and are also heedless of the consequences that may follow their actions. Lesser degrees of damage to the brain may be associated with mood changes, in particular depression or anxiety. Some cases involving damage to the frontal lobes may go on to develop bipolar affective disorder.

2.12 HEAD INJURY – POST-CONCUSSIONAL STATE

An intriguing form of a post-head injury psychiatric condition involves the post-concussional state. This may follow a minor or even trivial head injury. As a rule no neurological lesion is demonstrated despite extensive investigation involving a panoply of tests and scans. In this state are to be found numerous symptoms, some vague, some described with greater precision, which include headache, giddiness, irritability, fatigue, depression, sleep disturbance, frustration, restlessness, excessive sensitivity to noise, blurred vision, double vision, excessive sensitivity to light, nausea, tinnitus, poor attention and concentration with impaired short-term memory and an intolerance of alcohol. Mild organic dysfunction is not uncommon in the early days following minor head injury and the subsequent few months. Post-traumatic epilepsy may also be found although that is more common with penetrating wounds of the head where up to 50 per cent of patients may develop this condition. During this time psychological features can develop and/or pre-existing psychological vulnerabilities may be activated. When post-concussion syndrome persists, psychological factors may entirely account for the symptoms in some individuals, and organic or quasi-organic features will entirely account for the symptoms in others. Most patients will be found in between these extreme situations. A complicating feature in symptoms persisting over six months may be the expectations from a claim for compensation. Treatment of the post-traumatic state is often difficult partly because the patient is convinced that there is organic pathology underlying his symptoms, partly as the symptoms are often so vague and also in part because the personality of the patient may be the most important factor behind the symptoms and, accordingly, so much harder to deal with.

King[1] has reviewed the post-concussion syndrome which appears to have intrigued clinicians for 130 years. 75 per cent of all head injuries are mild, half of these experience some post-concussion symptoms. Most recover completely within three months of injury but around one-third have some persisting symptoms beyond this time. Around eight per cent have significant symptoms at one year and in some cases the symptoms are possibly permanent. There is also good evidence from the literature that early intervention, within the first few weeks of mild head injury, does significantly reduce post-concussion symptoms and limits the emergence of persisting problems. There is an association between the severity of post-concussion symptoms or time taken off work after mild head injury and the seeking of compensation. It should be noted, however, that although twice as many patients seeking compensation have post-concussion symptoms compared to those who are not, few show significant improvement following settlement of their case, even a few years afterwards.

Personality change following concussion or more serious injury to the brain is occasionally to be found. Sometimes the change in personality can take a dramatic turn as a previously peaceable and respectable citizen commences a career of psychopathic excess. A couple of examples of this phenomenon are given in Chapter 7 where personality disorders are discussed. Those are personality changes of a fairly gross kind but many patients following head injury leaving little or nothing by way of obvious physical sequelae complain they are not 'the same person' following an episode of trauma involving their heads.

---

[1]   See N S King 'Post-concussion syndrome: clarity among the controversy?' (2003) *British Journal of Psychiatry – Editorial* (October).

2.13   HEAD INJURY – RISKS

As we shall discuss in detail in Part II of this book, post-concussional states feature heavily in personal injury and employment cases where the recalcitrance of the symptoms is a consideration in the assessment of persisting disability. Symptoms such as irritability, apathy, poor tolerance of frustration and the hypersensitivity to light and, in particular, to sounds are features which bring these cases to the attention of those also in the fields of family and child law and, occasionally, the criminal law.

2.14   SUMMARY

- The risk of developing one of the commoner dementias appears to be age-related, the risk rising from five per cent at the age of 65 to 20 per cent at the age of 80. Dementia is associated with disinhibited and occasionally aggressive behaviour which could become a matter of concern for those caring for these patients. As a result of impaired memory and intellectual functioning, capacity to look after one's property and affairs may be adversely affected which has implications, in particular, for the issue of testamentary capacity. Dementing patients are also susceptible to infections which may cause a confusional state thereby worsening the mental state and further impairing capacity. Most confusional states can be reversed with the successful treatment of the relevant infection, which may then result in the mental state of the patient demonstrating what appears to be a fluctuating cognitive state.

- Confusional states are mostly due to infections and other physical causes. These states are also related to age and also to sensory impairment. It leads to very changeable mental states in which agitation, aggression and grossly impaired cognitive states may be seen. Capacity is invariably lost but is usually regained when the cause of the confusional state is corrected. Many drugs, both prescribed and unprescribed, can induce a confusional state and details of their consumption must always be sought.

- Minor head injuries can lead to the post-concussional state in which vague and indefinite symptoms may be seen. The pre-existing personality appears to play a significant part in this condition which is, therefore, similar in this respect to the neurotic conditions. These symptoms may be resistant to conventional treatment and may become chronic. Active rehabilitation reduces these risks. This state carries major implications for the outcome in cases involving employment and personal injury for there appears also to be an association between litigation and the prolongation of symptoms and disability.

CHAPTER 3

THE PSYCHOTIC DISORDERS

3.1   INTRODUCTION

These psychotic disorders – and those that follow in the next chapter – are the major psychiatric disorders and involve the patient losing touch with reality, with also loss of insight, and displaying symptoms such as delusions, hallucinations, and disorders of thinking and speech. As such, these features demonstrate a quite fundamental disruption of the higher functions of an individual and it is easy to see how many branches of the law including criminal law and family and child law practice may become involved with an individual who suffers from such a condition. In this chapter we shall concern ourselves with schizophrenia and related conditions but not with those affective disorders of a psychotic kind which we shall leave for consideration in the next chapter.

3.2   SCHIZOPHRENIA

Schizophrenia refers to a group of disorders which is a major worldwide cause of psychiatric disability. It is best considered as a form of brain dysfunction whose neurological lineaments are still far from well understood thereby reducing us to a study of the illness (or, more accurately, the group of illnesses) at a descriptive rather than at any deep pathological level. One matter we shall summarily dispose of at the outset. Lay persons – encouraged by the more thoughtless elements in the media – appear to hold onto a notion that schizophrenia involves some entity called a 'split personality'. It is nothing of the kind. The 'split' in schizophrenia refers to the dissociation between the various functions of the mind such as thinking, feeling, behaviour and perception so that contact with reality comes to be lost. This is a serious medical condition, far removed from any form of personality disorder.

3.3   SCHIZOPHRENIA – CLINICAL FEATURES

The mode of onset of the illness may be variable. Some patients may harbour the illness for months or years and come only casually to medical attention. Others may suffer an explosive presentation which is drawn to the attention first of the police or the criminal justice system. Symptoms used to be described as being positive (such as hallucinations) or negative (such as apathy and social withdrawal) and extensive classificatory systems used to be drawn up with many sub-categories but these are of little practical help nowadays. The symptoms may nevertheless still be varied in presentation. Self-neglect or a bizarre appearance and behaviour may be in evidence. Speech disorders indicating disordered thought were believed to be virtually pathognomonic of schizophrenia. Concrete thinking, neologistic constructions, irrelevant sentence structures and illogical speech patterns may be seen. Disorders of thinking may be further manifested by the possession of delusions, usually persecutory in kind. A delusion may be defined as a false unshakeable belief held despite the evidence to the contrary and out of keeping with the social norms and the cultural practices of the individual in question. Discussion of the features of a delusion arising in terms of such a definition has kept phenomenologists and philosophers happily occupied for years. It is plain that no false belief by itself necessarily amounts to a delusion. A belief in God may not appear rational by the usual standards but, quite apart from there being lack of definite proof to the contrary, it is also a belief sanctioned by social norms and cultural practices. Patients from parts of Asia and Africa may hold varying beliefs in 'evil spirits' or witchcraft but these may also be appropriate according to the norms obtaining in their cultures. More problematical diagnostic considerations may arise when an individual complains, say, of being hounded by the security services which, on investigation, turns out to be true. He may still be mentally ill if the means by which he arrived at his belief are shown to be pathological. This matter does not feature in the definition of a delusion given above but one needs also to enquire in practice as to how the belief was come by. Thus, the story is told of the man who, having paused at a red traffic light, came to the overwhelming conclusion that his wife was being unfaithful to him on account of the colours changing from red to amber. That state of affairs was true, as it happened, but the way the belief arose suggested it being pathological. So, one may say that just because they are really after you does not necessarily rule you out as also being paranoid. The usual form of delusion seen in schizophrenia is a persecutory delusion although grandiose delusions may also be encountered.

The other dramatic symptom is auditory hallucination. A hallucination is a perception experienced as real in the absence of a sensory stimulus. Thus, any of the senses may be involved in the manifestation of a hallucination. The commonest of these in schizophrenia is an auditory hallucination, ie one involving the hearing of voices. In this disorder it may take the distinctive form with voices talking about the individual in the third person, even offering a running commentary, the tone often being derogatory, and there may also be voices commenting on the individual's actions and thoughts.

Mood changes may not be remarkable in this condition but depression not uncommonly co-exists with other phenomena. Whether the behaviour is related or not to this mood change, there is an increased risk of suicide in schizophrenia, especially in the early phase of the illness when the changes in the mental processes may be bewilderingly incomprehensible and therefore distressing to the still insightful patient. There has been considerable recent interest in suicidal behaviour among schizophrenic patients. Previously, a depressive component in schizophrenia was believed responsible for this behaviour. Then it became known that the disorder, without any obvious depressive element, could also give rise to this phenomenon. The incidence of suicide in schizophrenia was put at about 10 per cent. Recent studies have shown this figure to have been exaggerated and, at any rate in the pre-community care age, does not seem to have exceeded one per cent. What the post-community care era will bring forth remains to be seen for it is believed that the single most important factor determining suicide rates in patients with schizophrenia is deinstitutionalisation – that is, the protective asylum function of institutions having now been lost – although drug treatment seems also to make a contribution to increasing risk. It seems a patient in the community has also to assume the cares of the community.

Schizophrenia may also be associated with cognitive changes, in particular with impairment of memory. The precise cause of this change, or its significance, is not understood with any precision but it may, of course, illustrate the ultimate cerebral provenance of the disorder and usually also indicates a poorer prognosis.

Insight, by which one means in this situation an appreciation by the patient that he is ill, that the illness is caused by a mental disorder that is the cause of his problems, and that he should seek and receive treatment, may be lost when the illness progresses but it is often preserved in the early stages, a feature which, as we said, compounds the distress experienced. Cultural factors, as we have already noted, may inform the issue of insight. In many cultures, especially of Asia and Africa, there is a notable lack of enthusiasm for acknowledging mental disorder, whether on the part of the patient or his family and the wider community. It is customary among these persons to try to understand the phenomena of disease in physical terms. In such cases it would be wrong to suggest that insight has been lost when all the patient is trying to do is trying to understand and explain his symptoms in terms of the acceptable cultural norms he subscribes to.

3.4   SCHIZOPHRENIA – CAUSATION – GENETICS

The schizophrenic disorders are found the world over in virtually all communities and in fairly uniform distribution apart from a few pockets of increased incidence. They affect young men and women in late adolescence or early adult life. Men have the more severe illness and the worse prognosis. It is a not uncommon condition with about five in every thousand of the public affected. Although nowadays there is not believed to be a social class difference in the affliction, the tendency of patients with these conditions to drift socially downwards may suggest a preferential poorer class distribution in surveys. There is sufficient evidence now of a genetic predisposition although the precise mechanisms still elude us. The closer the relationship to a schizophrenic patient a person has, the higher the risk that individual runs of developing the illness. The risk appears to increase with the closeness of the familial relationship – twin studies and adoption studies have confirmed this point. There appear to be multiple genetic foci involved rather than a single gene. However, the genetic risk is not 100 per cent which allows scope for environmental influences, both good and bad, to affect both onset and outcome. In fact, it appears it is a predisposition or vulnerabilty that is inherited rather than the illness itself. It has long intrigued observers that some of those who could have inherited this predisposition often tend to be gifted and highly creative individuals who, moreover, do not go on to develop the illness. There is a suggestion therefore of evolutionary advantage to be had in possessing some of this genetic material which is thereby propagated and kept in circulation. Schizophrenic patients themselves traditionally have had low fertility. There appears to be interaction between genetic vulnerability and environmental influences. It is these environmental influences – such as stresses of a diverse kind, illicit drug consumption, trauma, physical injury or illness – that may help to steer a vulnerable individual over the threshold. There may be overlap between true schizophrenia, the paranoid disorders to be discussed later in this chapter and the stress-induced schizophrenic illnesses which are sometimes referred to as the schizophreniform disorders. With the recent fashion for the use of the term, we could say there may even be a schizophrenic spectrum of disorders.

3.5   SCHIZOPHRENIA – CAUSATION – THE ENVIRONMENT

The environmental influences remain unclear. However, that the environment does play some part in the causation of schizophrenia has long been suspected. A viral theory has been mooted, viruses having been in the frame, so to speak, for a long time. Over the past generation or two the condition appears to have become milder in presentation, at least in some cultures, and less chronic in outcome. The kind of inhabitant seen in the old lunatic asylums – still to be recalled by an older generation of psychiatrists – is now rare and the change is exemplified also by the 'care in the community' approach, much traduced on account of its shortcomings, but an infinitely better and more humane way of dealing with the appropriate patient than incarcerating him, perhaps for ever, in primitive institutions offering little by way of comfort or treatment. The diminished severity of the condition has suggested to some observers that there could be a possible infective aetiology since viruses, in common with other micro-organisms, have a well recognised tendency to mutate rapidly to greater or lesser virulence. That apart, there have been some neurological changes noted on brain studies of patients with schizophrenia although these findings, as yet, do not provide any reliable basis for diagnostic purposes. The role of environmental pollutants also remains unclear. There have also been a reduced incidence of some symptoms of schizophrenia which were common in earlier years. One of these is catatonia which in the past was considered to be a characteristic symptom of the condition and, indeed, attracted a subcategory to itself in classificatory systems. The symptom is now rarely found in the developed world and, even then, appears to be preferentially distributed among patients from migrant communities. There is also the phenomenon that antibodies to various viruses such as the herpes simplex virus are found in the blood of patients with schizophrenia although the precise significance of this has not yet been explained. Closer to home, pathological and dysfunctional family relationships have been suggested both as being aetiological as well as relapse-inducing elements. Finally, some presentations of schizophrenia-like conditions are virtually indistinguishable from the traditional presentations of the illness and may arise in the presence of systemic illness or following some illicit drug taking. The strong association between self-reported cannabis use and the earlier onset of psychosis provides further evidence that schizophrenia may be precipitated by cannabis use and/or that early onset of symptoms is a risk factor for cannabis use. One study showed that half of all patients treated for cannabis-induced psychosis will develop a schizophrenia-like disorder and that almost one-third will be diagnosed with paranoid schizophrenia. The first episode of schizophrenia occurs several years earlier in these patients compared with those with no history of cannabis-induced psychosis. Another study has suggested that compliance with antipsychotic medication by someone with schizophrenia may not prevent a relapse or worsening of psychotic symptoms if stimulant drugs (such as the amphetamines and cocaine) are used. Another study has reported that cannabis use in adolescence leads to a two to three-fold increase in relative risk for schizophrenia or schizophreniform disorder in adulthood. The earlier the onset of cannabis use, the greater appears to be the risk for psychotic outcomes. Cannabis does not appear to represent a sufficient or necessary cause for the development of psychosis but seems to form a part of a causal constellation. A minority of individuals therefore experience a harmful outcome consequent on their use of cannabis. However, this minority is significant from a clinical point of view as well as at a population level. It is estimated that about eight per cent of cases of schizophrenia could be prevented by elimination of cannabis users in the population. Given all this evidence, it is tempting to believe that the picture of schizophrenia one sees in a clinical setting is but the result of some 'final common pathway' of brain dysfunction which may be instigated by diverse means.

3.6 SCHIZOPHRENIA – TREATMENT

The cornerstone of modern treatment of schizophrenia is drug treatment. In broad terms, the drugs used may be classified as the 'old' type and the 'new' type of drugs. The older drugs – the stalwarts among them were chlorpromazine, haloperidol and trifluoperazine – tended to be effective but were also sedative and in addition caused movement difficulties, some of which became permanent, causing a considerable degree of secondary disability. Versions of injectable depot preparations of these types of drugs, by which a patient may be given periodic injections thereby reducing the risk of non-compliance (a notoriously intractable problem in all medical practice), were also available.

The newer type of antipsychotic drugs include agents such as amisulpride, clozapine, olanzapine, quetiapine, risperidone, sertindole and zotepine. These drugs, it is claimed, have fewer of the adverse effects, especially the atypical movement disorders, associated with the older drugs. By and large the efficacy of both sets of drugs is comparable. Special mention may be made of clozapine which is said to have properties against the 'negative' symptoms of schizophrenia – apathy, lack of motivation etc – which appear to be largely beyond the reach of the other agents more commonly used. However, clozapine is a notably toxic drug capable of producing lethal adverse effects by causing bone marrow suppression of white cell formation. It is therefore never to be considered as a first-line treatment in the average case of schizophrenia, its utility being rather in its availability when the conventional drugs have failed to produce improvement especially with the negative symptoms which may also be present. It has to be used under strict medical supervision with periodic blood testing being a mandatory requirement. It goes without saying its use is limited to those who are specialists in this field who are able to weigh up the balance of benefits and risks. The patients being considered for this treatment must show motivation – however apathetic they may be – to take the drug as well as being able to submit themselves to regular blood testing.

If a firm diagnosis is made of schizophrenia, drug treatment, following a first episode of illness, is normally required for a period of at least two years. If there have been recurrent episodes of illness this period of treatment may have to be extended. If stresses are present – whether personal or social – longer periods of treatment may need to be advised to avail of the protective functions of drug treatment. Therapeutic drugs have been shown to have a prophylactic function in the face of most stressful situations but not, it appears, against persistent illicit drug use. Recourse should be had, wherever possible, to depot antipsychotic injections which will also ensure a reliable record being kept of compliance with medication. Contact with doctors, community nurses and other members of the mental health team is advantageous as is the prompt reinstatement of vigorous treatment early in the course of any relapse. Modern drugs, including clozapine, offer alternative choices which were not available in the past.

The drugs commonly used today are usually successful in controlling the acute symptoms of the illness and, unlike in the past, in-patient treatment is not always necessary. This shift of treatment to the community has also the supplementary benefit that rehabilitation can be started straightaway. This is essential for one can be successful in treating the disease and yet end up with a patient who becomes a chronic invalid and tends to make the most of his illness for conscious and unconscious motives. The rule should always be to aim for as rapid a return as is safely possible to the patient's pre-morbid state of physical and psychological functioning and minimise, as far as possible, the dangers of secondary disability and chronic invalidism.

3.7 SCHIZOPHRENIA – PROGNOSIS

The prognosis of schizophrenia has notably improved in the past generation or two. The starkly disabled, shuffling, muttering and disengaged patients seen in such vast numbers inhabiting the Victorian lunatic asylums – and their more recent successors – is a thing now of the increasingly distant past although if the theory of viral infection as a possible cause of schizophrenia holds any water it is not wholly inconceivable that the condition could once again in the future regain its previous severity – viruses, after all, are known to mutate in all directions. The improvement in prognosis cannot be attributed, to any significant degree, to the drugs used or the diagnostic or treatment approaches employed although the importance of early rehabilitation is better appreciated now than in the past. It used to be believed that a schizophrenic illness of early onset and of insidious progression, associated with prominent negative symptoms, heralded a poorer prognosis than an illness which came on at a later stage of life, announcing itself with an acute onset and the spectacular presence of positive symptoms such as delusions and hallucinations. A clearly identifiable stress factor acting as a precipitant, good compliance with medication, satisfactory social support and a sympathetic family environment are all known to improve prognosis. Good recovery from a few episodes of illness presages a reasonably sound prognosis while recurrent bouts of illness may be associated with a poorer prognosis. Abuse of alcohol or illicit drugs – along with non-compliance with prescribed drugs – remains a potent cause of future relapse and consequently of a poorer prognosis. However, most patients with this condition, with treatment and support, could reasonably expect to reclaim the life they used to lead before the illness struck. It used also to be believed that few sufferers from a schizophrenic illness could successfully resume professional, academic or social life. This is no longer necessarily true – a function of the reduced severity of the illness and the generally good prognosis it carries now

3.8   SCHIZOPHRENIA – THE RISKS

As will be expanded on in Part II of this book, such is the universal nature of schizophrenic illness that it will come as no surprise that practitioners in several branches of the law may find themselves involved with patients suffering from such an illness. Their unpredictable and occasionally aggressive behaviour interests the criminal law as it does family and child practice. The latter branch of the law is also concerned with schizophrenic parents or spouses or partners who show poor motivation, apathy and the presence of negative symptoms to an extent that leads to their functioning and duties concerning these risks being compromised. These negative symptoms may also impair their status as employees. The lack of active rehabilitation carries many risks for the schizophrenic patient including the failure to resume employment.

3.9   OTHER PARANOID DISORDERS

There are paranoid disorders – usually involving persecutory delusions with little or nothing else by way of other psychotic symptoms – which for a long time have been observed not to fit into the diagnostic categories reserved for the schizophrenic illnesses. The primacy of delusions was always evident in these cases. When the onset of these paranoid disorders is acute there is present an acute delusional disorder in which may be seen persecutory delusions with a mood of suspicion. The cause of these states may be illicit or prescribed drugs, and adverse life stresses are not uncommonly implicated as precipitants. The more chronic or more persistent form of delusional disorders involve systematised delusions – meaning these exist as a near complete system within the patient's mind and usually involve a belief in conspiracies against him – and there is little other impairment, intelligence and the personality in other respects being well preserved. These delusional beliefs and systems may also exist in isolation – they are then referred to as being encapsulated – and there is usually little other impairment in functioning or of the personality in other respects. A famous case – and a patient of Freud's – involved a German judge who apparently carried out his judicial tasks satisfactorily even while harbouring such a delusional system in his mind. The term paranoia used to be given to this class of paranoid disorders. Another kind of paranoid disorder afflicts the elderly in whom it showed virtually all the features of a paranoid schizophrenic illness, apart from the obviously late onset, and this condition usually carries a good prognosis. This condition was referred to as paraphrenia or, where appropriate, as senile paraphrenia. All these conditions have now been brought under the heading of persistent delusional disorders which are to be diagnosed in the absence of brain damage or schizophrenia. There are a handful of other paranoid disorders such as morbid jealousy which will be considered in Chapter 9 alongside other unusual conditions. Their treatment is essentially on the lines taken in cases of schizophrenia. This involves the use of antipsychotic drugs. The acute forms of the illness respond reasonably well to treatment and the patient should be able to make an uneventful recovery. Good results are usually also to be expected in those cases previously called paraphrenia but there is usually little impact on well established cases of chronic or persistent delusional disorders, or paranoia, as they used to be called, and these patients carry on with their life with their delusions well encapsulated in their minds.

3.10   OTHER PARANOID DISORDERS – THE RISKS

The risks are as for schizophrenia with the difference that apathy and poor motivation are not usually associated with the paranoid disorders. The criminal law and family and child law are usually involved in litigation with these patients although they may occasionally be involved in employment and housing law disputes on account of their unreasonable behaviour.

3.11   SUMMARY

- Schizophrenia is essentially an illness which afflicts young adults. There is known genetic risk, susceptibility to the illness rising according to how closely related one is to an affected family member. Schizophrenia-like conditions may be produced by some physical causes including the use of illicit drugs. There has been recent interest in how cannabis may cause or contribute to the development of the condition. The prognosis of schizophrenia appears to have improved in recent years. Its symptoms are amenable to drug treatment and active rehabilitation should prevent secondary disability arising. There is a known relationship between schizophrenia and aggressive behaviour but the relationship is complex. The personality of the patient and the concurrent misuse of substances may play a part in the violence associated with these patients. Apathy and lack of motivation are occasional features of the illness, made worse for want of active rehabilitation. There is evidence that with adequate rehabilitation patients will become less disabled and more capable of employment.

- The risks associated with the paranoid disorder are similar to those involved with schizophrenic illness. Interpersonal relationships may be affected with problems arising in respect of employment and housing. Aggression may also be involved. The acute state is susceptible to drug treatment and good results may be anticipated. The underlying personality may be a significant factor in the long-term prognosis.

CHAPTER 4

DISORDERS OF MOOD

4.1 INTRODUCTION

As far as the psychoses are concerned, the modern understanding of mood disorders is that it involves mania, depression or a combination of the two conditions which are called bipolar affective disorders or manic-depressive illness. These conditions are all characterised by pathological mood changes, usually in the form of depression or elation. In fact, it is a useful rule of thumb to remind oneself that the symptoms found in mood disorders should generally be capable of being explained by the central change in mood, whether downward or upward.

4.2 DEPRESSIVE ILLNESS – CLINICAL FEATURES

The term depression, used without qualification, is not wholly satisfactory for it is capable of bearing many meanings. It could refer to a mood state, a personality type or the constellation of symptoms that makes up a depressive disorder. These symptoms can involve bodily or physiological changes such as those concerning sleep, appetite, sexual desire, gastro-intestinal function or the menstrual rhythm. Symptoms may also involve psychomotor function.

The mood change in depressive illness must involve a pathological diminution of mood. This refers to a significant and sustained reduction of mood which transcends the regular variations of mood that all human beings (indeed, probably all animals) are subject to. Where normal variation ends and pathological change begins remains a problematical area of definition for there are no objective measures available to discern this shift, unlike, say, with the measurement of body temperature or blood pressure. There is no alternative to a detailed enquiry being undertaken into the individual's perceptions of changes in mood for different persons may also differ in their habitual setting of mood. Any change must be sustained and persistent, normally lasting for at least four weeks. The mood change may lead to a variety of ancillary subjective changes such as the inability to enjoy the things the individual habitually previously used to. There may also be present a pervasive feeling of gloom, pessimism and dark foreboding which is not in keeping with the previous character of the individual concerned. The sufferer may echo Shakespeare by saying:

> 'How weary, stale, flat and unprofitable / Seem to me all the uses of this world.'

These feelings may intensify to accommodate ideas of guilt and worthlessness which may extend even, in severe cases, to expressing delusions of guilt and worthlessness such as being convinced that one is responsible for all the ills, sins and wickedness found in the world. A related delusion is one involving a sense of nihilism in which the patient believes he does not exist, that his mind and body do not exist and that the world itself does not exist. As these delusions are to be derived from a pathological lowering of the mood, these ideas far transcend any philosophical notion one can hold that the world and the individuals within it are but an illusion. As might be imagined, these pathological ideas may co-exist with a sense of bleak hopelessness which leads on, with perverted logic, to suicide, an ever present risk in any patient with a depressed mood.

The changes in physiology or bodily function are common in depressive illness and have long indicated to some observers the ultimate biological provenance of any significant depressive disorder. The sleep rhythm may be early upset in the course of the illness. Although the classical feature is noted to be early wakening, that is waking two or more hours before the usual time of awakening for the patient, in practice sleep may be disturbed in diverse ways. There could be difficulty in getting to sleep, repeated wakening during the course of sleep, waking early or a combination of all these disruptions over several nights. Sleep may also be disturbed by intrusive dreaming. The upshot is disrupted sleep of poor quality which leaves the patient unrefreshed even after he has apparently been sleeping for several hours. This ensures the next day is started off on a shaky footing and, thereby, a vicious circle is also set in train, making the consequences of a depressed mood worse through a lack of any 'balm of sleep'. Many patients complain it is their poor sleep, above all other symptoms, that contributes most to their feelings of black despair and demoralisation. However, a small minority of patients tend to oversleep, giving the impression to observers that they could be attempting to escape their torments in a periodic loss of consciousness. These patients do not, however, appear to enjoy much refreshment as a result of their prolonged somnolence.

Parallel biological change may be seen in respect of appetite. Loss of appetite is common and may be severe with consequent weight loss which, in graver cases, could come to cause a medical emergency through loss of nutrition and hydration. Changes in bowel function may reflect poor appetite with ensuing constipation the common feature although diarrhoea may also be present when it is usual to attribute it to features of anxiety which are commonly found in depressed states. There could in some cases be a paradoxical feature of over eating when with the over consumption of what is called 'comfort food' there could be excessive, even gross, weight gain. Reduction in sexual interests – as with other appetites and sources of pleasure – is a common feature in depressive illness as are changes in menstrual rhythm.

Psychomotor retardation refers to slowness of both mental and physical activity. It is a common observation that patients with depressive illness often appear to be functioning like an under-powered engine, being laboured in thought, word and movement. In extreme cases – rarely seen these days – stupor can overcome patients when, mute and immobile, they enter into a catatonic state. On the other hand, minds can, in equally severe depressive illness, become seemingly overactive when agitation may be an accompanying feature. In severe psychotic forms of depressive illness, delusions of a kind already mentioned could be seen along with auditory hallucinations – the voices characteristically saying things in keeping with the patient's mood, abusing him, invoking feelings of guilt and, sometimes urging him to suicide to put an end to a worthless existence. In these cases the differential diagnosis must also consider other psychotic conditions such as schizophrenia.

An invariable feature in a depressive illness of any significant severity is loss of attention and concentration. Patients may report having difficulty keeping track of events when following popular pastimes such as watching the television. Serious intellectual activity may become impossible. Commonly complaint is also made of a poor short-term memory, of being forgetful and mislaying objects. A picture of dementia may be presented to the world. However, there is usually no evidence of anything unduly serious underlying these memory difficulties which are attributable to poor attention and concentration, and full recovery can be confidently predicted with successful treatment of the depressive illness.

4.3 MANIA – CLINICAL FEATURES

What is popularly regarded as being the mirror image of depressive illness is mania which appears to sit on the other pole of bipolar illness, although this stark distinction between 'polar opposites' is not by any means entirely accurate either in description or in terms of an analysis of underlying pathology. As with depressive illness, it should be possible, at a superficial level at any rate, to derive all the features of a manic illness from the central pathological elevation of mood. In mania this elevation of mood is elation, a sustained elevation of mood. It must be stated, however, that in many cases what strikes (occasionally possibly in more senses than one) the observer is not elation or pathological happiness but a mood of aggression mixed with irritability and hostility. Nevertheless, many of these patients do appear unduly cheerful, for a time at least, with a limitless supply of energy which – in stark contrast to the more severe cases of depression – causes them to act like an overpowered engines, fuelled by rocket fuel, being in constant overdrive, humming with activity and exhausting those around them. These patients may talk without end, make endless and increasingly ambitious plans and are pathologically optimistic. The future is scanned by them with lofty regard, money may be scattered on all and sundry, extravagant purchases (including the fabled elephant ordered through Harrod's, other exotic creatures, jewellery) made, largesse bestowed. Relations usually have to pick up the pieces at the end of the episode of illness.

Their excessive talk is characterised by what is referred to as a pressure of speech and the overpowered mind may give rise to a 'flight of ideas' which means a form of speech disorder is present.

So active are some of these patients that they have little time for food, drink or sleep and very occasionally they may collapse into utter exhaustion. Elation of mood is also mirrored in the patient having a grandiose or even fantastic conception of himself, occasionally believing he is of noble or royal birth, possessing special talents or powers and given also to possessing limitless wealth. There is also disinhibition in sexual matters and unwanted pregnancies in women patients is not uncommon. With the lack of any insight being present, all these excesses may appear to give the impression of behaviour by a celebrity albeit one who actually possesses little or no talent, which may not, of course, be unusual these days.

4.4   BIPOLAR DISORDER

Depressive and manic illness may be, indeed are commonly, found as separate and discrete illnesses. However, when serially combined, for instance, when depression and mania alternate or appear in irregular series in the same patient, the appellation bipolar affective disorder, replacing the formerly used manic-depressive disorder, is given.

4.5   BIPOLAR DISORDER – CAUSATION

As with schizophrenia, all the evidence suggests that pathological disturbances of mood originate in brain dysfunction although the precise mechanisms are far from clear in the present state of knowledge. The structure of the brain, especially in the parts below the cerebral cortex, appears to be implicated, the lesion detectable by scanning of the brain. It is believed that where obvious lesions exist the prognosis is poorer. At the neurochemical level changes have long been known to exist although the precise mechanisms involved continue to elude us. The finding of chemical disturbance of some kind being present offers the rationale for drug treatment. There is a discernible genetic influence (greater in bipolar than in unipolar disorders) and close family relations may show an increased tendency to these disorders. Relations of patients with a bipolar disorder have a higher risk of both bipolar and unipolar depressive disorder. The risk of depressive disorder in women is higher although the risk of bipolar disorder is comparable in men and women. But the environmental effect, as might be imagined, is also strong and in any given case of these disorders it is not uncommon to find an interaction between genetic susceptibility and environmental effects (eg an individual with genetic susceptibility falling ill having experienced some adverse life event) bearing responsibility for the illness. The role of life events may be particularly decisive. It appears to be the case that it is not so much the effect of the adverse life events themselves – which, after all, everyone is heir to – but the impact they could have on a person who might have been rendered vulnerable as a result of genetic and prior psychological influences. An intriguing question is to what extent genetics and the environment, in combination or separately, determine not merely how an individual faces up to stressful life events but how he has got into the situation of having to experience them, the so-called 'nature or nurture' argument. Among the psychological factors deemed significant in making an individual vulnerable to disorders of mood (especially depressive illness), are unemployment, having several young children living at home and having no confiding or intimate relationship to sustain the individual. Other psychological factors include parental loss, emotional deprivation or abuse and abnormal personality. Those with disordered personalities may appear to be drawn into situations which lead to mood disorders, in particular depressive illness, as a result of their reactions to these situations. Alcohol misuse may lead to a depressive mood and both depressed and manic patients may drink heavily as well as consuming illicit drugs. Many of these patients have low self-esteem and may be hypersensitive to criticism and not a few have a tendency to think negatively about themselves and the world, the focus of cognitive behavioural therapy.

Neither depressive illness nor mania needs to be of primarily psychiatric origin. These disorders can follow a host of medical or surgical conditions or the treatment given for those. The primary cause in such cases could be systemic illness of infective, metabolic, endocrine, haematological or neoplastic origins. Some of the conditions involved include cerebrovascular disease, brain tumours, hypothyroidism, steroid drugs, amphetamine and other stimulant abuse and multiple sclerosis. Treatment of the underlying condition may be sufficient in some cases to improve the mood disorder although, not uncommonly, both the secondary depressive illness or mania requires treatment in its own right whatever other condition might have been primarily causative of the mood disturbance.

4.6   BIPOLAR DISORDER – TREATMENT

The treatment of depressive illness usually involves some combination of drug and psychological therapy. The mainstay of drug treatment for many decades used to be the tricyclic group of antidepressant drugs. This group includes such drugs as amitryptiline and dothiepin. Their efficacy was, on the whole, acceptable but their adverse effects occasionally proved tiresome. They could be unduly sedating and thus be inconvenient for use in situations requiring alertness and, more crucially, they could be dangerous (even lethally so) in overdose, a situation that is potentially capable of arising in every case of a depressive illness. These drawbacks led to a search for drugs with different modes of action and in time was born the group of drugs called the selective serotonin reuptake inhibiting agents (SSRIs). As the name suggests, their biochemical action is to block the reuptake of an important brain chemical called serotonin, thereby, in effect, flooding the nerve endings where this chemical is believed to modulate mood function. Some other drugs are known to have analogous effects in respect of noradrenaline metabolism. These drugs do not have the same sedating properties as the older tricyclic agents and, more pertinently, are believed to be far less dangerous in overdose. Among their number are fluoxetine, citalopram, paroxetine and sertraline. In time other atypical drugs such as mirtazepine, nefazodone, reboxetine and venlafaxine also made their way to the market place. There is no doubt that we now possess a considerably improved armoury of drugs for use in depressive illness but in all drug treatment there is a cautionary tale to be told and remembered when it comes to the use of any pharmaceutical agent.

These newer atypical drugs were taken up with an almost messianic zeal, the drug fluoxetine (Prozac) in particular achieving notoriety by being promiscuously exhibited in subjects for whom it was never intended – very young children, domestic pets, not to mention individuals who were disaffected with life rather than suffering from a depressive illness – and the term Prozac nearly came to signify a synonym for panacea. Over a period of time adverse reports gathered and there is some evidence now that these newer agents may not be as risk-free, never mind of universal benefit, as they were once believed to be. In particular this group of drugs has been implicated as a possible cause in some cases of suicide and homicide where it is believed they might have enhanced aggressive tendencies already present in some depressed patients – might even have precipitated these tendencies in other patients – causing them to turn on themselves or towards others with violence. Litigation was mooted. The caution that was enjoined following these reports was wholly beneficial, for in all medicine a balance has to be struck in every patient between the reward and risks possible with any treatment that is being contemplated. The result now is that a more balanced view appears to be once again taken of all antidepressant drug treatment. Treatment is usually required for at least six months after which the drug dose may be gradually reduced and the drug treatment may be stopped altogether. Gradual reduction in medication reduces the risk of relapse and also prevents withdrawal effects, seen with some drugs, emerging. It has been shown that maintenance drug treatment reduces relapse rates by 50 per cent in cases of recurrent depressive illness.

Drug treatment works most effectively when allied to some form of psychological treatment. The role of conventional counselling and therapy is probably overestimated. Psychological treatment is labour – and, therefore, time and cost – intensive and resources are scarce. The motivation of the patient is the paramount requirement and relatively few patients appear to have the patience and the commitment necessary to achieve good results. As up to 50 per cent of patients are non-compliant even with medication, simple enough to consume, a great deal of motivation is demanded of any patient being offered psychotherapy. Where litigation is involved, there are two additional factors also to be taken into account. First, the motivation always required of the patient becomes mixed if he engages in treatment so as to impress a court. Second, litigation usually envisages a short timescale for treatment which may be insufficient for success. Most forms of psychotherapy are therefore to be ruled out for parties involved in the usual forms of litigation. Nevertheless, in carefully selected patients, considerable benefit may be reaped through the deployment of psychological methods of treatment used as an adjunct to drug treatment. The role of cognitive behavioural treatment (CBT) in particular has been studied with interest and there is no doubt that in suitable groups of patients better results may be obtained by the use of this technique with medication than by drug treatment alone. The purpose of CBT is, to put it at its simplest, to attempt to refocus a patient's approach to thinking. A patient's problem may not be due to some objective and inherent property in the problem itself but the way his thoughts or cognitions come habitually to interpret the situation. The patient and therapist work out methods of challenging unhelpful and negative thoughts in relation to situations and to focus instead on thinking in positive and helpful ways. There may be role-play, homework (the keeping of diaries involving cognitions) and practice involving situations that the patient could encounter then and also in the future. An associated form of treatment is what may be called social therapy. There is often little doubt that in a significant number of depressed patients underlying the disorder are adverse social factors such as uncongenial or non-existent employment, unmanageable debt, poor marital relationships, adverse housing and a host of similar influences. If anything can be done to ameliorate these adverse influences there is greater scope for successful treatment and rehabilitation involving these patients.

Brief mention must be made of electroconvulsive treatment (ECT) given the notoriety the procedure has attracted over many years. It is a procedure that is not without its risks but there is no gainsaying its potent efficacy in the most severe forms of depressive illness involving a seemingly intractable disorder that could be leading the patient into a serious state of ill health. It can be a life saving intervention. Its use lies in specialist hands and with carefully selected cases.

The treatment of mania involves the use of the kind of antipsychotic agents that were discussed in the management of the schizophrenic disorders. The essence of treatment is to bring symptomatic relief and curb the various excesses involving the case of a manic patient. But in the case of depressive illness or mania or both (bipolar states) there is also scope for prophylactic treatment, that is attempting to prevent the recurrence of these conditions. The primary agent available for use for such purposes are the salts of the metal lithium which has now been employed for this purpose for four decades. The benefit from lithium use can be considerable but, once again, it is not without risk, especially in terms of kidney and thyroid functions. There are also other adverse effects associated with this drug. Further, it is safely and satisfactorily used only with regular blood level monitoring available to the patient and accepted by him. The demands on the patient may be considerable and some selection as to who might be suitable is necessary. Risk of relapse, when the drug is used, may be reduced by up to 30 per cent, results being better with the prevention of manic relapse than the prevention of depressive relapse. Other drugs pressed into service in this regard are carbamazepine, valproic acid and lamotrigine. There is some evidence that the course of the natural history of bipolar affective disorder can be advantageously altered by the use of lithium. Hence, the tendency now to embark on prophylactic treatment after even one episode of illness rather than wait for recurrence which was the approach previously taken.

4.7   BIPOLAR DISORDER – PROGNOSIS

The prognosis for individual episodes of illness, whether of depression or mania, is generally good these days. Fairly rapid response to modern drug treatment may be expected. If recovery from a depressive illness appears to be slow, apart from non-response to medication (which may necessitate a change of drug), other factors may need to be considered or reviewed, in particular the personality and the social elements in the patient's life. Alcohol and illicit drug misuse are important factors interfering with successful treatment. Recurrence of illness is always possible. It is usual to advise that drug treatment be continued for six months following full recovery from symptoms so as to minimise the risks of relapse. The role of lithium in prophylaxis has been mentioned above. Recurrence following specific risk factors, eg the post-partum state is always possible (see Chapter 9 below).

4.8   BIPOLAR DISORDER – RISKS

As will be discussed in detail in Part II of this book, both depressive and manic illness have implications for the law. Both conditions are associated with the risk of violence which explains the interest of the criminal law and family and child law in these conditions. Recurrent depressive and manic illness also have implications for continuing employment, and depressive illness, given its close relationship to physical disorders and injuries, commonly features in cases of post-traumatic personal injury.

4.9   SUMMARY

- The risk of developing an affective disorder such as depressive illness or mania is affected by genetic factors, there being greater risk of developing bipolar disorder when the genetic loading is elevated. Environmental factors also play a significant part in causing or contributing to the onset of these conditions. These disorders are also associated with physical and systemic illness. There is also a well known relationship between the affective disorders and the misuse of alcohol and illicit substances. Modern treatment is generally successful in containing symptoms and also in the prevention of further episodes of these disorders.

- While the risk of violence associated with mania is well appreciated it appears not to be with depressive illness, with a result that the prospects for violence with depressive illness have come to be underestimated. Suicide is an ever present risk with any depressive illness or where depressed mood is present in another condition. But there may also be appreciable risk of violence directed outwards also associated with depressive illness. Murder followed by suicide is well established in cases of depressive illness. The symptoms of depressive illness may also lead to impaired functioning which has major implications in family and child practice and also in regard to employment. As with all psychiatric conditions, active rehabilitation is crucial if secondary handicap is to be avoided.

CHAPTER 5

THE NEUROSES

5.1 INTRODUCTION

The neuroses refer to those conditions which make up the minor psychiatric disorders. The qualifying term 'minor' refers to the presentation of symptoms as seen from the perspective of a detached professional observer who finds the symptoms associated with these conditions to be less severe than the features of a psychotic disorder. To a patient with a neurotic condition it may be anything but minor as he carries around pressing symptoms of greater or lesser chronicity which respond poorly to conventional treatment and causes him to become the despair of doctors. The old joke with an American flavour – that 'the neurotic builds castles in the air, the psychotic lives in them and the psychiatrist collects the rent' – conveys much truth as jokes often do. A neurotic patient, whatever his symptoms may be and however inexplicable they are, usually has some grasp on reality and, generally, some measure of insight; the psychotic patient may invariably fall down on both scores. A cardinal rule with most neurotic disorders is that there is also a strong contribution made to neurotic conditions by the personality of the patient whereas psychotic conditions are usually studied as 'true' disease conditions with distinct biological origins and with the disease condition usually overwhelming any observable feature in the habitual personality and forming a distinguishable break from it. The neuroses may also be approached from the point of view of conditions that arise from the interaction between a patient's personality and the impact upon it of some external stressful event.

5.2 MINOR DEPRESSIVE ILLNESS

The first of the conditions to be considered under this heading are the minor depressive illnesses. Already considered have been depressive illnesses under the psychotic conditions and, at one level, the differences between the conditions appearing under the two rubrics is merely quantitative – depressive neurosis may appear to be a less severe illness and is not usually associated with a bipolar affective disorder. If the term is to be taken literally, depressive neurosis will also be expected to lack psychotic features such as delusions and hallucinations which may be a feature in some very severe depressive illnesses. These patients also keep a good hold on reality and their insight could be considerable and, in fact, contribute to their perception of their disorder. However, it is usual also to observe other differences between the two forms of depressive disorder. One of these, as already suggested, is the contribution made by the patient's personality to his disorder which may be of greater significance than with cases of 'psychotic' depressive illness where the illness element is usually the more prominent observable feature. That apart, the symptoms may appear to be similar, with, as stated, the obvious absence of any psychotic features. Onset of illness may be less marked and there is a 'grumbling' (in all senses) feel to the condition as reported by the patient. In other words, the distinction between the patient's habitual mood state and the way he usually feels and the state of disorder seen at an objective examination may be far from clearly drawn. It is a feature of the neuroses that there is considerable interaction between personality and response to stress or life events in the causation of the conditions and this is usually seen in cases of the depressive neuroses. The management of the condition is on similar lines to any other depressive illness with the difference that more obvious attention should be paid to psychological approaches to deal with elements in the personality once the symptoms have been dispersed, or at any rate controlled, with the help of medication. Cognitive behavioural therapy is probably the approach of choice and holds far greater promise than any assault directed at the core personality where attempts at amelioration usually result in, at best, equivocal results. The prognosis for this condition is invariably guarded. Where personality is so intimately involved in symptom formation and even influences the patient's attitude to life and the situations that he finds himself in, little else can be said with any confidence. As with all personality disorders, and defects in the personality not amounting to the disorder, the suspicion remains that the patient's clinical improvement or deterioration will depend largely on the prevailing circumstances of his life.

5.3　ANXIETY STATES

One of the more common neurotic states involves the presence in the patient of pathological levels of anxiety. Anxiety in this context refers to unnatural and inappropriate feelings of fear. It is normal – and an important part of survival, both personal and collective, in the evolutionary sense – to feel fear. Most animals keep an eye watchfully open for predators. The human animal is naturally concerned for its personal security when living in its modern habitation and is understandably concerned for the future. Even a measure of anxiety – short of pathological levels – appears necessary for success in life for it fuels motivation. In anxiety states this natural and appropriate fearfulness appears translated into an overwhelming sense of fear in regard to ordinary and seemingly normal situations. A patient may feel a sense of impending disaster when seated indoors, behind locked doors and in the absence of any obvious threatening stimulus. Another patient may become fearful about walking outdoors among people going about their routine and unremarkable business. A third may become exceedingly fearful in ordinary situations or in the presence of mundane objects or common and generally harmless creatures such as domestic pets where, in no obvious way, is such feeling serving any protective purpose. Anxiety states may be classified as being generalised anxiety states, panic states or as phobic disorders.

5.4   GENERALISED ANXIETY STATES

In generalised anxiety states the patient is subject to 'free floating' anxiety which may arise without any provocation or warning and in the absence of obvious stimuli. There is a feeling of great unease and of foreboding, a sense of some disaster waiting to strike imminently. The feeling of persistent anxiety differs from the episodic or paroxysmal feelings of anxiety which occur in panic disorders and are unrelated to specific situations as happens with the phobic disorders. This feeling is accompanied by physical symptoms such as palpitations, a dry mouth, a tightening in the chest, excessive sweating, a tremor of the extremities, sleep disturbance (characteristically an inability to get off to sleep), diarrhoea and an increased feelings of urgency and frequency of the urge to urinate and evacuate the bowels. There are also symptoms of physical tension such as a particular type of headache (usually described as feeling like a band around the head) and stiffness in the region of the back and neck. There is loss also of attention and concentration which, in turn, may lead to poor short-term memory. Insight is normally preserved, meaning the patient can recognise all these effects (will, indeed, complain about them and ask for help), attribute them to a nervous or mental phenomenon and confirm that something has definitely gone wrong with the mechanisms.

5.5   PANIC STATES

Panic attacks were previously considered to be part of any state of generalised anxiety but are now believed to occupy a discrete subcategory among the anxiety states. The symptoms of a panic state are well known and combine the physical symptoms seen in generalised anxiety states with an overpowering mental reaction – as a result of severe, periodic and paroxysmal attacks of anxiety – which may give rise also to feelings in which the patient's life may seem unreal or the world itself may appear unreal (depersonalisation and derealisation). Attacks tend to recur and are unpredictable, a state of affairs leading to much distress and also tending to feed the anxiety.

5.6   PHOBIC DISORDERS

In phobic disorders the anxiety is experienced in relation to a situation and is usually restricted to the experience of, or anticipation of, the stimuli associated with that situation. Phobic anxiety states refer to pathological and irrational fearfulness experienced in these specific situations. There is both quantitative and qualitative elements distinguishing these phobic states from normal responses. Children may fear the dark as a normal response and anxious adults become apprehensive in unlit locations. These fears do not usually handicap them in their daily existence, is a response shared by several persons and may, in fact, both be seen to be normal and sensible responses to reality. Phobic anxiety states are of a different order for the fear may be out of proportion to any threat inherent in the situation, it cannot be reasoned away, is beyond the control of the individual and leads to the avoidance of these situations. These fears are not shared by any large number of other citizens and, on occasion, may be socially disabling. Common phobias involve outside locations (agoraphobia), confined spaces (claustrophobia), social settings (social phobia) and such situations as heights, flying, spiders, domestic animals, needles and of contracting illnesses.

One of the most common of the phobias is agoraphobia (whose name is derived from the Greek for fear of the market place) involves intense fear of open spaces or large spaces which are built up and difficult to escape from such as supermarkets and shopping centres. It appears, at any rate in some cases, it is not so much the market but the situation of social contact that provokes the anxiety experienced indicating an overlap with social phobia. The phobia may also involve the fear of physical symptoms of anxiety and panic attacks in which case there is also overlap with the panic disorders. Young women appear to be preferentially involved and in extreme cases the patient may be reduced to being housebound. Social phobia extends well beyond normal shyness and bears all the hallmarks of an anxiety disorder. There could be difficulties in the personalities of these patients, with a lack of confidence and self-esteem and there is commonly a history of involvement in some incident or situation in the course of which the patient had not appeared to his best advantage. (One recalls the story about the eminent Cambridge economist whose arguments had been comprehensively demolished in a coruscating attack in a learned journal. He had not returned to Cambridge for some time afterward, pleading plaintively: 'I dare not return. Even the porters at the station will be laughing at me.' Happily he recovered without further incident.)

5.7   ANXIETY STATES – CAUSATION

Anxiety states are common and their prevalence comfortably outstrips the distribution of the psychotic conditions. The symptoms of anxiety are strongly suggestive of involvement of a part of a brain called the limbic system. There is a significant genetic component and features of anxiety may be seen to run in families where sometimes psychological contagion may also be implicated as a cause, unnaturally fearful parents infecting children under their influence. The environment undeniably plays a part. Anecdotal observation suggests that the modern overprotective parent can induce unnatural fearfulness in children so much so that a child today appears to be more apprehensive of situations, especially concerning outdoor activities, than its predecessor of a few generations ago (similar explanations are given for the apparent increase in allergies to all manner of stimuli among children and young adults believed to have been reared in excessively sanitary conditions). The other psychological explanation of note regarding causation involves faults in attachment in childhood, where early feelings of insecurity may be reactivated later in the form of anxiety in relation to the world and the objects within it. Whatever the suggested explanations, it seems certain that the primary foci responsible for these disorders will be found in some part of the brain.

5.8   ANXIETY STATES – TREATMENT

Treatment of the anxiety states involves both pharmacological and psychological approaches. The best known drugs for use in anxiety states are the benzodiazepine group including such agents as diazepam (Valium) and lorazepam. There is no doubt these drugs are effective in treatment in virtually all forms of anxiety but for some considerable time now their primary adverse effect has become all too well known – that they are also remarkably addictive. In fact, the anxiety in the patient having been successfully dealt with, the problem then arises that the patient needs to be weaned off these drugs, a process which sometimes causes far greater trauma to the patient than the symptoms of anxiety did in the first place. There is still a place for these drugs in the treatment of anxiety but that lies in the hands of specialist practitioners who may use it under strictly observed conditions – for short periods of time and as an adjunct to other treatments. These drugs may also have a place in the treatment of some phobic anxiety states where the anxiety-provoking situation is only met with occasionally, eg when the prospect of air travel looms to a patient suffering from anxiety in such a situation or a visit to a dental surgeon beckons for another who becomes anxious in those situations.

Other drugs have useful anxiety-relieving properties as side effects of their primary therapeutic use. The tricyclic antidepressant drugs discussed in the previous chapter have such effects which can be usefully mobilised in the treatment of anxiety. However, the more serious adverse effects of these drugs such as a fatal result in overdose constrain their widespread use. The modern SSRI group of drugs such as paroxetine and citalopram also have well recognised effects in reducing anxiety, although the paradoxical effect of making anxiety worse in some susceptible cases must be borne in mind. For all these reasons drug treatment of anxiety should be approached with care and left in specialist hands. Another group of drugs with useful anxiety-reducing features are the beta-blocking group of drugs such as propranolol. Their effects are on the physical manifestations of anxiety such as palpitations which they may be successful in reducing. The mind-body relationship may well be in evidence in these situations for it is believed a reduction in physical symptoms may lead in turn to an amelioration of the psychological effects and a virtuous circle is thereby caused to come into being.

Psychological treatment is well established in the management of anxiety states. At its simplest the procedures involve techniques of relaxation and anxiety-management being taught to the patient. Phobic anxiety states, in particular, submit well to psychological approaches. Perhaps the best known of the techniques employed with cases of phobic anxiety is called graded exposure by which the patient very gradually becomes attuned to approaching the object or situation that has caused dread previously and either comes to deal with the situation with greater equanimity or has his previous feelings replaced by not too disabling nervousness. Panic attacks and phobic anxiety states may also respond well to cognitive behavioural treatment which involves shifting – by means of reframing – the existing cognitive bias of the patient in a more positive direction. Social approaches must not be neglected as the patient's personal and social circumstances could, at least in part, be responsible for his anxiety state, causing it or maintaining it. It is necessary to deal with the mundane stresses the patient may be experiencing for his personality is, by and large, beyond correction.

5.9   ANXIETY STATES – PROGNOSIS

The prognosis of anxiety states is variable but is generally satisfactory. If an anxiety state is of acute onset and has followed discrete trauma such as, say, a road traffic accident leading to a phobic state about driving or travelling in a motor car, and the patient has a reasonably stable personality, the results are generally good if treatment is undertaken swiftly. As a general rule, the longer the symptom persists the less good is the outcome with any treatment, for symptoms can become entrenched through delay. Chronic anxiety states are much harder to deal with and delays in offering treatment may worsen the prognosis. An important point to bear in mind – as with all psychiatric disorders – is the danger of secondary disability supervening and exacerbating the primary difficulty. For unconscious and conscious reasons of gain – relief from some inner anxiety or some more obvious profit – the patient's symptoms could worsen, become entrenched and become unresponsive to treatment. The rule therefore is always to treat with vigour and to rehabilitate the patient promptly. With generalised anxiety states the previous personality of the patient may intrude upon treatment and may be a bar to successful recovery. Such patients may continue to be predisposed to relapse even while temporary short-term improvement can be produced. As might be imagined, the exigencies of the modern world inform the anxieties of many patients. Relationship insecurities, financial difficulties, employment uncertainties, poor housing or a run of misfortune, eg being a victim of street crime when one is recovering from a previous assault (something not unknown to happen in certain neighbourhoods) may defeat the best efforts of the most skilful of therapists.

5.10 ANXIETY STATES – RISKS

As will be discussed further in the next part of this book, the anxiety states are so pervasive in the community that many branches of the may become involved with patients suffering from anxiety states. Chronic disabling anxiety may impair employment duties and family and child law practitioners may come across a spouse, partner or parent whose duties have become compromised through the symptoms of anxiety. Anxiety states are also well known to lead to substance misuse, especially alcohol and cannabis misuse, which may bring about complications that attract the attention of the criminal law.

5.11 OBSESSIVE-COMPULSIVE DISORDER

A relatively uncommon neurosis but one which has become better appreciated in recent years is obsessive-compulsive disorder. This condition is characterised by obsessional thinking and/or compulsive actions. The former involves persistent and intrusive thoughts which are unwelcome to the patient who attempts to resist them and yet fails. This is not to be confused with being preoccupied with some thought, a common enough and perfectly normal experience. Compulsions or rituals are their motor equivalents leading to repetitive, usually non-productive or inefficient, behaviour. The patient may spend many hours engaged in rituals of diverse kinds which are meaningless to the observer. The commonest feature among these patients involves repeated handwashing. Thoughts and actions of this kind involving a patient can cause immense distress to the patient and eventually lead to destruction of family, social and occupational life.

An obsessive-compulsive disorder may exist in its own right or it could be part of the symptomatology of a depressive illness. Also, as some forms of brain damage can cause the features of obsessions and compulsions to emerge, it is believed the locus for pathology in this condition exists somewhere in the brain (very severe forms of the disorder are one of the rare indications for modern psychosurgery which may achieve good results where all other treatment has failed). However, as with all neuroses, the personality of the patient cannot be ignored when evaluating this disorder for a substantial majority of patients do have a pre-morbid obsessional personality which is characterised by a tendency to unusual orderliness and conscientious attention to detail, admirable characteristics in those in clerical or administrative occupation but not always tolerable when it forms the basis for pathology of this kind. It is common to see some stressful life event precipitating the neurosis in a susceptible individual who previously might only have displayed the features of an obsessional personality. Treatment involves both drugs and psychological approaches. Antidepressants, both of the SSRI group as well as the tricyclic agent clomipramine, have been shown to be useful. Behaviour therapy is also effective and a combination of drug and psychological treatment may well be the most effective approaches to the management of the condition. Untreated, there is risk of the condition becoming chronic. Treatment undertaken reasonably promptly after onset can achieve reasonably good results in the average case, although recurrence is not uncommon.

5.12   STRESS REACTIONS

While all neurotic conditions may generally be understood as being the reactions of vulnerable personalities to stress of some kind as perceived by them, stress reactions involve situations where the stress has been overwhelming or threatening in some way to the patient. It can be an acute reaction, arising immediately after the stressful event, or it could be delayed.

Acute stress reactions are emotional reactions that follow in close temporal proximity to some stressful event. The patient may become dazed or distressed with little recollection of the precipitating event and he could react by withdrawing himself or, conversely, by becoming excessively active. Many of the features of an acute anxiety state may be present. Treatment is by means of removing or alleviating the effects of the stressors, reassurance and a short course of medication which, in this instance, could be a member of the benzodiazepine group of drugs such as diazepam.

A more prolonged reaction to stress may lead to an adjustment disorder. The symptoms, similar to those found with the acute stress reactions, may last up to six months. There is a clearer presentation with symptoms such as anxiety and depression being present. Treatment approaches are similar although the use of standard antidepressant drugs may be more appropriate than employment of the benzodiazepine group of drugs. Counselling may be offered in addition to reassurance.

A more serious form of stress reaction is what is commonly referred to as post-traumatic stress disorder (PTSD). The probably much overused diagnosis remains controversial. It is moot whether a severe acute anxiety state associated with depressive symptoms is truly distinguishable from what is called PTSD, and whether the latter term adds anything to an understanding of the severe emotional reactions which have been long been known to follow exceptionally traumatic events, eg 'shell shock'.

PTSD follows serious trauma, eg major disasters, violent personal assaults, grave road traffic accidents and its association with war continues – with its modern description being born out of the Vietnam war. This condition may be defined as:

> 'a delayed and/or protracted response to a stressful event or situation of an exceptionally threatening or catastrophic nature.'

One of the more common features of the condition is the tendency of patients to re-live the experiences of the traumatic event either in nightmares or as 'flashback' phenomena during their waking hours. There may be present the more usual symptoms of anxiety and depression along with a detachment displayed by the patient from ordinary concerns. There may also be avoidance of situations related to the precipitating trauma and the anxiety may provoke hypersensitivity to light and sound and cause also a startle response. There is a common association with misuse of alcohol and illicit drugs. If it is to be diagnosed at all strict diagnostic guidelines should be followed.

Treatment of the condition, as previously mentioned, has raised surprising controversy given its widespread diagnosis in recent years. There is a place for drug treatment in the form of antidepressant agents such as paroxetine and sertraline. Cognitive behavioural therapy is known to be effective, especially in combination with drugs. The technique of eye movement desensitisation and reprocessing (EMDR) in which the patient is encouraged to think of an image of the trauma while his eyes move from side to side has been claimed to be effective, but it is still not clear what form psychological intervention should take. The extensive 'debriefing' that was routinely practised soon after the victim had emerged in the immediate aftermath of the tragedy has been questioned in some quarters with some holding this activity may tend to make things worse or even retard recovery. Some others have even gone as far as saying these victims should be left alone to recover with the help of their 'stiff upper lips'. The truth, no doubt, will appear in the course of time as to what, if any, approach should be taken although clinical experience already suggests that, as with any clinical procedure, there should be careful sifting of victims to see who is most likely to benefit from counselling. Statutory agencies, charities and commercial organisations often automatically offer their services to victims following traumatic events. Fearing litigation, some companies require their employees to undergo 'debriefing' following certain incidents. More promising are studies which show good results when the intervention was not offered to everyone indiscriminately but only to a minority with acute stress disorders who are at higher risk of developing subsequent psychiatric disorder. The interventions in this successful situation involved multiple sessions and was based on a cognitive-behavioural model. Another study involved work with the Marines. All ranks had been offered simple training so that when disasters happened the 'therapist' and 'patient' shared a common culture and outlook which gets over the problem of using strangers unknown to the patient and invariably coming from another 'culture'. What form any mental disorder following trauma has taken is a matter for detailed clinical analysis rather than short-hand diagnostic descriptions such as PTSD. What treatment, if any, should be given to the patient in these cases will depend on the precise delineation of symptoms present, the past history and an evaluation of the patient's previous personality, and not on any diagnosis alone. A study undertaken among service personnel found that PTSD and post-traumatic stress symptoms were not associated with consequent disability. Rather, it was the co-morbid symptoms of depression that were significantly associated with disability. The clinical importance of PTSD and post-traumatic stress symptoms may therefore become questionable if they are not a cause of disability.

The prognosis for stress reactions is in general good. An impaired prognosis is associated with delay in treatment, where there is misuse of substances following the reaction to stress and where there has been a delay in rehabilitation when in common with most psychiatric conditions of this type, a disabling secondary handicap can supervene.

Stress reactions can cause risk-associated behaviour to arise, in many situations involving the law. The criminal law, family and child law, employment law and, of course, personal injury law may all become involved. These matters will be taken up in detail in Part II of this book.

5.13 HYSTERIA

History justifies the inclusion of hysterical reactions in a book of this nature in that it has historical sanction and the condition, in its way, helped to define both neurology and psychiatry. The disorder involves unconscious mechanisms which, perhaps as a result of their subterranean presence, are far from clearly understood despite several years of study. There is undeniably a strong cultural and social background to the condition for gross examples of hysteria are now rare in the West although still observable in many parts of the developing world and also in migrant communities in the developed world. Hysterical symptoms are usually diagnosed in the absence of so-called 'organic' features of illness. These symptoms, subdivided into dissociative symptoms and conversion symptoms, are therefore diagnosed by exclusion, dissociative symptoms are believed to represent a loss of normal correspondence between different mental processes. Conversion refers to the translation of anxieties into physical symptoms. The short explanation to be proffered in seeking an understanding of this condition is to say that when a patient is confronted by unbearable and irresolvable anxiety as a result of some inner conflict, the unconscious mechanisms at work translate this conflict into physical symptoms thereby giving the patient what is called primary gain through relief from anxiety. Secondary gain may then arise from any practical advantage to be accrued by sporting the symptom to the world.

The symptoms in question are manifold and may include amnesia, wandering (the fugue state), stupor, trance and possession states, motor paralysis and sensory loss and, in extreme cases, multiple personality disorder. The other symptom of note is *la belle indifference* which refers to an apparent lack of concern shown by some patients towards their symptoms and is often regarded as being characteristic of conversion/dissociative states. Recent studies, in fact, have shown that true 'organic' illness may underlie conversion symptoms and that this finding of indifference actually discriminates poorly between 'organic' and 'functional' symptoms. In fact, serious physical illness such as multiple sclerosis may initially present with symptoms which, as they often non-plus the clinician in the early stages of the disorder, are not uncommonly damned as being hysterical. Treatment is by way of intensive psychological investigation for which relatively few of these patients are suitable. Notwithstanding this, the results in the acute state, ie where symptoms are short-lived, may be surprisingly good although recurrence is not uncommon.

5.14   SOMATOFORM DISORDERS

In this category exist those conditions where patients present with somatic or physical symptoms which have no obvious basis in a known physical disorder and which cannot be explained as being features of other psychiatric conditions such as depressive illness or anxiety states. The cultural background of the patient must be taken into account for, as stated before, it is common for patients from African and Asian communities to present with physical symptoms even when the underlying condition is one such a depressive illness.

The concern about physical symptoms may involve the presence of an illness or deformity or may involve only preoccupation about a symptom or some group of symptoms. By definition, these concerns or symptoms must have no basis in some obvious physical condition or be disproportionate in relation to some actual condition. Other psychiatric conditions involving mood changes, delusions or hysterical reactions need to be excluded also. These conditions may appear to have a strong environmental bias in that deprivation or abuse in childhood or an upbringing by anxious parents may be risk factors.

Patients with hypochondriasis are preoccupied with the idea that they are suffering from a serious physical condition. Recurrent complaints of physical symptoms yield little or nothing by way of physical investigation which, in some of these cases, can be extensive and prolonged. There is no alternative to full investigation of these symptoms for the elusive 'real' cause of the symptoms; the skill comes in knowing when to put a stop to investigation and to resist the entreaties and importunities of the patient. Closely related to this condition is another where the preoccupation is with bodily appearance (dysmorphic disorder). The patient's life may become very restricted as a result of preoccupation with, say, the notion that one's nose is grossly misshapen and demands may be made for a referral for cosmetic surgery.

Closely related, at any rate in appearance, is the condition referred to as the chronic fatigue syndrome. The main complaint here is that of a persistent and disabling mental and physical fatigue. One cause of this condition appears to be myalgic encephalomyelitis (ME). As said repeatedly throughout this book, all these conditions are likely to have their origins in some form of brain dysfunction but present day knowledge does not as yet allow any formulation in those terms. This outcome appears to be especially upsetting to ME sufferers who, caught up in medieval distinctions between body and mind, actively resent and resist any suggestion their symptoms are 'all in the mind', implying that they are second-class patients. Treatment of all these conditions is difficult. There appears to be some scope for antidepressant treatment although results with CBT, if and when accepted by patients, are often better. The prognosis is variable, better results being obtained in hypochondriacal states (where the patient may at least be persuaded to remain socially active despite the symptoms, with the help of apt references being made to public figures who discharge their functions despite suffering apparently disabling conditions) than with sufferers of the chronic fatigue syndrome where the preoccupation with proving a 'physical' basis is often associated with a poor outcome. For what it is worth, the overriding approach should be to encourage patients to lead as full and active a life as is possible.

5.15   SUMMARY

- The risk of developing any of the neurotic conditions is that they are due to, and their natural history is heavily influenced by, the personality of the individual concerned. As personality is for all practical purposes beyond any fundamental correction, treatment in many cases may only have a limited impact. A simple method for understanding these disorders is to consider them to be the result of an interaction between an individual's personality and his reaction to some stressful event. Where the personality is stable, and the impact of some discrete stressful event a relatively powerful one, the results from treatment appear to be appreciably better.

- Although the neurotic conditions are described as minor psychiatric disorders their consequences can be serious. Both depressive illness and anxiety states are well known to lead to misuse of alcohol and illicit drugs resulting in the individual's behaviour impinging on the subject matter of both the criminal law and family and child law. Chronic neurotic conditions may prove so disabling that sustained employment could be compromised. Obsessive-compulsive states could also become disabling with implications for an individual's overall functioning. The somatoform disorders may prove wasteful of resources including clinicians' time.

CHAPTER 6

DISORDERS OF DEPENDENCE AND APPETITE

6.1   INTRODUCTION

Substance abuse, the term used to collectively designate misuse of alcohol and illicit substances, is much misunderstood which is paradoxical given the prominence the subject attracts in the media. One reason for this is that, despite the vast resources given to the study of the problem, objective scientific evidence in respect of many aspects of the difficulties concerning these substances is still sparse.

6.2   ALCOHOL

Alcohol is easily the most widely used of the common intoxicants. Some 90 per cent of the British public use the substance while the figure for the United States is around 60 per cent, a preliminary indication of the differences between cultures in the use of alcohol. While alcohol-related problems are far commoner than those associated with illicit substances, the extent of alcohol misuse is not known with any certainty. Up to 10 per cent of the British public are perhaps heavy consumers of alcohol, if one takes the recommended 'safe' limits (see below) as being 21 units per week for the adult male and 14 units per week for an adult female as the guide. An example was given[1] of how even a teetotaller or novice could get caught up in a variety of complications associated with even a one-off heavy use and come to display the features of alcohol-related problems. The example also illustrated the importance of looking at the facts in any individual case. It is not always the quantity of alcohol or drug abused or the prolonged history of misuse that may be in point but the behaviours engaged in by the individual which are recorded in the facts of the case. A practical definition, based upon one given by the World Health Organisation itself, is that abuse of alcohol occurs in those who drink excessively to such an extent that alcohol use has attained a degree which shows noticeable disturbance or an interference with their bodily and mental health, their personal relationships and smooth economic functioning or who show prodromal signs of such a development and, therefore, require treatment.

---

[1]   See B Mahendra *Adult Psychiatry in Family and Child Law* (Family Law, 2006).

6.3   ALCOHOL – THE EFFECTS

There are various categories of misuse of alcohol. The simplest to
understand is intoxication which is an acute effect of consuming too
much (for a particular individual). There is then 'at risk' consumption
where physical, mental or social harm may follow from persistently
exceeding the recommended 'safe' limits. Then comes harmful use where,
in the absence of dependence or addiction, there is misuse associated with
health and social consequences. Thereafter comes true addiction. Alcohol
can cause physical dependence. By this is meant tolerance has developed,
in other words, more and more needs to be drunk to obtain the same
behavioural effect. This also means a hardened drinker can consume
considerable quantities before showing signs of intoxication whereas
someone like the novice mentioned above needs only a few drinks before
showing obvious changes in behaviour. Next, there may be withdrawal
effects in the absence of sufficient alcohol in the system which include
tremor, agitation, sweating, nausea, irritability and feelings of anxiety and
panic along with a craving for more drink. These withdrawal symptoms
can be quelled by drinking a sufficient quantity of alcohol which leads to
a vicious circle being brought into operation. Regular drinking to avoid
the symptoms of withdrawal sets in, the individual becomes preoccupied
with drinking and drink-related behaviour. Soon, if measures are not
taken to curb the consumption of alcohol, drinking becomes the primary
activity in the individual's life at the expense of all others.

Physical and mental effects follow persistent drinking. Bodily effects
include damage to the liver. At first, fat infiltrates the liver cells. Later, the
liver shrinks with the onset of cirrhosis. Alcoholic hepatitis may present
itself. If drinking continues in these circumstances the liver may fail
altogether in its functions, and coma and death supervene. If abstinence
can be brought about, and sustained, repair of the liver can take place for
the organ has remarkable powers of recovery and regeneration. Effects
may also be seen in the gastro-intestinal system with oesophageal and
peptic ulceration. Bleeding from oesophageal varices leads to the
well-known symptom of vomiting of blood in these patients, who also
eliminate dark coloured faeces (melaena). The blood present in the gut
helps turn it darker in the course of its passage through the bowel. Heart
and circulatory problems may also follow with an enlarged heart and
elevated blood pressure in consequence. Considerable disturbance may
also be seen in both the central and peripheral nervous systems. Effects on
the brain may lead to blackouts, amnesia and fits. Peripheral neuropathy
may give rise to motor and sensory deficits along with paralysis later on.
It is no exaggeration to say that every bodily function may be adversely
affected through persistent alcohol abuse.

Running in parallel are the mental complications due to persistent alcohol
abuse. The symptoms due to states of withdrawal have been noted above.
Fits may follow as well as the dangerous and potentially lethal condition

called delirium tremens in which consciousness fluctuates and, classically, visual hallucinations involving usually small animals (rats or insects) but occasionally larger creatures ('pink elephants') are seen. Fleeting persecutory ideas may be present. Alcoholic psychosis of a more sustained kind may also be seen later. There is a notorious connection between alcohol and depression. Alcohol is a depressant, a fact not always recognised by those who mainly see its disinhibiting properties. The depression it induces leads usually to more drinking in an attempt to dull the senses and, thereby, more depression ensues which means there is another vicious circle also in operation. About 10 per cent of patients with alcohol dependence commit suicide. Sexual dysfunction ('it provokes the desire but takes away the performance') and deterioration in personality and social functioning are common consequences. The impact on social life can prove considerable. Apart from involvement with the criminal law, there are also consequences for employment, and accidents are more common. The impact on family life may also be substantial and these matters will be taken up later.

6.4   ALCOHOL – THE RISK FACTORS

Despite many years of intensive study, those at risk of developing alcohol-related problems cannot be pinpointed with any accuracy. There is a clear genetic factor but this generally shows a predisposition not only to alcohol abuse but also to depressive illness, in other words there may be 'alcohol equivalents', a predisposed individual going on to suffer depressive illness rather than having problems with alcohol. Environmental factors are dominant influences. Cultural influences may also play a part. In rural communities alcohol was used for the purpose of celebration, especially at the time of the gathering in of the harvest. As society industrialised, grew more urban and prospered, the form of alcohol-related problems became more uniform. There may also be racial differences in the way alcohol is metabolised and in the occurrence of phenomena such as hangovers and withdrawal effects which could lead to excessive drinking in some communities. There seems no doubt that the ready availability of alcoholic beverages in the community can contribute significantly to an increased prevalence of problems concerning alcohol misuse. Economic factors are also important. It has been shown that alcohol has become cheaper in 'real terms' over time, making its routine use within the reach of most pockets. Thus, there seems to be a close relationship between per capita alcohol consumption and alcohol-related problems and an inverse correlation between the 'real' price of drink (as a percentage of average disposable income) and national per capita consumption of alcohol. Finland is among several countries where relaxation of previously restrictive licensing laws had been shown to cause significant increases in alcohol consumption. As the recent debate on the relaxation of the licensing laws showed, there are also quite considerable cultural and subcultural influences at work. As has been repeatedly pointed out, the patterns of drinking in Continental Europe are appreciably different to those found in Britain. In those countries there is still much stigma attached to public drunkenness (whose manifestations, even without disorderly conduct, attract official sanctions in those parts) and there appears to be an altogether socially more appropriate and responsible approach to the consumption of alcohol compared to the excesses which habitually mark and disfigure British life.

There is no hard and fast rule pointing to any community or group that may be preferentially at risk of developing alcohol-related problems. Social change had rendered out of date the assertions that certain occupations – bar staff, journalists, manual workers, mariners – were preferentially at higher risk. Clinical practice reveals virtually all trades and professions now represented, not to mention those who have no occupation. The professional bodies concerned with both doctors and lawyers have expressed their alarm at the prevalence of alcohol-related problems among their members and have established formal assistance for those affected. One striking social change is the presence now of women and, increasingly, younger children among the ranks of problem drinkers. The advice, which is somewhat conservative in its import it has to be admitted, as to what might constitute 'safe' drinking allows 21 units of alcohol per week for adult males and 14 units of alcohol for adult females. Common observation shows that large numbers of individuals comfortably exceed the conservative limits proposed and suffer no discernible harm. Even the consumption of a bottle of wine a day – easily achievable in the circumstances of modern life – may mean the individual concerned may be consuming more than three times the recommended limit if a man and up to five times the limit if a woman. What constitutes a unit of alcohol is not without controversy. A half-pint of standard bitter beer, a measure of spirits or a glass of wine were conventionally deemed to make up a unit of alcohol. But this assumption has been undermined by the growing alcoholic strength of beverages and also by social and cultural change such as the growing preference for New World wine and lager beer which may be much stronger in alcohol strength than the counterpart beverages. It seems a matter of urgency that more realistic advice is proffered to citizens if mass disobedience, seemingly openly practised, is to be corrected.

6.5   ALCOHOL – TREATMENT

The actual treatment is more problematical than allowed for by many lay persons. The truth is that there is little by way of any specific treatment for alcohol-related problems. What there is is advice and support to assist such a person to bring his problems under control. It is *par excellence* a problem which requires self-help. It follows that the single most important determinant of success in treatment is the motivation and attitude shown by the individual. Without this, all help will be futile and fail. The patient must accept with true insight – mere lip service is insufficient – that he or she has a problem with alcohol and has to take steps to counter this problem and bring it under control. This means the patient must also feel he or she has the necessary incentive to 'turn over a new leaf'.

Results of treatment of alcohol misuse are far from satisfactory. Where dependency exists, the first requirement is detoxification, by which means alcohol is leached from the system through abstinence. This can be achieved in the community but a hospital setting is favoured when community detoxification has previously failed and in cases in which intercurrent physical or psychiatric conditions are also found. Detoxification may be supported through treatment with benzodiazepine drugs such as chlordiazepoxide. Vitamins are prescribed as ancillary agents to forestall some neurological complications that may follow withdrawal. That, in most cases, is the easy part of the management. The altogether more challenging task is to maintain the state of abstinence or of controlled drinking. Some drugs may be of use – disulfiram and acamprosate are two of the agents used – but the treatment at this stage is predominantly psychological. Support and advice are the key elements. Cognitive behavioural therapy, social skills training and motivational enhancement may assist.

There appears also to be considerable interest in objective indices of alcohol abuse. Liver function tests are commonly utilised for this purpose. As a snapshot of current heavy drinking they may have some use but their limitations must be understood. Increased liver enzymes, in the absence of liver disease or concurrent medication, may be indicative of heavy persistent drinking. But the liver, as we have seen, has substantial powers of recuperation and regeneration and absence of disordered liver function may denote little more than a temporary period of abstinence. There is little alternative to taking a holistic view in relation to any patient suspected of heavy drinking, clinical observation being supplemented by the reports of witnesses. Heavy drinking, in itself, can be concealed but its effects – on domestic life, child care, social activity, occupation – can rarely be kept hidden over any period of time. Any deficiency in behaviour will usually be apparent if observation continues long enough.

Too much emphasis is often laid on the 'treatment' aspect of management of alcohol-related problems. In truth, specific help by means of pharmacological treatment is very limited, being reserved for some select and exceptional cases and has no application in the vast majority of cases seen in practice. Treatment therefore ordinarily means counsel, advice and support deployed through community-based agencies. Counselling provided by public agencies may be complemented with attendance at Alcoholics Anonymous, an organisation that is sometimes mocked but which has a useful ancillary part to play in assisting the motivated patient with his rehabilitation.

6.6   ALCOHOL – THE PROGNOSIS

Since the disease concept of alcoholism is largely a matter of form and convenience, and the specific medical element in any treatment is so small, it is a somewhat artificial exercise to talk of prognosis in any accepted medical sense. However, over a period of years, clinicians have utilised their experience of these cases and the accumulated knowledge to arrive at a 'rule of thumb'. It is believed two years usually have to elapse – involving either abstinence or controlled drinking – before one can sign off a patient as being 'cured' of the disease of alcoholism, albeit perhaps only for the time being. The danger period is in the early phase of abstinence. Nobody knows for certain how many 'fall off the wagon' – that is, drop out of treatment – but it is believed that in the first six months following abstinence some 50 per cent of patients will relapse. There are those who argue that a tendency to alcohol misuse is a life long affliction and that as a result one can only speak of remissions and exacerbations. Be that as it may, the patient has to show evidence that he has attained mastery over drink, however temporarily. Whether he can aim for controlled drinking in the future rather than settle for the somewhat monastic existence involving total abstinence is usually determined entirely on an individual basis, by trial and error in most cases, and there can be no hard and fast rule as to who could aim for moderate social drinking and who should aim for abstinence for life. Some individuals will not be able to touch another drop, others may be able to develop a much more socially appropriate modus vivendi with alcohol. It is one of those decisions that patient and counsellor need to work out following a course of treatment.

Once alcohol has been defeated, on however short-term a basis, the patient needs to be reassessed in terms of his mental state. Alcohol can mask many problems and once it is out of the picture one may be able to see if there remain difficulties such as depressive illness, anxiety states, chronic pain etc which might have induced, or contributed to, the original bout of heavy drinking. It is obviously more rational to treat any underlying condition which might have been a significant causative factor in the previous drinking in its own right rather than leave the patient at risk of relapse into further drinking. More ordinary social repair work can also be contemplated for such matters as marital or relationship difficulties, financial problems, poor housing or occupational concerns.

In the ultimate analysis, any prognosis to be given, as might be expected, is very variable. The only valid point to make is that if there is any underlying problem, and if this remains or recurs, the danger of relapse could be high. In the end one is reduced to saying that if the patient derives greater satisfaction from alcohol – or, at any rate, greater relief from emotional pain from drinking – than from more normal social pursuits and satisfactions then he may have greater incentive to take or return to drinking. On the other hand, if the physical and mental well-being associated with a freedom from excessive drinking enables him to pursue worthwhile and rewarding social goals, it is likely the balance will shift in the opposite direction. The concerned professional, confronted with a patient or client with alcohol-related problems will do well to see how the balance sheet in respect of these matters reads.

6.7　ILLICIT DRUGS

There are many drugs that are in common use. Some of these drugs include those which are legitimately prescribed and have genuine medical properties for use in those cases for which there is a need for them to be prescribed but which, occasionally, find their way in large quantities into the hands of patients (whether those for whom they were originally prescribed or others). We are not here concerned with these prescribed drugs. Rather, we shall concentrate our attentions here on cannabis, the opiate drugs, the amphetamines and cocaine which, in the public eye and in respect of public health, are the illicit drugs, so to speak, of substance. The problem involving illicit substances is not at all uncommon. It has been estimated that at least three per cent of the population, that is about two million people in Britain, will take illicit drugs at any given time. In the nature of things this figure is likely to be an underestimate, apart from causing the mental and behavioural consequences of misuse in their own right their association with mental disorder (co-morbidity, as it is called) is significant. More than 40 per cent of patients managed by community mental health teams reported problem drug use and/or harmful alcohol use among the patients in the previous year. The general perception among professionals is that co-morbidity has a much greater impact on services than its single components with increased psychiatric admission, violence and poor treatment outcomes.

6.8　CANNABIS

This is probably the most commonly used of the illicit drugs. It is used as marijuana, hashish and ganja and consumed on virtually every continent on the globe. It is imported from the tropics (an area said to be increasing in extent on account of climate change) although Cannabis sativa, the hemp plant from which these substances are derived, can be grown with success in Britain and aficionados of the drug relish the superior quality of the home-grown product. The main psychoactive component is delta-9-tetrahydrocannabinol (THC) which acts on susceptible receptors in the brain. Cannabis is usually smoked neat or combined with tobacco, but can also be eaten on its own or after being baked into cakes and biscuits. Its fumes have a distinctive odour when smoked, nowadays to be considered as part of the smells of the street. It has been a drug which has been used in some cultures for centuries and has the status of a staple recreational agent much as tobacco used to have elsewhere. Its effects are very variable and dependent on the purity of the source, the amount taken, the route through which it is absorbed, the personality of the consumer and the social and cultural expectations in play. In cultures where its use is traditional it is accepted as a relaxant and as an aid to social intercourse and conviviality. It has a tendency to exaggerate the mood existing at the time of consumption – the calm become mellow, the forceful more aggressive. There may be a tendency to distort space and time and judgment may be impaired in relation to many matters including motor performance (the word used in its widest sense to include vehicular propulsion). In some users increased anxiety may progress to agitation and even paranoid behaviour. However, it has long also been associated with apathy and lack of motivation, and debate has raged as to whether it is the laid-back individual who is drawn to its use or if the drug itself induces feelings of relaxed indifference and insouciance. These effects are deemed to be psychological and it is not clear whether physical dependence can also arise as with alcohol or the opiate drugs.

There have been reports of pulmonary complications following prolonged use though confirmation of this is awaited. However, what is of renewed psychiatric interest is the implication of cannabis in cases of psychotic breakdown where it has been alleged that the drug can precipitate or induce psychotic symptoms in a predisposed individual. Similar claims have also been made for the precipitation of violence following its use. Neither the inducement of psychosis nor the production of violence is a universal feature and it appears to be the case that a susceptibility, probably of the genetic kind, is required as a pre-condition for psychosis and/or violence to arise. Concurrent other substance misuse may also be a contributory factor. Nevertheless, it is probably true to say the drug is by no means as benign as claimed by those who campaigned for its decriminalisation, a revised point of view now seemingly accepted by the authorities who fear another problem drug may have fallen into their hands and are now preparing to advance its status back to being a Class B substance, the category it occupied until it was relegated to Class C.

6.9   THE OPIATE DRUGS

Like many drugs that are now abused socially, the opiates have had a parallel history of having been very valuable weapons in the medical armamentarium for decades. Morphine, heroin (diamorphine) and codeine along with synthetic derivatives such as pethidine and dextropropoxyphene continue to have legitimate medical use. Opium has, of course, been used and abused for centuries and a subculture of abusers, some intellectuals, others mere addicts, has existed probably in every age and in every society. The most important illicit use nowadays concerns heroin which finds its way into the streets of Britain from origins in Afghanistan and Pakistan (an important reason for the maintenance of the current war in the former country). As with cocaine, commerce is difficult to control in large part because of the importance of the substance to the local economies; intricate networks of supply supplemented by the financial infrastructure needed to support the trade are in place. The effects of the drug are virtually indistinguishable from those seen when it is used in some form in legitimate medical practice save for the complications due to contaminants. Purity is variable and when a pure supply of the drug occasionally hits the streets many deaths not uncommonly occur as users do not allow for the strength of the uncontaminated product when they unwittingly consume it. The drug may be smoked, inhaled or injected. Dependence of the physical type can supervene – sometimes following single use – and withdrawal effects are similar to those seen in alcohol deprivation with an added element of more intense craving, a state in which the individual is prepared to sacrifice everything, including his liberty and even his life, in the pursuit of the drug. The feelings experienced on use include euphoria. With chronic use there could be malaise (which may lead to repeated use in an attempt to regain the experience of euphoria), loss of appetite and interest and libido, constipation and the tell-tale sign of pinpoint pupils. Tolerance is usual as in all substances leading to physical dependence. The euphoric feeling which follows its immediate use is difficult to replicate with the same repeated dose, so the amount taken needs to be increased, resulting in the phenomenon of tolerance. Death follows overdose which leads to respiratory depression. Other complications include the high risk of infections and thrombosis following intravenous use. The use of needles also leads to the risk of contracting hepatitis B and C and HIV infections. In general the severity and length of withdrawal depends on the nature of the drug being abused, shorter acting drugs tending to have more severe withdrawal symptoms over shorter periods as compared to longer acting drugs. The symptoms noted on withdrawal may include anxiety and agitation, sleeplessness, sweating, muscle pains and cramps, diarrhoea and vomiting, dilated pupils, a running nose and a sense of feeling cold. The onset of withdrawal symptoms is usually within 8–12 hours of the last dose, with the most intense withdrawal symptoms experienced over 24–48 hours and subsiding over 7–10 days.

The opiates, when used outside of medical supervision, are as socially destructive as any substance that can be imagined and life expectancy used to be drastically reduced in untreated cases, quite apart from the complications arising from infections due to contaminated needles, intercurrent infection and concurrent medical disorders. Two-thirds of heroin users have had drug overdoses and one-third of them have done so in the previous year. Part of the reason attributed to this is that, as we have seen, the purity of heroin can vary so that, especially when injecting, the exact dose being taken is unpredictable. It has also been suggested as an alternative explanation that near-death experience may form part of the desired euphoric effect due to heroin. Methadone overdose has also been reported to be on the increase.

6.10   AMPHETAMINES

These drugs also had legitimate medical use in the days before standard antidepressant drugs came into being to elevate the mood in depressive illness and more recently for conditions such as attention deficit hyperactivity disorder (ADHD) and narcolepsy. It is freely available on the streets nowadays – methyl amphetamine use is now said to be the biggest public health hazard in terms of illicit drug use – and its commonplace nature sometimes leads to these drugs being treated with disdain and contempt among the authorities. Its effects are initially to produce euphoria along with the appearance of increased physical and mental energy. However, persecutory ideas along with paranoid states (indistinguishable from the usual run of paranoid disorders) may also be seen and convulsions are not unknown. The actions of the drug are short-lived – no more than a few hours – and, if the effect is not sustained by repeat use, there is the 'downer' element in which depression and lethargy supervene. Sleep and appetite, both suppressed with use, may remain permanently impaired.

6.11   COCAINE

This drug has effects similar to the amphetamines. It is derived from the coca plant in South America and the substance is a mainstay of the economy of countries such as Colombia. A more powerful part-synthetic derivative is called 'crack cocaine', which is notoriously even more addictive than native cocaine. The substance is conventionally inhaled, snorted or 'piped' (a form of inhalation using glass vessels in which holes are drilled to convey fumes drawn from cocaine which has been ignited on top). Its effects, though more dramatic than those seen with the amphetamines, last an even shorter time than the amphetamines and repeat use has to be resorted to. There is an increase in physical and mental energy and feeling of euphoria following use. As with the amphetamines, a complication of recurrent use can be paranoid psychosis and there may be present a combination of psychological and physical dependence. A stimulant dependence syndrome – usually involving the amphetamines but increasingly also cocaine and 'crack' cocaine – has been mooted.

6.12   SOME OTHER ILLICIT DRUGS

Ecstasy is a synthetic amphetamine derivative (3,4-methylene-dioxymethamphetamine) which is in part stimulant and part hallucinogen. Its use is commonplace among significant numbers of teenage children part of whose 'clubbing' experience the drug provides. Its adverse effects include hyperpyrexia (elevated body temperature) and acute renal failure due to dehydration as well as water intoxication following attempts to compensate for water loss. Acute psychotic conditions may also be seen. Concern has been expressed that long term emotional and cognitive effects could persist even after cessation of use.

Hallucinogenic drugs include 'magic mushrooms' and the synthetic preparation lysergic acid diethylamide (LSD). Hallucinations and other sensory distortions are the usual feature following use of these substances with distorted sense of time and space and changes in body image. Dependence is psychological but there is the possibility of 'flashback' phenomena, that is, the sensations due to the drug being re-lived even after a good deal of time has passed since the drug was last consumed.

6.13   ILLICIT DRUGS – TREATMENT

The assessment and treatment of illicit drug abuse follows the principles set out in regard to the treatment of alcohol misuse. In general terms there is little by way of an underlying medical reason – save those cases where opiate dependence has followed therapeutic use of these drugs – for becoming dependent on or abusing these substances. Social conditions are now such that problematical abuse of these drugs now mostly follows the casual or recreational use of these substances. Medical complications may, of course, follow their use. Dependence in the physical sense is common with the opiates and is occasionally probable with amphetamine and cocaine use but only psychological dependence is normally seen with cannabis use. Psychological dependence means, broadly speaking, the patient feels he can take or leave the substance, but its effects being such – the sense of relaxation, increased sociability, confidence and well-being – that the patient is drawn into continuing use of the drug. It may be thought that a distinction between physical and psychological dependence in these circumstances is little more than academic.

The actual medical treatment of cases of misuse of illicit substances is limited, being restricted in the main to the management of opiate dependence. Detoxification may be carried out in an in-patient setting or in the community. The former is probably the preferable option as control is easier to maintain and there is the added bonus that concurrent physical and mental disorder can be investigated and, where possible, treated. Maintenance (or substitution) therapy is now a common feature of long-term treatment of opiate misuse although not all practitioners are convinced of the efficacy of maintenance treatment. The purpose of maintenance drug treatment is to achieve some control over the patient's drug use by prescribing him maintenance drugs rather than leaving him to seek these or other drugs on the street. By such means his use of the drug may become stabilised, he may be able to give up such hazardous means of consumption as injecting himself, with all the complications that could follow such a course, and be able to divert himself from criminal conduct which he usually has to engage in to fund his habit. The majority of patients with opiate dependency tend to be managed, at least at some point, in a maintenance programme. It is said that maintenance treatment of this kind retains patients in treatment, reduces illicit drug use, diminishes criminal activity and may also lower the incidence of HIV, hepatitis B and hepatitis C infection. It may also improve the chances of resocialisation. The substitute prescribing usually involves oral methadone in a dose necessary to control withdrawal symptoms. The aim generally is to reduce the methadone over time and cease its prescription altogether but there will always be patients who will need long-term substitution drug prescription and dispensing. Bupronorphine (Subutex) is an alternative drug used on similar principles.

The rest of the treatment consists essentially of advice, support and counsel. A variety of treatment approaches have been tried with little by way of consistent results. The timescales used in measuring prognosis are as for treatment of alcohol misuse. The prognosis in the short-term is probably comparable to that achieved in cases of alcohol misuse, the longer term prognosis could be worse, though sharp individual variations are to be found. Motivation is the key to the stopping the use of all substances when misused and for keeping away from them. Progress in treatment may be monitored with the aid of objective measurements such as by testing hair strands for the presence of illicit substances. These measures are most useful when a patient is under treatment and regular hair strand testing for drugs can be undertaken to see if progress is being made in respect of controlling the use of the drug and, later, to ensure abstinence is maintained. Random drug tests are occasionally undertaken in family and child proceedings and are of limited value, whether positive or negative values are obtained. It cannot be overemphasised that, as in the case of alcohol misuse, what is really in point in these proceedings is the actual behaviour of an individual. As will be discussed in detail in Part II of this book, the matter that normally concerns the law is the actual behaviour of an individual, not simply the extent of his substance misuse.

An important aspect of alcohol and drug use is the social scene in which these substances are indulged, in other words the social relationships and networks fostered among users, along with the sense of camaraderie which follows any involvement in what could be seen to be daring and unlawful activity. This may mean breaking away from the illicit drug scene is difficult – conveying also perhaps a sense of betrayal or treachery in respect of one's comrades – even when the patient is otherwise motivated and has the incentive to desist from further use.

Untreated, the picture can be dire. Apart from accidents and suicide, intercurrent infections and those complications directly attributable usually to intravenous drug use, there is the ever present risk of entanglement with the criminal law as these substances remain unlawful to possess or distribute and the cost of their consumption is not negligible. Apart from medical and legal complications there is also always the risk of social and personal degradation involving the patient.

However, all is not lost if the patient seriously engages in treatment. Recent studies have shown that some hope is permissible in cases of opiate dependence. On a 30-year follow up of patients who had suffered injected heroin abuse, 42 per cent of patients had been abstinent for at least 10 years following treatment, 10 per cent of patients were continuing to take methadone and 22 per cent of patients were dead.

6.14   PATHOLOGICAL GAMBLING

A few words need to be said about this condition in view of the social and legislative changes that have led to the easing of previous restrictions on gambling. Pathological gambling is a hidden menace for indulgence in gambling, at any rate in Britain, is not unlawful, is seemingly encouraged by the state and its effects are not as obvious as may be, say, with problematical alcohol use. There are believed to be approximately 300,000 persons who could be described as problem gamblers in Britain and the amount is believed to be growing. Problem gambling, in the clinical sense, does not usually involve such glamorous activities as playing the roulette wheel or engaging in the activities of well appointed clubs in Mayfair. It normally involves an impecunious individual who has become pathologically dependent on such humble activities as playing the lottery and scratch cards besides engaging in the more traditional pastime of backing horses and dogs in insane hope. Other areas of dependence are found increasingly through activities of gambling on the internet. It is as pernicious a form of addiction as any other mentioned in this chapter and the personal and social cost can be immense and lead to the destruction of a not insubstantial number of individual lives and those of families. The poor are selectively more afflicted because they are the least likely to afford the inevitable losses associated with gambling. The point made earlier about the self-absorption and the relentless pursuit of personal gratification at the cost of all else, in respect of alcohol and illicit drug use applies equally well here, helping to bring the subject within the purview of the family and child lawyer. Treatment is entirely by psychological means – unless there is some underlying medical condition such as mania or bipolar affective disorder predisposing the individual to pathological gambling – and success of any therapeutic endeavour depends, once more, on the motivation and the desire for change exhibited by the affected individual.

6.15   SUBSTANCE MISUSE – THE RISKS

The issue of risk involving individuals caught up in the misuse of substances or pathological gambling will be discussed in detail in Part II of this book but it is easy to see how affected individuals may come to interest various areas of the law. Broadly speaking, the risks involve the direct result of the misused substances as may be manifested by physical, mental or behavioural changes. Secondly, there are also risks associated with the pursuit by these individuals of the means by which these substances of abuse are acquired. Pathological gambling usually only involves the second of these aspects of dependence behaviour. One way or another the criminal law becomes involved in cases of substance abuse. Such is the impact of the behaviour of these individuals on others, including those who are members of their families, that the subject is of lively interest to practitioners in family and child law. Employment may, of course, be affected and nuisance behaviour may be engaged in the form of antisocial conduct.

6.16   DISORDERS OF APPETITE

These disorders are included in this chapter for completeness and as they appear to have at least a superficial resemblance to the kinds of perverted appetites found in the cases involving alcohol and illicit drug misuse. We leave obesity from any consideration here – this is no doubt a subject of considerable and expanding medical importance but shall here concentrate instead on anorexia and bulimia nervosa while also noting that there are several forms of atypical eating disorders which, while not meeting the diagnostic criteria of the conventional disorders, may yet be of clinical significance.

Anorexia nervosa is a condition that has been known for some centuries but has become more prominent in recent generations. There is a 'fear of fatness' in the individuals who suffer from these disorders – the vast majority being adolescent girls and young women – which leads to their imposing a low weight threshold upon themselves. The disorders are characterised by the refusal of the individual to maintain a minimum normal body weight, often to the point of starvation. The core feature is an intense fear of gaining weight. This lower body weight is maintained at least 15 per cent below the standard norm applicable to such an individual. The behaviour aimed at achieving this self-imposed target includes the avoidance of high calorific foodstuffs, self-induced vomiting, self-induced purging, excessive exercise, and the use of appetite suppressants (the attraction of these properties of amphetamine drugs is obvious) and diuretic agents. There may also be a loss of the menstrual cycle. The medical consequences of starving may be serious and not uncommonly life threatening in graver cases especially if the unwillingness to consume food is compounded by the simultaneous use of laxatives and diuretics and the effects of vomiting. There may also be some features of depressive illness including obsessional symptoms and irritability. Social withdrawal follows in the wake of the preoccupation with eating behaviour.

A variant of the condition is bulimia nervosa which involves binge-eating and has some similarities to episodic heavy alcohol intake or dipsomania. There is a history of anorexia nervosa in many who later become bulimic and indeed patients may move from one condition to the other. One of the features in this condition is that normal body weight may be retained, indeed some subjects can be overweight. Binges of eating may be followed by the use of laxatives, diuretics and excessive exercise and vomiting. Complications could arise as a result of the abuse of substances.

6.17   EATING DISORDERS – CAUSATION

The onset of the condition is in early adolescence and a feature is the preoccupation with food in all its aspects apart from eating it. The condition may go unnoticed for many years for a preoccupation with figure and weight is otherwise considered normal in young girls. The female predominance in anorexia nervosa is notable and there is no doubt that, at present, this is a condition found primarily in the developed world. The eating disorders, as conventionally understood, have been viewed as a culture-bound disorder, rare or absent except in Western cultures, where there is pervasive pressure to diet to obtain a socially desirable weight and/or shape. There is a tradition of self-starvation in some cultures but the motivation of individuals undertaking this ritual is quite different. An intriguing recent study from Ghana questions, however, the Western view of these disorders. First, it says, there are historical descriptions of cases of self-starvation without concerns about weight in cultures in which there is no emphasis on slimness. Second, cross-cultural comparison has suggested that the eating disorders do not necessarily follow the accepted Western form. Starvation in these cultures may be an end in itself, often undertaken for purposes of religious devotion. Weight concern as in the usual case of anorexia nervosa may become more common as the degree of Westernisation increases. The Ghana study suggests that anorexia nervosa may take different forms in different cultures and the patients studied there had a form of anorexia nervosa without concerns about weight. Studies examining eating disorders in developing countries seem to have assumed that the psychopathology of anorexia nervosa follows the recognised 'Western' form. The authors of this study suggest that a unifying theme of the diverse cultural presentation of the disorder is morbid self-starvation which may be driven in many ways and that self-starvation may, in fact, be the core feature of anorexia nervosa with the attribution for the self-starvation behaviour varying between cultures. However, there is also evidence that incidence of conventional cases of eating disorders is rising in those parts of the world where the major preoccupation has traditionally been with finding enough food to eat. An interesting phenomenon awaits us if, with growing prosperity and the advances towards globalisation, these disorders became as common in those parts of the world as other psychiatric disorders have usually done. There may also be growing parity between the sexes as roles become blurred as between men and women and the former also start becoming preoccupied with appearance and weight, a feature also believed to be on the increase (one has already noted the behaviour concerning alcohol consumption in women has approximated to that seen in men in recent years). This does not make these conditions solely those of social and cultural origins for an intriguing involvement of the brain is found in some of these cases. It is believed, at least in some of these cases, the problem is primarily one concerning body image, that is, of the view that one comes to achieve of one's body, a matter of perception and therefore capable of being traced back to the brain. Social and cultural factors – such as the pictorial depiction of the desirable female form and build – may well provide the raw material for the brain to work on. It has also long been known that complex endocrine changes associated with such symptoms as the loss of menstrual periods are found in this condition, and aberrations in the levels of hormones have also been noted. Whether these are causal phenomena or are effects secondary to the disorder are not always clear. There is a genetic influence that can be seen but the effects of this are not pronounced. Family conflict is often elicited. Childhood trauma, especially involving sexual abuse, has been discovered in a minority of cases. Bulimia nervosa is rarer than anorexia but shares many of the aetilogical features of the other. The major difference between the two conditions appears to be the greater genetic risk present with bulimia nervosa.

6.18   EATING DISORDERS – TREATMENT

Treatment of these conditions is far from satisfactory or indeed of finding a consensus among therapists. Measures include both practical steps – a regime of controlled re-feeding – and psychological treatment. The latter may involve individual or group psychotherapy and also family therapy. Cognitive behavioural therapy may have some merit and has its advocates. The aim with psychological treatment is to attempt to alter the individual's attitude to weight and body shape. Drug treatment is of limited value. Severe weight-loss may necessitate in-patient treatment which may also be required if the risk of suicidal behaviour or medical complications becomes appreciable. The prognosis is variable dependent as it is on so many factors peculiar to each patient and on account of the poor understanding as yet achieved of these disorders. The severity of the occasional case involving the eating disorders is often underestimated and it is believed that five per cent of these patients will die, either through starving themselves or by suicide. Severe cases may need to be treated in hospital and specialised units now exist in an attempt to achieve the best possible result. The prognosis of bulimia nervosa appears to be better.

6.19   SUMMARY

• Substance misuse, other forms of addictive behaviour and the eating disorders appear to be heavily influenced by prevailing social and cultural conditions and attitudes. Depending on the substance involved, physical or psychological dependence could be encountered. The complications arising out of these conditions could be considerable, involving physical and mental disorder and also impairment of relationships within the family and the community.

- Substance misuse behaviour may lead to involvement of the individual with the criminal law (through behaviours involving the substances directly as well as in the attempts made to fund use) and family and child law and is also a major consideration in personal injury and employment practice. These conditions are also implicated in changing mental states and with nuisance behaviour. Thereby, they involve every form of risk that is considered in Part II of this book. The absence of any reliable form of treatment for the common forms of addictive behaviour compounds the problem.

CHAPTER 7

DISORDERS OF PERSONALITY AND PSYCHOPATHY

7.1   INTRODUCTION

No other condition in all psychiatric practice leads to such confusion, disagreement and dissent as do those conditions making up this category of mental disorder. The essence of personality disorder is a failure on the part of an individual to adjust to the norms and standards of society. Many definitions have been given, though no single one is satisfactory. The ICD-10 defines personality disorder as:

> 'deeply ingrained and enduring behaviour patterns, manifesting themselves as inflexible responses to a broad range of personal and social situations. They represent either extreme or significant deviations from the way the average individual in a given culture perceives, thinks, feels and particularly relates to others. Such behaviour patterns tend to be stable and to encompass multiple domains of behaviour and psychological functioning. They are frequently, but not always, associated with various degrees of subjective distress and problems in social functioning and performance.'

Not surprisingly these difficulties often spill over into the law, in particular the criminal law, but family and child law as well as other branches of the law also consistently encounter these patients.

7.2   PERSONALITY DISORDERS – GENERAL FEATURES

Some points may be made in trying to break down the kind of compendious definition of personality disorder such as the one given above:

(1)   The abnormal behaviour pattern is persistent and enduring, in other words it is not episodic as may happen with most forms of formal psychiatric illness. Even in saying that, a word of caution must be uttered since chronic illness, such as some forms of schizophrenia or depressive illness, may itself lead to personality change which may be difficult to distinguish from the disease process, although the history may suggest normal development up to the first onset of the illness. While personality disorders amount to mental disorders, conditions

such as schizophrenia and depressive illness are considered to be true
disease entities and, as such, are forms of formal mental illness.

(2)   Personality disorders are mental disorders in their own right but
      these are to be seen as separate from formal mental illness such as
      depressive illness to which many personality disordered individuals
      are subject. Similarly, alcohol and illicit drug misuse these
      individuals frequently indulge in may found a diagnosis of mental
      disorder in their own right and must be kept separate from
      personality disorder as far as one can do so.

(3)   The crux of the problem is the element of 'rule breaking' in relation
      to the norms and standards of society. This lack of harmony with
      their surroundings and the inability to conform may be due to
      several elements in their psychological functioning, eg their poor
      impulse control, their often high levels of anxiety and arousal, their
      ways of thinking and perceiving, their view of another person etc.

(4)   It follows the abnormal behaviour pattern may be pervasive and may
      lead to maladaptive responses in many areas of personal and social
      behaviour.

(5)   Although the diagnosis is not to be made until maturity is reached,
      at least in chronological terms, problems of adjustment and conduct
      are invariably seen in childhood and adolescence and persist into
      adult life.

(6)   The condition is usually associated with significant problems in the
      social and occupational spheres.

(7)   The disorder may lead to significant personal distress although this
      may happen only later in its course and may not always be detected,
      especially if contact with the patient has not been made by
      professionals.

The distinction to be made between the personality disorders and formal
illness, briefly touched on above, may be usefully expanded along with a
discussion on the inter-relationship between the two conditions. First,
personality disorders can predispose to formal mental illness. An anxious
or obsessional personality is more prone to suffer the corresponding
neurotic condition than an individual with a more normal personality.
Second, personality disorder and formal illness may co-exist. This state is
commonly found in situations involving misuse of alcohol and illicit
drugs where the mental disorder due to substance abuse may be found
alongside a personality disorder which may make the patient vulnerable
to other disorders. This is an example of the state of co-morbidity. Third,
as already noted, personality changes, sometimes amounting to disorder,
may follow from illness. As shall be discussed, personality deterioration

may follow head injury and there is the possibility of adverse personality change in cases of chronic schizophrenia. Fourth, the features of formal illness and the behaviours associated with it can be modified by a personality disorder. Violence (that is, suicidal behaviour or violence directed against others) involving the mentally disordered is commonly suspected to be the result of some mental illness per se but, in fact, may actually flow from the underlying personality of the individual concerned.

7.3 PERSONALITY DISORDERS – CLASSIFICATION

We consider here a practical psychiatric classification of the common forms of personality disorders. A psychological approach to the classification of these conditions is considered in Van Rooyen and Mahendra.[1] Given the state of current knowledge, personality disorder is only amenable to description and the classification of subtypes – themselves subject to change over the course of years as diagnostic methods become refined – are based on clusters of descriptive features. Many subtypes are recognised and we consider briefly here only those commonly seen in medico-legal practice:

(1) One such type is the *dependent* personality disorder, referring to an individual who encourages or allows others to make most of one's important life decisions, subordinates one's own needs to the wishes and demands of others, has a feeling of helplessness, is insecure on account of fearing desertion and requires excessive amounts of advice and reassurance from others. It has an association with borderline personality disorder and the aetiology is thought to be the outcome of early social processes within the family environment.

(2) Closely related to the *dependent* type is the *anxious (avoidant)* type who has persistent and pervasive feelings of anxiety and tension, believes he is socially inept, physically unattractive and inferior to others, is over-sensitive to being criticised or rejected in social situations, unwilling to become involved in situations unless certain of acceptance, leads a restricted lifestyle in order to have security and avoids social or occupational activities that involve significant interpersonal contact because of fear of criticism, disapproval or rejection. It is also associated with phobic disorders, specifically social phobia which has similar clinical features.

(3) The *histrionic* type of personality disorder involves an individual given to self-dramatisation and exaggerated expression of emotion, is suggestible and easily influenced by others, is shallow with changeable emotions, is continually craving excitement, appreciation of others and the need to be the centre of attraction, is

---

[1] See C L Van Rooyen and B Mahendra *Psychology in Family and Child Law* (Family Law, 2007).

inappropriately seductive in appearance or dress and is unduly concerned with physical appearance, is egocentric, self-indulgent and manipulative. Although traditionally believed to be commoner in women, more recent studies show the gender ratio to be 50:50. It is more commonly found in divorced and separated persons and is associated with parasuicidal behaviour. It is associated also with women who suffer unexplained medical conditions and in men with substance misuse.

(4)   The *paranoid* personality type is excessively sensitive to setbacks and rebuffs, has a tendency to bear grudges persistently, is suspicious and with a tendency to distort experiences through misconstruction of the words and actions of others, is combative and tenacious in regard to personal rights, has a tendency to experience excessive self-importance and is given to suspecting conspiracies in regard to personal matters as well as in the world at large. It is more commonly found in males and persons of a lower social class, and also more common among relations of patients with schizophrenia. It exists with antisocial personality disorder and is associated with violent crime.

(5)   The *schizoid* subtype is more prevalent in offender populations. It has been suggested that this category may be better classified as a neurodevelopmental disorder than a personality disorder, possibly within the spectrum of autistic disorders.

(6)   The *obsessive-compulsive* type finds grouped within it 'high functioning' individuals, more commonly white males who are highly educated, married and employed. It has an association with anxiety states.

(7)   An important subcategory, which may have significant implications for medico-legal practice concerning the patients within it, is the *emotionally unstable* type. This kind of personality is governed by his or her impulses without any considerations of consequences or repercussions. The ability to plan ahead is much reduced and there may be outbursts or explosions of anger sometimes leading to violence. These individuals may be unduly provoked when they are thwarted. There are two variants of this subcategory. One is the *impulsive* type characterised by emotional instability and lack of impulse control. Outbursts of violence or threatening behaviour are commonly found here. The other is the *borderline* type which also is characterised by emotional instability, with disturbed behaviour, a chronic feeling of emptiness within and with a liability to become involved in intense and unstable relationships which are associated with repeated emotional crises which lead to violence (whether directed against oneself or others). It is not unknown for this – and perhaps subtypes such as the paranoid personality – to tip over

fleetingly into displaying the features of psychosis including delusions, hallucinations and losses of insight and a sense of reality. It is said to be more prevalent in younger age groups (19–34), white females, associated also with a poor work history and single marital status and also more common in urban areas. It is further associated with substance misuse, phobic and anxiety states and has a nine per cent suicide rate. It is associated in forensic samples with antisocial personality disorder. There is also an association with depressive illness. It is most severe in individuals aged in their mid-twenties with improvement noted in those aged in their late-thirties and beyond.

7.4 PSYCHOPATHY

Psychopathy may be referred to as the 'turbo-charged' version of personality disorder. It has achieved notoriety and invariably attracts a bad press. The highest in the land may be caught up in its coils as is exemplified by the government's seeming inability to know how to deal with some of the more violent members of this group – what is called dangerous and severe personality disorder – and the ensuing debate that held up the reform of the Mental Health Act 1983 which will now be amended rather than repealed. Traditional classificatory systems used to mark these patients as being inadequate, creative or aggressive. Sociopath is the favoured term in the United States where intensive studies have been undertaken on them with little enlightenment forthcoming. It is believed there is a prevalence of psychopathy of two to three per cent in most Western societies and it is four to five times more common in men than in women. The highest prevalence is in the 25–44 age group. It is associated with school drop out, homelessness and raised mortality in early adult life. Prevalence is raised in inner-city areas and is lower in rural populations. It has a high association with substance misuse. The symptoms of antisocial personality disorder or psychopathy diminish in middle age but about 20 per cent of sufferers are still said to meet the criteria for diagnosis at the age of 45 years.

Most of the remarks addressed above to personality disordered individuals will also find application to those suffering from psychopathy. The condition remains a matter for observation and classification with little by way of any objective measurement as yet feasible. Some of the features seen in these individuals include a marked unconcern for the feelings of others, a gross and persistent attitude of irresponsibility in terms of 'rule-breaking' to be discussed below, an incapacity to maintain any enduring relationships, a very low tolerance to frustration and boredom with a corresponding low threshold for unleashing aggression and violence, an inability to learn from experience including punishment (whether officially or informally meted out to them), a marked inability to accept responsibility, a tendency to blame others and the possession of a dogged capacity for rationalisation of the usually deplorable acts they have been engaged in.

As with the personality disorders, the causes of psychopathy remain largely mysterious. It is a condition found in every culture and society and even where, say, aggression and assertiveness are more socially acceptable than in cultures where restraint and moderation are the preferred approach to life it is noteworthy how denizens of the former societies can still point to individuals who have overstepped an even higher threshold. A rule-breaker remains a rule-breaker even when the rules may appear to have been adjusted to accommodate his like.

7.5 PERSONALITY DISORDERS – CAUSATION

These patients, as has been said, are rule-breakers. They are also abnormal individuals in the statistical sense. Truly it could be said of them, employing Thoreau's words for the purpose:

> 'If a man does not keep pace with his companions perhaps it is because he hears a different drummer.'

Perhaps in trying to make sense of these patients a good starting point may be the normal personality, the one from which these patients are deemed to deviate. Although personality has long been studied, many gaps still remain in our knowledge. We do know there are significant genetic influences although, as with many conditions or states or attributes, normal, abnormal and pathological, the precise genetic mechanisms elude us. The genetic contribution to personality traits appears to be modest. As for personality disorder, there are widely and wildly varying figures given according to the populations and groups selected for study. There are rare chromosomal abnormalities implicated in aggressive behaviour. Brain studies have shown from time to time – through abnormal scans, aberrant electroencephalographic and blood-flow studies – that there could be some abnormality in function, perhaps even in structure, of various regions of the brain but these studies are far too indefinite, and on occasion contradictory, to serve any practical explanatory or diagnostic purpose. In any event the manifestations of these disorders are so wide-ranging it seems unlikely there could be one specific lesion. A high level of autonomic nervous system arousal is sometimes posited in these individuals to account for their impulsive actions. Environmental factors, at first sight, hold greater promise for purposes of trying to explain these conditions but, once again, the available studies prove too contradictory – too much, too little, parental attention, deprivation in childhood, or, on the contrary, being 'spoilt', too comfortable or too spartan an upbringing, too much or too little caring – to have much value in terms of reliability and validity. All that can be said is that those with personality disorder or psychopathy appear able to spring from any kind of soil – social class, parental background, cultures can be of any kind. In other words, those who desire to turn out well balanced, responsible citizens have little to work with and almost never can predict with any great confidence how young persons will turn out as adult citizens. Personality disorder and psychopathy are usually diagnoses made with hindsight as the 'back-tracking' to detect childhood and adolescent misbehaviour shows. In most cases, of course, children and adolescents outgrow their years of rebellion and are transformed into model citizens.

We suspect, nonetheless, that the social as well as the physical environment very probably do play an often decisive part in moulding an individual's personality characteristics. While the definitive personality emerges at maturity – which, with some arbitrariness, for these are not matters of precise chronological calculation, we may set at the age of 18 – many of the characteristics found in adult life are found surprisingly early in life, even possibly in the first few months of life according to closely observant parents. Numerous studies have shown that persistent and pervasive aggressive and disruptive behaviours seen before the age of 11 are strongly associated with persistence of antisocial behaviours through adolescence and into adult life. The risk extends far beyond antisocial behaviours to unstable relationships, unreliable parenting and underachievement in education and at work. Furthermore, children who do not have conduct problems are very unlikely to subsequently develop antisocial personality disorder which is rare without a history of conduct problems in childhood. The brain obviously plays a crucial role and its own growth, development and maturity appears to underlie the personality the individual comes to present to the world. Therefore, any insult to the brain, while causing also possible intellectual deficiency,[2] may also hinder the normal development of the personality. These injurious factors may include infections such as encephalitis or meningitis, head injuries, environmental toxins (one recalls the recent impassioned debate on whether or not mercury could have an impact on childhood mental development when used as a vehicle for vaccines), the foetal environment itself (subject as it is to maternal health, drugs taken etc) and more obvious socio-economic influences such as poor diet and housing. One must say, however, that the vast majority of patients with personality disorder have no discernible cause for their condition and, even when they suggest one of the above factors for their condition, the examiner remains sceptical for the precise role, if any, for any such causative agent is usually far from clear. If all children suffer infections, some of which are bound to be serious, how does one know which of these children has had its personality development adversely affected by the infection it suffered? These imponderables also affect the analysis of the psychological development of children such as the quality of their upbringing, the nature and number of their attachments etc. Children brought up in dire deprivation may turn out to be well adjusted adults and with the ground

---

[2] See Chapter 8.

well prepared for success in all spheres of life. Equally well, those whose lives appear to be little more than a non-ending march to and from the criminal courts and prisons may reveal they had every advantage in their upbringing. The subject of personality development therefore remains one for speculation at the present day. However, an audience of lawyers will be able to appreciate the facts in a case which involved personality change in an adult person following head injury. The case was *Meah v McCreamer*[3] and the primary legal interest was on the issue of remoteness in tort. The plaintiff (as these used to be called) was an estimable member of society who, however, foolishly accepted a lift from a drunken driver who proceeded to cause an accident. This passenger suffered head injury. What is of peculiar interest was what the consequences of the claimant's head injury turned out to be. He suffered a calamitous personality change which led him to committing a series of vicious sexual assaults one of which led him into being imprisoned for life. It was held he could recover for this 'loss of amenity' (subject to a reduction for contributory negligence) and that his criminal actions following head injury were reasonably foreseeable. Another man, aged in his forties, involved in both personal injury and child care litigation, on similar facts turned from being a dutiful partner and devoted father into a drunken lout who came to lose all he had following a series of violent assaults. Fortunately, his aggression abated with time and the court could entertain a claim to his right to have renewed contact with his child with some equanimity.

While it has been said already that personality disorder (and psychopathy) can only be diagnosed after maturity, once personality has been deemed to be fully formed, when such diagnoses are being considered it is still believed to be necessary to 'track-back', so to speak, and look at the picture that obtained in childhood and adolescence of the individual concerned. When that is done, it is invariably the case that behavioural disorders are discovered to have been manifested at an early stage in life. Precursors of an antisocial life style are said to include antisocial behaviour in childhood, impulsivity, school failure, antisocial family, poor parenting and economic deprivation. Turning points away from an antisocial life style include finding employment, getting married, moving to a better area for residence, and joining the army. Weak bonds to society and individuals, self-centredness, low empathy and lack of religious belief are all associated with substance misuse and an antisocial life style. Early contact with the police, truancy, school misconduct and divorce are significant predictors of premature death. There is often a history of such activities as truanting, fighting, lying, bullying, insubordination, indiscipline, thieving and other features of juvenile delinquency to be found. In other words, personality disorders and psychopathy do not appear to arise de novo in adult life but have already laid down patterns considerably early in childhood. All aspects of social and personal life come to be affected in these individuals and often they may leave behind a trail of destruction. Relationships – personal as well as with officialdom –

---

3   [1985] 1 All ER 367; [1986] 1 All ER 943.

are usually superficial, brittle and unstable. Repeated marriages, along with illegitimate children from numerous extra-marital relationships are not uncommon. The occupational record is equally chequered with much difficulty shown in relationships with colleagues and superiors and much disruption in the work place as these individuals have a genius for creating chaos. Confrontations, in a repeated pattern, with the law are commonplace as these individuals often have what the law has called 'abnormally aggressive' and 'seriously irresponsible' attitudes leading to involvement with the criminal law following assaults on the person as well as property and, on occasion, for acts of dishonesty. Resort is readily had to abuse of alcohol and indulgence in illicit substances. Their career appears to be one of an individual looking back on the ruins of one relationship and contemplating the next. In early middle-age it is customary for these individuals to show some signs of settling down, the convictions and spells of incarceration ease and a modus vivendi appears to have been reached with the world. It is often suggested that by that age these individuals could be running out of the animal energy that sustained their destructive and disruptive careers and that some measure of stability is often restored although some individuals may proceed to cause havoc in their lives and those of others right through life.

The older classification into inadequate, aggressive and creative psychopaths had some merit in helping to understand the life and works of these patients. The inadequate individual is the one commonly found to have a poor interpersonal and occupational record. The aggressive individual is the one who had entangled himself with the criminal law and the penal services. The creative individual becomes the renowned businessman or artist in occupations where 'rule-breaking' is the norm, where, in fact, success and progress is not possible if existing rules are not broken, although fulfilment or stability in their personal lives do not regularly match the material or artistic success they come to achieve, a matter readily explored by a study of the biographies of many gifted individuals.

7.6 PERSONALITY DISORDERS – MANAGEMENT

Treatment of these conditions remains problematical. The Butler Committee (1975) concluded:

> 'the great weight of evidence presented to us tends to support the conclusion that psychopaths are not, in general, treatable, at least in medical terms.'

Over three decades later that sentiment remains, by and large, true. There is no specific drug treatment available for these conditions as such although therapeutic drugs may be useful in dealing with the symptoms of formal psychiatric disorder these patients, like anyone else, may develop. It is often glibly asserted that psychological approaches by way of psychotherapy – individual, group or even institutional – may produce significant results. The results, in fact, are almost uniformly poor within any timescales envisaged in medico-legal practice. Psychotherapy is a time, labour and, hence, cash intensive treatment procedure. As these lines are being written, the Henderson Hospital (one of only two institutions in the country able to offer institutional treatment for cases of severe personality disorder) contemplates the threat of closure. There simply were not sufficient numbers of cases referred to it and bringing the necessary funding with them. Using the phrase employed in demotic usage, the money seemingly was not in the mouths of those who had clamoured for this form of intensive specialised treatment.

However, other specialist institutions such as the Cassel Hospital (the counterpart of the Henderson Hospital) have claimed reasonably positive results in cases of personality disorder. Specialist psychosocial treatment for personality disorder, they say, can show appreciable and reliable in improvement in symptomatology, social adjustment and global assessment of mental health over a 36-month follow-up period. Improvement is said also to continue after discharge, a proportion of patients showing stable and durable change two years after termination of treatment. A phased programme that included a community-based stage of treatment was found to yield more stable improvement than a purely hospital-based programme, as shown by the greater reduction in self-mutilation, attempts at suicide and readmission rates. There is at present a co-operative venture involving the Prison Department, the Home Office and the Department of Health in a number of locations to see how the most irresponsible of psychopaths – the most dangerously violent – can be dealt with, if at all, therapeutically. No studies have yet emerged to show any promise. It appears there is as yet no treatment or management programme that is compatible with personal liberty in a civilised society which can yet be formulated to deal with these individuals. Secure units and special hospitals remain the institutions for those individuals with these conditions who seriously transgress the criminal law. As far as timescales normally envisaged in most legal proceedings are concerned, any real treatment of psychopathy is, it is safe to say, not yet in the realm of practical politics.

7.7 PERSONALITY DISORDERS – PROGNOSIS

The remarks made above may suggest that the prognosis for cases of personality disorder is uniformly hopeless. This is not always the case. Apart from the factor of maturation mentioned above – many of these individuals do settle down in middle age – they are also subject to circumstances that could be positive. Employment, marriage, or some other new challenge may all engage them and lead to an improvement in their functioning. It is striking how well some of these patients acquit themselves when they face a real challenge such as the conditions of war. It is also repeatedly stressed how the Empire came to be built on the backs of misfits who, while they idled at home, had seemingly been undone by the mundane nature of their ordinary existence. It is invariably seen in clinical settings that the single most important factor in the improvement of the clinical functioning of these patients is their capacity to lead a settled life. As these matters remain unpredictable, and largely out of the hands of clinicians, the prognosis for these patients is mostly said to be guarded.

7.8 PERSONALITY DISORDERS – THE RISKS

As will be discussed further in the second half of this book, individuals suffering from personality disorders and psychopathy find themselves involved in many situations of risk. Consequently, they are also active participants in many fields of the law.

7.9 SUMMARY

- How personality disorders arise is far from well understood. There appears to be an interaction between genetic factors and environmental influences but the impact of genetics appears to be weaker in personality disorders than with the formal mental illnesses. The environment, therefore, appears to play a more decisive role but it is not clear how. Head injury and systemic illness and its treatment may be occasional causes of changed personality. These conditions are usually beyond all conventional treatment although amelioration is to be expected with age and especially if they manage to lead a settled existence. Complications include the misuse of substances.

- Given the nature of the condition, many of these patients are actively involved in litigation. Aggression and violence involves the criminal law. These behaviours as well as impulsive and unreliable conduct may lead to their participation in family and child proceedings. Difficulties in interpersonal relationships may lead to problems in employment. Delayed recovery from psychiatric injuries sustained following trauma may complicate personal injury litigation. Changing mental states seen in some patients may be attributable, at least in part, to their personalities. Their behaviour may be such that nuisance is caused to the public.

CHAPTER 8

LEARNING DISABILITIES AND DEVELOPMENTAL DISORDERS

8.1 LEARNING DISABILITIES

The term learning disabilities has been evolving for some time. At various periods in recent history the terms mental retardation, mental subnormality, mental handicap or mental impairment have all been employed to describe this phenomenon and some of these terms still find favour with official sources such as the International Classification of Disorders (1992, mental retardation) or the Mental Health Act 1983 (mental impairment). At an earlier period in history the terms used included those such as idiocy, imbecility and feeblemindedness which nowadays are considered to be too pejorative. The primary problem in this disorder has long been considered to be one of an intellectual shortfall, although the more enlightened attitudes of today also give proper attention to the more social and emotional aspects of the processes of learning whose deficiency is now believed to be the core handicap. The ICD defines these conditions as being characterised by:

> 'arrested or incomplete development of the mind, which is especially characterised by impairment of skills manifested during the developmental period, which contributes to the overall level of intelligence.'

Intelligence, therefore, still remains a central issue with learning disabilities. The conventional measure of this is the IQ (intelligence quotient) test. Intelligence in the ordinary population is said to have a normal distribution by which is meant that with a modal score of 100, and a standard deviation of 15, two standard deviations from the mode in either direction would cover 95 per cent of the population. In other words, all but five per cent of the public would score between 70 and 130 on an IQ test. A borderline score is about 70, mild learning disabilities would cover scores between 50 and 70, moderate learning disabilities will be found between 35 and 50, severe and profound learning disabilities involve lower scores. The practical difference between those with higher scores – involving the vast majority of patients with learning disabilities – and the lower scores is that the former can hope to live in the community with some support while the latter may come to require institutional care of some kind. There are other distinguishing features found between those suffering from mild, moderate or severe handicap. Those with mild

handicap or disability – who account for some 85 per cent of the total
number with learning disabilities – may have reasonable language skills
with a measure of literacy, possess ordinary social skills, hold down
employment (usually involving jobs of an unskilled or semi-skilled nature)
and have conditions rarely associated with physical illness. In other words,
these individuals are little different from members of the normal
population. Those with moderate or severe deficits have, however,
generally limited language skills, are employed, if at all, in unskilled or
sheltered employment, may be deficient in social skills and suffer more
often from associated physical disorders.

For historical reasons the study of learning disabilities has fallen, in the
medical sense, to the specialist psychiatrist. It is a condition which is
distinct from formal mental illness although associations between
learning disabilities and other mental disorder are not uncommon.
Learning disabilities, of whatever origins, always arise in childhood. A
distinction needs to be made between these conditions and dementia,
where intellectual impairment is acquired in adult life.

These conditions may first attract the attention of those involved with the
education of the individual or those called upon to deal with the
behavioural problems of childhood at which stage problems involving
conduct may at first mask the intellectual deficits that may also be
present.

8.2   LEARNING DISABILITIES – CAUSATION

The prevalence of learning disabilities within any population is about
two per cent with a slight male preponderance. Despite some of the
commoner causes of intellectual handicap having been tamed – for
example, childhood infections being better controlled through pro-
grammes of immunisation – prevalence appears to have remained stable.
It is probable that mild forms of handicap are constant the world over.
These are usually associated with socio-economic factors, less easy to
eradicate than infections. In many undeveloped rural communities
learning disabilities, as commonly understood, may not even be seen to be
an obvious handicap whereas in complex developed societies it is only all
too clear that such an affected individual may be at substantial
disadvantage in coping with ordinary existence. This is especially well
observed in the sphere of employment. An agrarian society has a supply
of work and a supporting social network for individuals at all ranges of
intellectual functioning while a modern industrialised society demands
increasing skills and may exclude even those who are only mildly impaired
in intellectual terms.

The disorders leading to learning disabilities show clear evidence of both
genetic and environmental influences. Plainly, the brain must ultimately
be affected in some fashion to bring about disability and impairment. As

a general rule, the more severely afflicted tend to have a known genetic cause for their condition while the mildly disabled have no obvious genetic causation but are believed to be affected to a greater or lesser extent by socio-cultural influences. There are obvious exceptions to this rule for severe brain damage due to a clear environmental cause, eg trauma or infection can lead to grave affliction while a condition such as Down's syndrome can lead to variable levels of intellectual difficulties.

The causes, where known, of learning disabilities are numerous. An example already given involving chromosomal abnormality is Down's syndrome. Genetic disorders include phenylketonuria (involving the metabolism of phenylalanine). More than 1000 genetic causes of learning disabilities are known to exist. Other causes include maternal infections in the course of pregnancy (eg rubella) or other complications of pregnancy and it is also believed the maternal consumption of alcohol, tobacco or prescribed drugs could be important, though as yet unquantifiable, causal factors. Birth injury and childhood infection such as meningitis are well established causes as are later head injuries. One area whose causative potential is as yet little understood involves the role of adverse social and cultural factors such as poor diet and material deprivation. How these elements affect the developing brain remains unclear for there are children developing in conditions of extreme poverty and privation who yet emerge, as far as can be ascertained, normally into the world with their intellectual inheritance intact.

8.3   LEARNING DISABILITIES – MANAGEMENT

As the modern term learning disabilities suggests, the disabilities of individuals suffering from this condition go well beyond intellectual difficulties and may include also those problems associated with social and educational functioning in a wider sense. The assessment of the needs of these patients is a complex exercise and may involve a variety of agencies including the educational services, the local authority and the health authority. The modern trend is to have these patients functioning as far as possible in the community with appropriate support, which may include supported lodgings. The days of traditional institutionalisation are long over, the older institutions now believed to have significantly added to the handicaps suffered by these patients by adding secondary disabilities due to the institutions themselves. Even when some form of residential care may become necessary, emphasis is placed on encouraging independence and fostering self-sufficiency among these individuals.

Intervention may become necessary when a patient with learning disabilities develops a formal mental illness. Assessment needs to be made of the requirements of the service needs of each individual. Care for these individuals, where needed, is usually shared between the local authority and the health service, as the learning disabilities need to draw on the services of both, occasionally a source of tension as scarce resources and budgets are jealously protected.

8.4   LEARNING DISABILITIES – PROGNOSIS

The prognosis is invariably poor as the underlying conditions causing learning disabilities are usually beyond any treatment available today. However, improvement in functioning of the individual patient can be brought about through successful treatment of some co-existing physical disorder such as by the control of epilepsy or by the treatment of depressive illness. Appropriate social support, eg the instruction given in budgeting their finances or settling these patients in appropriate supported lodgings can increase confidence and self-esteem and thereby improve functioning as well as protecting these often vulnerable patients from exploitation.

8.5   LEARNING DISABILITIES – THE RISKS

Given the pervasive nature of their disabilities, many of these individuals find themselves in situations of risk, a matter to be considered in Part II of this book. Of particular importance is the need to appreciate their possible lack of capacity in various situations and also their exaggerated vulnerability in situations involving stress.

8.6   OTHER DEVELOPMENTAL DISORDERS – CHILDHOOD AUTISM

Intellectual deficits as found in the learning disabilities are due to one form (though involving many varieties) of developmental disorder. Another form could preferentially lead to impairment in personality development resulting in the personality disorders and psychopathy which we dealt with in the previous chapter. Here we take up a form of developmental disorder which leads to problems of behaviour, emotion and social interaction called the autistic spectrum disorders. These conditions have been prominent in the public mind in recent years on account of the controversy surrounding the triple MMR vaccine (used for protection against measles, mumps and rubella) administered in childhood. It was being alleged in some quarters, with little or no scientific foundation in fact, that the MMR vaccine had led to an increase in the incidence of these forms of autistic disorder. This was plainly not the case but it is still legitimate to ask whether the seeming increase in the incidence of these disorders is real or apparent. There is no conclusive answer forthcoming as yet. It has been suggested that it is the increased awareness of the condition among the general public as well as among the professionals, along with more refined diagnostic methods that had caused the apparent rise in numbers. Disorders that had previously been considered as being the usual forms of behavioural problems in childhood were now being dignified, it is said, by the diagnosis of autistic spectrum disorder. As so often happens – with attention deficit hyperactivity disorder (ADHD) when medication became available for its treatment, bipolar or manic depressive disorder when lithium treatment first became established – the advent of new therapeutic possibilities raises awareness and leads to a reconsideration of previous diagnoses. In those situations there may be a tendency to overdiagnose some conditions that might previously have been underdiagnosed. The curious feature with the autistic spectrum disorders is that there is as yet no specific treatment available and the greater awareness (and possible overdiagnosis) therefore does not appear to have any pressing therapeutic impetus behind it. For once the pharmaceutical companies could not be convincingly blamed for attempting to raise awareness of a condition so as to promote and be able to sell their therapeutic products.

Childhood autism has been known to exist for a long time and was formally recognised in 1943. It is a condition of childhood and is recognised before the child is three years of age. It has a male preponderance in its prevalence. It afflicts all social classes and the earlier suggestion it had a preferential higher social class distribution is now known to be false. In fact, this previous assertion was cruel in its further implication that it was 'cold' parents – mostly professionals, some academics – who, by their somehow repressed methods of child rearing, had caused the condition to arise. Looked at now, this suggestions sounds as absurd as it was offensive. There is little doubt that the condition – or the spectrum of disorders – is likely to be shown to be caused by brain dysfunction, the brain being in some way disrupted in its normal development. Several findings have been made on studies of autistic brains though no result is conclusive. Brain size appears to be larger early in life of autistic individuals and abnormalities in brain microstructure as well as in neurochemistry have been proposed as possible accompaniments of the pathology.

The cardinal features of the condition include a solitariness or aloofness found in the child, what is referred to as 'autistic aloneness'. Intimacy is difficult to achieve with these children who appear from early on to have an impaired capacity to form social relationships. So unresponsive can these children be that deafness or learning disabilities may at first be suspected. They lack the playfulness usually associated with children. The second feature is an impaired ability to communicate. This may be manifested by delayed speech, sometimes in a complete failure to talk. Speech, when it appears, is of poor quality and may be repetitive and incorrect in form and content. Comprehension of speech is also poor and language skills such as reading are imperfectly acquired, even then often in a mechanical way with little or no understanding. There is poor eye contact and non-verbal communication is also affected. The third diagnostic feature is the desire for sameness shown by the child with rituals and routines adopted with repetitive patterns of behaviour which, when thwarted, can lead to much distress being demonstrated. There is a mechanical element to play and social communication with little imaginative creativity or fantasy which reflects the rigidity in the thought processes of the child as well as in its behaviour. Associated features may include intellectual impairment (found in some three-quarters of affected individuals), epilepsy (found in about one-quarter) and behavioural problems. Abnormal movements are not uncommonly seen and severe behavioural problems including self-mutilation may be observed. Seizures, as noted, are found only in a minority of cases.

These abnormalities are associated with other intellectual and behavioural deficiencies. Many autistic children are also intellectually impaired and have the kind of learning disabilities previously described. However, the range of intellectual ability is variable and some autistic children are of normal abilities and in some cases celebrated examples of isolated areas of high accomplishment emerge. These areas of excellence usually involve mathematical or artistic abilities, eg being capable of undertaking prodigious feats of calculation which are usually in the province of advanced computers, accomplishing astonishing feats of memory, rising to incredible precision in drawing architectural structures after a mere glance at the building etc. These being isolated oases of high performance in an otherwise barren desert of serious disabilities, the term 'idiot savant' has come to be applied to these perversely gifted individuals.

There is evidence of some genetic influence although the impact of the environmental component in causation is suspected to be far greater in most cases. There is no specific treatment available for the condition and the best results are achieved through the deployment of specialised educational techniques. In fact, it has been said the only worthwhile advance in the management of autistic conditions in the past two generations has come by way of improved educational techniques. Residential care may have to be considered in the most severe cases of behaviour disorder. As might be expected, the prognosis is often poor, another indication that intractable forces in the brain are behind the condition. It is probably rare to see an individual suffering from the average case of childhood autistic disorder growing up to become a passably normal member of society. This makes the education and support of parents and teachers all the more important. The abnormal behaviours and the associated medical conditions may be amenable to more successful symptomatic treatment.

8.7   ASPERGER'S SYNDROME

Childhood autism exists at one end of the scale in the disorders of the autistic spectrum. Many atypical or less well defined cases of autism inhabit the rest of the spectrum which leads to, at this other end,

Asperger's syndrome. It may be considered to be a milder version of childhood autism – there may be a similar impairment in social communication with repetitive and isolated behaviour, the child remains aloof, solitary, clumsy and eccentric. However, unlike in the classical case of autism, intelligence and linguistic ability may appear unimpaired. It is rare also to find the associated medical complications such as epilepsy. What the causes are remain mysterious and its resemblance to classical autism in some aspects may only be coincidental. There is no specific treatment and the best hope lies in attention being paid to the improvement in social responses and communication. Individuals with this condition grow up to become not unlike those individuals who have developed some forms of personality disorder.

This is also a condition that seems to have caught the public imagination. Any mental abnormality in an otherwise reasonably successful individual appears capable of being attributed to Asperger's syndrome, as anyone with experience of family and child law, not to mention other branches of the law, knows. A galaxy of persons are now included among the suspects, in some cases posthumously with the help of tendentiously written (or interpreted) biographical studies. In fact, it is an uncommon form of disorder at the other end of the scale from childhood autism. There is no shortfall of intelligence (in fact, the opposite is usually true, as the public's view shows) and no difficulties with ordinary communication. The diagnosis turns on difficulties these individuals have in social and interpersonal interaction.

In view of the widespread misunderstanding of the condition it is well worth considering the diagnostic criteria – these suggest the following as being required:

- first, there may be marked impairment of nonverbal behaviour such as involving eye contact, facial expression, bodily posture and gestures;

- failure to develop appropriate social peer relationships, a lack of social or emotional reciprocity;

- possessing a restricted and repetitive stereotyped patterns of behaviour, interests and activities such as involvement with routines and rituals, stereotyped and repetitive behaviour;

- the disturbance must cause clinically significant impairment in social, occupational or other important areas of functioning;

- there is no clinically significant general delay in language;

- there is no clinically significant delay in cognitive development or in the development of age-appropriate self-help skills, adaptive behaviour (other than social interaction), and curiosity about the environment on childhood; and

- that criteria are not met for another pervasive development disorder or schizophrenia.

As is evident, there are strict criteria to be met before a diagnosis of the condition is arrived at. There is no place, it would appear, for casual suggestion that an individual could be suffering from the disorder. In one case the estranged female partner of a 35-year-old man suggested in private law child care proceedings that he could be suffering from Asperger's syndrome. On examination, the only findings were that he was highly qualified, was rather concerned with household security (he lived in North London in an area notorious for crime and was following police advice given to householders) and was somewhat of a stickler about things and detail. He had been to university which, when the relationship had run into difficulties, had been a point apparently used by the female partner's father as a possible foundation for the diagnosis (inevitably the man occupied a higher social position than the woman's family). A second case involved a 20-year-old woman, a mother in child care proceedings, had developed a schizophrenia-like illness and had suffered numerous breakdowns over the course of years. She was known to abuse illicit substances extensively and was non-compliant with medication. The urgent clinical question was whether or not she had true schizophrenic illness with all the implications for having the condition (see previous discussion on schizophrenia) or this was a drug-induced schizophreniform state. However, it became known that she had a half-brother who had severe childhood autism. Asperger's syndrome as being suffered by her became a preoccupation during the proceedings.

8.8   SUMMARY

- Learning disabilities, although they may involve most or all functions in a patient, are conventionally attributed to intellectual handicap. Minor forms are far more common than severe affliction and involve predominantly environmental factors in the form of personal and social deprivation of some kind whereas a clear genetic influence may be discernible in severe cases. While the condition is untreatable in conventional terms, support can enable patients to lead reasonably successful lives in the community. There is no place now for institutional care of the traditional kind.

- The provenance of the autistic disorders is still unclear although almost certainly some form of maldevelopment of the brain is involved. This spectrum of disorders contains individuals who may be near normal to those who suffer severe physical and mental disability. The condition is untreatable, the best results being obtained by special educational and behavioural measures.

- The nature of the handicap suffered by those with learning disabilities and autism leads them into various situations concerning the law. Offending may involve the criminal law while parental incapacity of various kinds interests family and child law practitioners. The intellectual shortfall is a consideration in employment while nuisance behaviour due to a lack of social awareness is not uncommon. The capacity of these patients to manage their property and affairs is always a consideration. They may also be unduly suggestible, a matter of interest to the criminal law when they become suspects, and they may also be at risk of abuse and exploitation.

CHAPTER 9

SPECIAL SITUATIONS AND UNUSUAL DISORDERS

9.1 INTRODUCTION

Some psychiatric conditions, although they could be accommodated within the diagnostic categories already considered, would benefit by separate treatment.

9.2 POST-PARTUM PSYCHIATRIC DISORDERS

This refers to mental disorders suffered in the period following childbirth. These conditions, at any rate in their clinical aspect, are indistinguishable from mental disorders suffered at any other time but for many reasons, including their importance in medico-legal situations, they will be taken up separately here.

The distinction to be made between physiology and pathology applies here as it does in all clinical psychiatric, indeed all medical, practice. Physiological states – such as unhappiness, uncomplicated grief reactions, psychological shock – are deemed normal responses. Up to 70 per cent of women suffer some changes in mood in the post-partum period, say within the first six weeks. These are the well-recognised 'maternity blues' with an onset normally in the first week following childbirth. Apart from this mood change in the direction of depression, there could also be anxiety, irritability and insomnia. Some negative feelings in respect of the newborn may be the result. These changes in the mood state are normal and do not require any active treatment. All that is usually required is reassurance (it seems to be more common after the first episode of childbirth) and support. As with the distinction to be made between normal unhappiness and a clinically significant depressive illness, the differences between 'maternity blues' and post-partum depressive illness appears to be quantitative, the psychotic depressive state being rare, however.

The physiological changes which, in part, cause the 'maternity blues' and other normal phenomena may be due to the hormonal changes occurring after the birth when the body begins the process of readjustment towards the normal physical state for the mother.

9.3   POST-PARTUM DEPRESSIVE ILLNESS

This is a clinically recognised condition, meaning it satisfies the criteria required for a depressive illness to be diagnosed with the only additional element being it happens to be found in the post-partum period. This period is variously defined, but up to six months is usually allowed although most cases of depressive illness appear to have their onset within the first three months, in particular in the first month after the birth of the child. Up to 15 per cent of mothers are noted to have this illness. The full significance of the clinical picture and, hence, the diagnosis could be missed because the symptoms come to be attributed to 'maternity blues' or a mother's natural anxiety in the care especially of a first born child. Tiredness and exhaustion following childbirth could also mask the clinical picture. Otherwise the clinical picture is as it is found in depressive illness afflicting women, and for that matter men, at other times. The treatment is also broadly similar although there is an additional urgency brought about by the need to ensure mother and baby can bond without too much disruption in their relationship. More severe cases are treated in 'mother and baby' units which are dedicated to treating mother and holding baby so that the processes of bonding continue even as the mother receives treatment. The prognosis, as with modern treatment of any depressive illness, is generally good. Post-partum depressive illness is common in mothers with a history of psychiatric disorder and in those in whom adverse personal and social factors operate. Social isolation, relationship difficulties and worries concerning finance and housing are commonly to be found. The obvious risk emanating from the mother is to the baby, an issue to be addressed in the second part of this book.

9.4   POST-PARTUM OR PUERPERAL PSYCHOSIS

Like depressive illness, the psychoses may also make an appearance in the post-partum period. The first months following birth is the time when women appear to be most at risk and a significant proportion of these (up to 25 per cent) give a history of previous mental illness. Women with bipolar disorder are at particularly high risk of puerperal psychosis, with episodes following 25 to 50 per cent of deliveries. In addition to a history of bipolar disorder, other important risk factors include having experienced a previous episode of puerperal psychosis, having a first degree relation who has experienced an episode of puerperal psychosis and having a first degree relation with bipolar disorder. It is, however, a far less common condition than depressive illness in the post-partum period. Only about 1 in 500 women is affected in this situation with this condition. The onset can be fairly sudden and acute with features of schizophrenia, a schizo-affective disorder, mania or psychotic depression all being possible. There is little or nothing that is distinctive in the symptoms seen in this period as opposed to a condition presenting at other times. There is obviously greater urgency with treatment and it is usual for admission to be sought to a 'mother and baby' unit. Some care has to be taken with medication as the mother may continue to breast feed and many drugs are known to be transmitted through breast milk. Treatment through modern drugs – and the judicious use of ECT in appropriate cases in the past – is generally successful and a good result may be anticipated. The prognosis is as good as in the non-puerperal case and when there is a protracted or chronic course run by the illness the adverse factors determining this are as for any other illness. Nothing specifically pathogenic or conducive to a poor prognosis has been conclusively shown to exist in the post-partum period in itself. However, as stated, women with a prior history of mental disorder are more vulnerable to mental illness of all kinds in the post-partum period and, if they have suffered one bout of post-partum mental illness, it is usual to predict they could be at higher risk after any subsequent childbirth. The chances of recurrence of illness after the next childbirth appear to be about 1 in 4.

The aetiology of the post-partum psychiatric disorders remains unclear. The obvious potential causative factors are the significant hormonal and chemical changes that occur during pregnancy and persist into the post-partum period. But these changes are common to all women in this condition and no convincing differences in endocrine or biochemical changes have been established between those women who fall ill and those mothers who do not. The prior history of the mental illness and the persisting risk in any future post-partum period has been noted already. Emphasis has been laid on psychosocial factors such as marital or relationship difficulties, ambivalence towards the pregnancy and the newly born child, and more general factors such as housing and financial worries. In fact, considering the available evidence as a whole, one must conclude the post-partum period (and the preceding pregnancy) probably act as a stressful life event to susceptible women. The fact that childbirth may generally be a desirable event in the minds of most women is not a particularly relevant consideration; a much anticipated move of house is known to be one of the most powerful adverse stressors to individuals. Prevention makes use of the fact of prior vulnerability in those who have suffered previous mental ill health. Careful monitoring during pregnancy and in the puerperium should be able to prevent the onset of more severe illness and disability. The obvious risk posed by these women to the newborn child is a consideration for the second half of this book.

Practitioners in family and child law are occasionally drawn into situations involving these cases. A mother who previously experienced difficulties in looking after a newborn may be deemed to be at risk after any subsequent pregnancy. Liaison between local and health authorities may mean information comes to be shared more sensibly. Prejudice is, however, to be avoided. Although there is evidence that a mother who falls ill once is at higher risk of becoming ill again in the course of a subsequent puerperium, it can never be the case that a mother's child care abilities should be deemed automatically to be or at risk of becoming impaired. In fact, the degree of illness and disability may vary widely and each situation needs careful consideration and analysis in its own right.

9.5   CULTURAL INFLUENCES

At first sight it may appear odd to separate culture from the general description given to psychiatric disorders for no disorder is free from the influence of culture, the term used in its broadest sense. We have already considered the impact of culture and subculture in the study of alcohol and illicit substance misuse. In this section, however, we shall use the term culture in its narrower meaning. With so many communities now displaced from their places of origin, it is widely accepted that diverse cultural influences may be in play when mental illness presents itself for examination and study. The subject is vast and here only the common influences with some impact on medico-legal situations will be taken up. Also, only those possible influences of psychiatric (ie medical) interest will be considered. Some further remarks will be made on the possible cultural aspects of aggression and violence with reference to risk assessment when this matter is touched on in the next part of this book.

Mental disorder, like all disease conditions, is universal and the signs and symptoms of disorders, at any rate in their technical aspects, are now increasingly studied according to standard criteria. It is, therefore, in the interpretation of these signs and symptoms that the challenge of culture-bound influences resides. The issue of cultural influences operating in any study of delusions has already been discussed in the chapter on psychotic disorders.[1] A delusion, it will be recalled, is not merely a false belief that is unshakeably held despite evidence to the contrary, it is also a belief which is out of keeping with the social and cultural beliefs of the patient. Thus, one finds persisting in many cultures beliefs in such phenomena as witchcraft and 'the evil eye' and an individual from such a culture may express a view that neighbours or family or some person in or outside of his culture has evil designs on him, has taken steps to put such designs into practice, that this person should be thwarted lest he succeed in his aim for illness or misfortune due to the machinations of such an individual may otherwise come to afflict him. If within the culture of such an individual such beliefs are commonplace it may not amount to a persecutory delusion and, therefore, is not a symptom of mental illness. Careful analysis of the facts, apart from the possession of a sound working knowledge of the culture in question, is required before one comes to this conclusion, for persecutory delusions can, of course, arise in such an individual in the course of schizophrenia or some other psychotic condition. The test, as we have seen before, is to see how any persecutory beliefs an individual possesses might have originated, what form the finished product has attained and, most

---

[1]   See Chapter 3.

importantly, what the interpretation or explanation given by family members or others in the community is for this phenomenon. As a rule of thumb, anything deemed abnormal within the family or the community is more suggestive of a true delusion than any belief accepted with equanimity by others within that community.

Two examples of apparently delusional beliefs have been discussed previously.[2] One involved a 26-year-old woman from Rwanda who had suffered horrific experiences including acts of multiple rape in the course of the civil war then prevailing in that country. She had become involved in child care proceedings in England after the child conceived as a result of a rape and born to her showed serious disabilities. It transpired she held strong cultural views on those who might continue to harm her and these beliefs were based on her experience of tribal rivalries. She had also spent time in Uganda where many of her compatriots had been displaced with her. Seeking asylum in Britain, she had also made contact with an evangelical church. She naturally sought comfort among the black community in Britain but her specifications for association with members of the black community were rather strict – she was prepared to trust and work with black Americans and those whose origins had been in the Caribbean or the West Indies but she continued to have the liveliest suspicion of any person originating from Africa.

Another example was an 18-year-old girl, of Bangladeshi origins but brought up from infancy in Britain, who became involved in child care proceedings on account of her very young child. The girl's lifestyle, notwithstanding the strict constraints of her native culture and the location she found herself in (which was predominantly Muslim) as a teenager and adolescent, could have been, on first impression, that of a certain type of native young girl of today – she drank alcohol and got drunk, she freely abused illicit substances and engaged in casual and, for a while, underage sex. Closer inspection showed, however, a more serious disturbance of conduct along with some psychotic features such as auditory hallucinations. In fact, there appeared to be much disruption to a still evolving personality in her case and although it was probably too early yet to arrive at a diagnosis of personality disorder the signs of such a condition were suggestive. What was, however, even more interesting from the clinical point of view, was her belief that her troubles – in particular the symptoms of mental disorder – had been brought about through consuming foodstuffs given to her by the 'the many enemies of the family.' She now took extreme care to examine the provenance of any food she consumed and shunned food that had been sent to her family from abroad. Thus, the outlook and attitudes of a thoroughly modern (if somewhat disturbed) young girl, whose behaviour was to all intents and purposes those of many denizens in the West, could co-exist with beliefs which are commonplace within the Bangladeshi culture. That is why her

---

[2]   See B Mahendra *Adult Psychiatry in Family and Child Law* (Family Law, 2006).

auditory hallucinations were clearly recognised as being features of a mental disorder but her persecutory ideas had not been.

Where psychotic illness is concerned the presence of some recognised symptoms of illness may be found in some cultures while being absent in others. Moreover, symptoms of illness may also show a change over a period of time. Until about a half century ago there was present, universally as far as one can judge these matters, a symptom of schizophrenia called catatonia. This involved both the phenomena of mutism (mute by visitation of God, in medico-legal parlance) and stupor, that is a severe psychomotor retardation. So common was this condition that a subcategory of schizophrenia called catatonic schizophrenia came to be recognised. Over some generations this condition has shown a dramatic decline in incidence in the nations of the West so much so the diagnosis (which is still in existence in the ICD-10 Classification of Mental Disorders) is largely made only in the developing parts of the world. This also means the condition may still be found in immigrant communities in the West. Why this decline should have taken place so selectively remains something of a mystery although there have been suggestions that an infectious process might be involved – a virus, perhaps, that mutated into innocuousness in some parts of the world. Whatever the explanation, catatonia remains a condition where a physical symptom appears now to be determined by a cultural influence of a more tangible kind.

In similar vein, the influence of known infection, especially in the causation of acute confusional states, including delirium, which could have been acquired in the cultures of origin is not to be disregarded when it comes to the evaluation of mental disorder in migrants. Other physical illness, now rare in the West, as possible causes of mental disorder should also be borne in mind when dealing with these patients.

In the chapter dealing with depressive illness the need to consider the patterns of presentation of depressive illness in various cultures was noted. In those patients originating especially from the cultures of Asia and Africa it is customary for them to emphasise the physical aspects of symptoms (such as the insomnia or the aches and pains associated with depressive illness) and deny or play down the psychical element such as the low mood or the reduced capacity to enjoy oneself. It is usual to ascribe this emphasis on the physical to the stigma still believed to prevail in many parts of the world against mental disorders. Notwithstanding this, it is important to recognise this cultural bias for it has a bearing on the issue of the kind of insight the patient possesses in respect of his disorder. In evaluating the presence of insight it is usual to seek evidence that the patient recognises that they are suffering from a mental or psychological problem. It can be readily appreciated that in a patient from these cultures denial of psychological causation or manifestation of disorder is not necessarily a sign of lack of insight as the term is understood. Further, given the apparent prominence of physical symptoms as reported by these patients, there is also the risk of over-investigation in the pursuit of supposed physical causes of the disorder. Unnecessary radiological or laboratory investigations are to be deprecated in the management of psychiatric disorder as they tend to reinforce the impression the patient may already have that what underlies his feeling of being ill is possibly something grave which could be identified if more energetic (and expensive) investigation were only undertaken. One runs the risk of converting someone suffering from a straightforward disorder such as a depressive illness into someone with a somatoform disorder or hypochondria.

This leads us naturally into considering the hysterical or conversion/dissociative disorders which were briefly dealt with in the chapter on the neuroses. The grosser manifestations – once very common and which helped to make the reputations of Freud and other psychoanalysts – are now rare in the West. However, the more florid examples of this condition – paralysis, blindness, trance states etc – are still to be found from time to time in persons from communities drawn from the developing world. Hysterical conditions are believed to be due to a neurotic reaction to stress which may be perceived or only unconsciously expressed. In many cultures gross mental disturbance in the form of psychosis – reactive or stress-related – may also be found. These are usually short-lived episodes of illness proximately related to stressful events, reasonably easily treated through symptom relief by antipsychotic agents and the treatment does not need to be prolonged. The prognoses of these conditions does not depend on any underlying disease process (as may occur with schizophrenia or the bipolar affective disorders) as such but in the capacity the individual possesses to deal with and cope with future stressful events.

There are many culture-bound, as opposed to culturally influenced, psychiatric disorders which are of little relevance to everyday psychiatric practice in the West. We mention here only 'amok' which has entered the language by way of such phrases as 'running amok'. This is a condition occasionally manifested in South East Asia and which is marked by extravagant behaviour in the face of stressful events and which may lead to homicidal or suicidal acts being committed unless the patient is restrained, usually with the help of a traditional local healer.

We are more interested here in a few otherwise uncommon disorders which nevertheless may have an impact on legal practice. The first of these is morbid jealousy.

9.6   MORBID JEALOUSY

This is referred to also as the Othello syndrome. The main symptom involves a state in which the patient may show a variation between demonstrating excessive suspicion of a spouse or partner's fidelity (males are more commonly afflicted) to possessing full-blown delusions, having symptoms in other words which make up a psychotic condition. There is often present an inadequacy in the personality of the sufferer even before the illness sets in and there is also an association with abuse of alcohol. The behaviours engaged in may be unreasonable, even extreme or bizarre. One recalls a middle-aged man who worked as a commissionaire at the doors of a financial institution in London. He sported colourful livery as his uniform. His jealous wife forbade him to wear this uniform on the underground, which he used to reach his place of employment, lest it turn women passengers' heads. There is usually a relentless pursuit of the truth the patient has become convinced of, namely that the spouse or partner has been unfaithful and all that is necessary for the evidence to emerge is to leave no stone unturned in looking for that proof. Investigation, interrogation and cross-examination may reach extraordinary levels with spying on movements, checking credit card slips or telephone bills, following the spouse wherever she goes, and examining her underwear and bed linen for evidence of sexual activity. Violence is not uncommon and it is one of the psychiatric disorders where in a small minority of cases the killing of a spouse or partner becomes a rather more predictable eventuality than in the usual run of psychiatric cases. Treatment is difficult for the interference of the personality is usually strong and the best results are probably obtained when morbid jealousy is a symptom of another condition such as schizophrenia, depressive illness or alcohol misuse rather than as a free-standing paranoid illness in its own right. The protection of the spouse or partner may become a matter of urgency. The subject is of obvious interest for consideration of risk in the second part of this book.

9.7   EROTOMANIA

Another condition, once believed to be a rare curiosity, has come into prominence on account of an association, at least in a few cases, with the phenomenon called 'stalking'. In its traditional form – called erotomania or De Clerambault's syndrome – spinsters of a certain age used to be affected. She would become deluded that a man, usually of exalted social status or distinguished standing, was in love with her. She would proceed to arrange her life accordingly and could remain chaste and faithful while waiting for him to come definitively into her life. At this stage things remain fairly innocent but the behaviour could extend to harassment and pursuit which could lead to social, personal and professional embarrassment for the victim (some male doctors have been hauled up before the GMC following a complaint by a spurned female patient suffering from this disorder that there had been an improper relationship between them). The criminal law could also become implicated. Injunctions, their breaches and ensuing incarceration are not unknown. Treatment is rarely straightforward unless, as in the case of morbid jealousy, the delusional belief is a symptom of another psychotic illness amenable to treatment, when there is a reasonable prospect of success although relapses are common. The free-standing psychosis is a form of paranoid disorder or a persistent delusional disorder. More recently, the phenomenon of stalking – a form of nuisance behaviour – with a male preponderance, has become recognised although few of the individuals involved in it have any recognised mental disorder. There is no conclusive explanation for the phenomenon though it could be suggested that the easy familiarity with the lives of, and imagined intimacy with, celebrities – encouraged by the media – makes it appear that anyone, however high, is now accessible to someone, however low. Treatment, if actually merited, is difficult and the law's protection may have to be sought by the victim. This condition, too, has obvious implications for the study of risk and the situations involved will be explored in Part II of this book.

9.8   MUNCHAUSEN'S SYNDROME

This topic has made several sensational appearances in connection with the law, especially by way of its alleged variant, Munchausen's syndrome by proxy, and therefore it seems appropriate to make passing reference to it in these pages. The syndrome in its classical form owes its name to an eighteenth century figure. Baron von Munchhausen (sic) (1720–1797) was a real enough person, a German soldier descended from ancient Hanoverian nobility. He served in military campaigns and was noted for his ridiculously exaggerated exploits. A collection of stories was attributed to him. However, much of the final form of the stories was due to the work of Erich Raspe (1737–1794), a scholar and curator of gems and medals at a museum. Accused of stealing and selling the medals he fled Germany for England. Here he engaged in further swindling and had to flee, in turn, to Ireland where he died.

The symptoms displayed in the classical form of the disorder have as much foundation as the baron's stories but display a more humdrum character which, paradoxically, succeeds in fooling doctors. Young men are preponderantly affected. They show the features of pathological lying, exaggeration (or manufacture) of symptoms and the presentation at various hospitals, especially in their casualty departments. Their symptoms may be described with such skill that extensive investigations may follow. The features of an acute abdominal emergency may be so convincingly described that they may come to have numerous operations and they walk about sporting 'criss-cross' patterns on their abdomen as stigmata of their adventures. Apart from the lying there is often also the skilful acting complete with the necessary props, eg simulation of bleeding, self-injury with swallowed objects and the convincing portrayal of physical and mental illness. They are deemed nuisance patients for they waste so much resource (while also putting themselves at risk of iatrogenic illness or injury) and their details may be transmitted across the land so as to alert hospitals to their existence and possible attendance at their doors.

The syndrome is probably best understood as a form of severe personality disorder although a hysterical basis cannot be ruled out (see case described below). A severe personality disorder is probably the most likely explanation also for the variant Munchausen syndrome by proxy which has achieved such notoriety that the diagnosis has been discredited. In this situation a parent (most usually the mother) repeatedly seeks medical intervention for a child by making up symptoms of disease or by deliberately inducing same in the child by any means including causing injury. In other words, the child is being made an instrument of the parent's psychopathology. Gross disorder of mental functioning may be seen in such parents. A 30-year-old woman with a young child – hence their involvement in child care proceedings – not only made up symptoms of illness for herself and her child but also consistently denied usually impeccable sources of factual information – the details on her birth certificate, marriage certificate, pictures of her wedding, letters written about the child by doctors and other documents in similar vein. She would not accept her recorded age or that for the child even when these had been established through official documentation. When the paternity of a second child was brought into question, she tampered with a sample being taken for DNA analysis and very nearly earned a conviction for attempting to pervert the course of justice. The diagnostic category most closely fitting her behaviour appeared to be mixed dissociative disorders (F.44.7 of the ICD-10). The condition, whether in its classical form or its variant, is untreatable for practical purposes

These conditions often have strong associations with matters genuinely involving health and the care of patients. A notorious case which made public headlines was that involving the paediatric nurse Beverley Allitt (another case involving a nurse recently was that of Benjamin Geen, a nurse in Oxford convicted in similar circumstances) who was convicted in May 1993 and sentenced to 13 life sentences for murder, attempted murder and serious assault. She was a nurse aged 24 who was said to have craved approval, attention and sympathy from colleagues and senior staff by raising alarms and helping to save the lives of child patients whose lives she had placed in jeopardy through her own actions. She had later shown no remorse, indulged in pathological lying and attention-seeking behaviour and had sought to be a member of the medical resuscitation team. It turned out she had herself made numerous visits to the casualty department of a local hospital in the course of a three-year period. She had been treated for various self-inflicted injuries and had made false complaints of pregnancy, gastric ulcer and brain tumour. She also alleged she had been sexually assaulted at knife-point and also had had treatment for anorexia nervosa.

9.9 SUMMARY

- Post-partum mental disorder is not uncommon although frequently missed on account of 'maternity blues' being so common. Various risks including a failure of attachment between the newborn and the mother and physical risk to the newborn may arise. Results with prompt and vigorous treatment are satisfactory. There is an increased risk of recurrence following future childbirth.

- 'Culture', the term used in its widest sense, influences the presentation of all mental disorders, in some cases conditions being confined to particular cultures. In some cultures the physical symptoms are given greater emphasis, which does not indicate loss of insight but is a manifestation of cultural belief. Treatment is influenced by beliefs of the individual affecting his attitudes to medication and psychological treatment.

- Morbid jealousy, a form of psychosis, is a potentially dangerous condition, a spouse or partner being at appreciable risk of being a victim of violence. Protective measures need to be taken in all cases. The results of treatment depend on whether the condition is a symptom of another condition when results may be relatively good or is free-standing psychotic condition when results are usually poor. There is a strong association with alcohol misuse.

- Munchausen's syndrome and any of its variants are to be seen as forms of severe personality disorder. The preoccupation these individuals have with matters concerning health may lead to harm being caused to themselves and also to those with whom they are intimate, especially their children.

PART II

RISK ASSESSMENT IN PSYCHIATRY

CHAPTER 10

RISK ASSESSMENT OF VIOLENCE

10.1   INTRODUCTION

This chapter considers aggressive conduct as it is directed against the self (suicidal behaviour and deliberate self-harm) as well as against other persons and property. The special case of sexual violence is also addressed. These behaviours form the basis for the risk assessment exercise concerning violence which involves all psychiatric practice.

10.2   SUICIDAL BEHAVIOUR

About one million people die by suicide worldwide each year. In England and Wales there are between 4,500 to 5,000 suicides per year. A distinction is to be made between suicidal behaviour (including attempts) and behaviour leading to deliberate self-harm. Suicidal behaviour is distinguished by the presence of intent as a mental state required for the act or omission involved. What 'intent' is may be explored by means of the proposals put forward by the Law Commission[1] which is a proposed attempt to statutorily define what is at present a common law concept. By this proposed definition a person acts intentionally with respect to a result when he or she acts either:

(1)   in order to bring it about; or

(2)   knowing that it will be virtually certain to occur;

(3)   knowing that it would be virtually certain to occur if he or she were to succeed in his or her purpose of causing some other result, with the proviso that a person is not to be deemed to have intended any result which it was his or her specific purpose to avoid.

In practice, whether there is suicidal intent is to be determined by the stated views of the individual if these are available (usually conveyed

[1]   *A New Homicide Act for England and Wales?* Consultation Paper No 177 of 2005.

orally or by the writing of a 'suicide note') and the surrounding behaviour of the individual which may perhaps be best illustrated by way of a couple of examples.

A 40-year-old single mother could no longer cope with the increasingly disturbed behaviour of her 14-year-old son who was later diagnosed to be suffering from one of the autistic spectrum disorders. She planned to kill herself. She left notes, also made elaborate plans for the future care of her 10-year-old daughter, settled her affairs and asked in a note for her possessions including her jewellery to be passed on to the daughter. Suicidal intent was therefore clear in this case but it may not be so clearly observed in many other cases, a fact explaining the reluctance of some coroners to bring in a verdict of suicide in the absence of incontrovertible evidence of intent being present.

The unusual facts of a second case also illustrate the concept of intent in these circumstances. A 39-year-old man, separated from his wife, had contact with his three-year-old son who resided with its mother. The man suffered from severe and enduring physical illness which necessitated treatment with methotrexate (a cancer drug which may occasionally be used to treat some intractable physical illnesses) and also a steroid drug. Both these agents may precipitate or exacerbate mood disorders and the man had, in any event, for many years suffered from depressive illness as a result, it was believed, of his chronic physical illness. Soon after the man separated from his wife he suffered a further bout of severe depressive illness. In a state of deep despair and depression he proposed to drive to an isolated spot and there gas himself and his child by means of the exhaust fumes emitted by his motor car. The car, a fairly up-to-date model, was equipped with a catalytic converter which is believed to prevent the normal kind of exhaust fumes, laden as they are with the lethal carbon monoxide gas, from emerging. This fact was not, however, known to the man at the time and he insisted at a later examination that his intention had all along been to die with his son. In the event no injury due to the actions of the father resulted to either father or son. However, the impossibility of bringing about an intended outcome does not preclude a genuine attempt having been made, with intent as the underlying mental state. This was, in fact, a genuine suicidal (and homicidal) attempt.

Pure chance might also have determined the end result in another case. A 40-year-old chartered accountant, beset by many problems and facing possible indictment on a charge of mortgage fraud, decided to end his life also through gassing himself by means of his car's exhaust fumes. The turmoil in his mind was such that he had failed to ensure the car had sufficient fuel in its tank for this purpose. The engine accordingly cut out in due course in the isolated woodland spot he had chosen for his deed and he was rescued by some sightseers. He was left with severe, uncorrectable brain damage which virtually completely destroyed his memory. Suicidal intent was nonetheless clearly present.

Contrary to popular notion, the fact of death or near death through dangerous behaviour does not necessarily distinguish between intentional behaviour and merely reckless action. It is perfectly possible to die following an impulsive act if the means employed are dangerous enough, eg swallowing a sufficient dosage of paracetamol tablets if they are to hand. Some tragic consequences have resulted even in situations where the victim probably did not intend to die but the circumstances were against her (females more commonly engage in reckless rather than intentional acts of self-harm). Even an apparently trivial consideration such as the day of the week when the act takes place may make a difference as to whether an individual lives or dies. If, say, towards the end of the week, when the supply of paracetamol tablets in the household drug cupboard is running low, an impulsive act takes place, it may well lead to the individual surviving. If the act had taken place, on the contrary, at the weekend, say, when the supply has been replenished after the week's shopping has been done, enough tablets may be available to make death the outcome as sufficient poison would then have been ingested. Recent legislation restricts the amount of paracetamol available for sale in packages; therefore stockpiling may be evidence of intent for the reckless self-harmer usually merely swallows what is to hand.

Risk factors for suicidal behaviour include male sex, unemployment, a single state, psychiatric disorder (especially depressive illness, schizophrenia, anorexia nervosa or abuse of alcohol and/or illicit drugs or the personality disorders), chronic physical disability, recent bereavement and personality malfunction not amounting to disorder. Some 50 per cent of successful suicides have previously made an attempt to end their life. Swinson et al[2] have shown that 25 per cent of suicides have been in recent contact with the mental health services. Between 160–200 psychiatric in-patients die by suicide annually, most commonly by hanging. The period of highest risk after discharge from hospital in-patient care appears to be in the first 14 days. Over one-fifth of individuals dying by suicide have not been adhering to their medication regime in the preceding month and nearly one-third appear to have disengaged themselves from the services.

Hunt et al[3] have shown the differences between younger and older suicides. Deaths of younger patients were characterised by jumping from a height or in front of a vehicle, and these patients suffered from schizophrenia, personality disorder, unemployment and substance misuse. In older patients, drowning, depression, living alone, physical illness,

---

[2]   See N Swinson et al 'National Confidential Inquiry into Suicide and Homicide by People with Mental illness: new directions' (2007) *Psychiatric Bulletin* 31, 161–163.

[3]   See I M Hunt et al 'Suicide within 12 months of mental health service contact in different age and diagnostic groups' (2006) *British Journal of Psychiatry* 188, 135–142.

recent bereavement and suicide pacts were more common. Individuals with schizophrenia were often in-patients and died by violent means. About one-third of individuals with depressive disorder died within a year of illness onset. Those with substance dependence or personality disorder had high rates of disengagement from services. Prevention measures likely to benefit young people including targeting patients who had schizophrenia or a dual diagnosis and had lost contact with the services; those measures aimed at depression, isolation and physical ill health were likely to have more effect on elderly individuals. Suicide prevention in those under 25 may require comprehensive care packages for patients with schizophrenia, co-morbid substance misuse and poor engagement with the services, whereas improving the recognition and treatment of depression, the care provided at times of bereavement and the mental health care of those with physical illness could reduce suicide among older patients.

In the assessment of suicidal risk the examination of the mental state appears to be the most important element. The presence of any psychiatric disorder (and not merely the conditions mentioned above) increases risk. A depressed mood – which may be found as a symptom in any psychiatric disorder – associated with feelings of pessimism, despair and worthlessness will elevate risk. The psychotic disorders are generally believed to carry a lower risk although, as already noted, an appreciable number of schizophrenic patients proceed to kill themselves. Auditory hallucinations may impel a patient to take his life by ordering him to do so. Suicidal ideation is an important sign to elicit in the mental state examination. There is a gradation in those thoughts and we shall consider them in an ascending order of risk. The most innocuous are fleeting thoughts that life may not be worth living. This is followed by momentary notions where actual suicide is contemplated. Next comes recurrent and persistent thoughts of putting an end to one's life. At the extreme end is found actual planning of the kind we have described. It has been shown that suicide attempts among patients with major depressive disorders are strongly associated with the presence and severity of depressive symptoms and predicted by lack of a partner, previous suicidal attempts and the time spent in being depressed. Suicidal thoughts must be actively sought and it is a false sense of propriety and delicacy that decides not to intrude into private matters or even causes one to be fearful of putting such thoughts into an innocent mind. The purpose of the enquiry is to be able to arm oneself with the information which may dictate the necessary responses to be made including, where the conditions merit it, compulsory hospital admission under the Mental Health Act 1983. The actual treatment to be given is, of course, dictated by the underlying disorder when it is treatable. Social measures are very useful in the long-term, even those involved in giving such simple information as the availability of the Samaritans organisation. As noted above, treatment, even in a hospital setting, does not always provide the necessary security for it is well known that the recovery phase in a depressive illness is a particularly dangerous period for further suicidal attempts The explanation usually given in respect of depressive illness is that the marked psychomotor retardation found in the acute stages of the illness is selectively eased with treatment, with improved physical activity coming before psychological uplift so that the patient previously physically incapable of carrying out a suicidal act now has the means as well as a still persisting intention, a case of the flesh becoming stronger while the spirit remains weak.

10.3   DELIBERATE SELF-HARM (DSH)

This is to be distinguished from attempted suicide which, as with any attempt, is marked by the possession of intent. In fact, the behaviour seen in DSH is usually characterised as reckless for the individual knows that some harm may befall him if he proceeds with the actions he is about to take but he continues with it nonetheless. It should be remembered that mental states, in both the medical and legal sense, can change and vary, and recklessness may give way in time to intentional behaviour. In fact, it is known that in the 12 months following an act of DSH there is increased incidence of both further acts of DSH (some 20 per cent of cases) as well as acts of completed suicide (one to two per cent of cases). While death may follow an unintentional act in ways described before, there is some evidence that the perpetrator of DSH might also have had some time before the intention to take his life.

Deliberate self-harm is a fairly recent phenomenon which, at one stage in the 1960s and 1970s, threatened to attain epidemic proportions. Even now there about 150,000 cases of DSH admitted to the casualty units each year. It is difficult to find many examples in the historical literature of deliberate self-harm unrelated to hysterical states (except, of course, as acts of mutilatory malingering to avoid going to war) while attempted suicide was, of course, not uncommon. Why this should be so is unclear although the identity of the perpetrators of self-harm – mostly adolescent and young women of lower social origins than is associated with suicidal behaviour – may furnish a clue. Perhaps it results from social emancipation from previously fairly tightly regulated lives. Whatever the cause may be, the methods used in DSH now involve prescribed and off-prescription drugs (which account for some 90 per cent of cases of DSH) and some form of self-mutilation which involves (usually) superficial cutting of parts of the body, chiefly the limbs.

The causes of this behaviour are not uniform. While a significant number of these individuals exhibit features of personality disorder (or behaviour disorder if younger than the age of deemed maturity), quite a few have no discernible psychiatric abnormality at all. The most common factor in the act is a precipitating event preceding the act which has caused distress or is perceived as threatening. As many of these acts are impulsive – done in 'moments of madness', as it is commonly described – it is difficult sometimes to identify any persisting personal or social difficulty but there is not uncommonly a pervasive or smouldering feelings of unhappiness or dissatisfaction – neither of which is, of course, a psychiatric symptom – which is waiting for some stimulus or spark to set it off by way of an act of self-harm. Alcohol is commonly involved as a disinhibiting agent.

The assessment of DSH is as for suicidal behaviour for no conclusions can be arrived at as to whether intent is or was present or the act followed recklessness without proper assessment. It is now routine for psychiatric assessments to take place in Accident and Emergency departments of hospitals to which the patient is taken in the first instance following an overdose. Transfer to a psychiatric unit takes place when there is an underlying disorder detectable or when there is uncertainty about the clinical picture and the patient is believed to be at risk of repeating such behaviour. Treatment is, as with suicidal behaviour, for any underlying psychiatric condition if one exists. Social and personal problems – some of it amenable to advice and practical help such as rehousing or debt management – is often more appropriate than formal psychiatric treatment. The risk of further DSH and suicidal behaviour is always present and the most useful duty of the attending psychiatrist is to detect the presence of some treatable condition in the individual who has engaged in DSH. It has been shown that those patients who display an escalating severity of self-poisoning episodes are at high risk of completed suicide. In a review by Crawford et al[4] it was shown that there was little evidence that additional psychosocial interventions following self-harm had a marked effect on the likelihood of subsequent suicide. Individual trials of psychosocial treatments might have demonstrated statistically significant reductions in the likelihood of repetitions of non-fatal self-harm, but such findings do not necessarily mean that these treatments would reduce the likelihood of subsequent suicide. These authors suggest that a range of public health measures should be pursued in an attempt to reduce rates of suicide.

10.4   AGGRESSION TURNED OUTWARDS

Violent behaviour is a complex subject and its roots go beyond the psychiatric, yet it is the professional in this field who is often asked to evaluate violent behaviour as part of a risk assessment.

10.5   VIOLENCE ASSOCIATED WITH MENTAL DISORDER

When formal mental illness can be identified, an understanding of the psychiatric origin of cases of violent behaviour may be achieved without

---

4   See M J Crawford et al 'Psychosocial interventions following self-harm. Systematic Review of their efficacy in preventing suicide' (2007) *British Journal of Psychiatry* 190, 11–17.

too much difficulty. Psychotic violence is not uncommon and conditions such as schizophrenia and mania may feature high in such violence although overall, despite popular prejudice, violence associated with mental disorders is comparatively rare. Perhaps reassuringly – for it confirms what has long been suspected by informed persons – a recent study from New Zealand has reported that homicides by the mentally ill has not increased as a rate and also that people in close relationship with the perpetrator, rather than strangers, are most at risk of being the victim. In schizophrenia the violence may be associated with underlying symptoms such as delusions (persecutory delusions may cause a patient to protect himself against his imagined tormentors) or hallucinations (voices may urge the patient to act violently) though violence may also remain an unexplained feature, indeed lead to the first presentation, of the condition. In the days when it used to be commonly seen, catatonic excitement (when the patient had roused himself or was roused from stupor) used to be a particularly frightening phenomenon and hard to control. Among states of psychotic violence one may also class the condition of delirium or acute confusional states in which lashing out on the part of the patient is not uncommonly seen. Confusional states may or may not be associated with dementia, another condition in which violence is occasionally seen when it may be associated with agitation and wandering behaviour and appears related also to the previous personality of the patient, a matter previously discussed. Both the carer and the cared in cases of dementia not uncommonly experience violence at each other's hands. As has also been discussed previously, the risk to the spouse or partner of a patient suffering from morbid jealousy is a very real one, a risk that requires to be taken seriously in all cases – for it brings together various strands involved in violent behaviour such as the victim being closely related to the assailant and therefore at the highest risk of violence from a psychotic patient and also the known statistical risk of violence to spouses or partners (a couple of whom are killed every week) – and must be acted on urgently.

The affective disorders may also lead to violence. Depressive illness, contrary to popular belief, is not all about slowed down physical and mental functions. There is an appreciable risk of violence in this condition, most often directed against the self as in suicidal behaviour but other aggressive, even homicidal, features are not unknown. One particular form of violence associated with depressive illness is murder followed by suicide, cases occasionally featured in the media, when a depressed individual kills one or more persons, usually those who have had an intimate relationship with him, before turning on himself, perhaps by using the same murderous weapon. As these words are being written one reads about the successful middle-aged man, estranged from his wife and waiting to be divorced, who had had a long history of depressive illness. He discharged himself from being a voluntary patient at a psychiatric hospital in the south of England, drove to the matrimonial home where he bludgeoned his wife to death before proceeding to kill himself by driving his car into a tree. These tragedies are also not uncommon especially where the father has been in dispute with the mother over their children who are then killed by the father before he kills himself. It is, of course, by no means the case that depression – in the form of illness – has been suffered in all these instances and there are, in addition, numerous other contributory factors usually involved but the features of an affective illness are not uncommonly reported in such individuals before the act. Affective disorders in the post-partum state, including the most common, namely post-partum depressive illness, are a source of risk to the newborn child and one must ensure the relatively common nature of the condition does not lead to the minimising of the need for risk assessment.

Systemic disorder is a possible cause of violent behaviour. Head injury, in particular where it involves personality change, as in the case of *Miah* discussed previously, could be a potent cause of such aggression. Brain tumours may present themselves with aggressive conduct. Epilepsy – especially in the post-fit state – is another cause and what used to be called 'post-epileptic furore' used to match catatonic excitement in its scope for and degree of violence. A well known physical state involved with violent and other uncharacteristic bouts of behaviour involves the hypoglycaemic state which follows over corrected diabetes mellitus, usually after the patient has taken his insulin or oral medication but has then failed to keep up his blood sugar levels by eating sufficiently or at regular intervals. One must also bear in mind the use of steroids – by renegade professional sportsmen or by body builders – which is a class of drug which can not uncommonly lead to aggressive behaviour.

By far the most common psychiatric condition associated with violent behaviour is personality disorder including its most severe form called psychopathy. Aggression in these individuals is commonly attributed to poor impulse control and lack of restraint though it has to be said their lack of remorse or feelings of guilt may also contribute by means of the absence of personal or social 'brakes' which are so vital for harmonious life in any community. Personality disorder is also commonly associated with the abuse of alcohol and illicit substances though an underlying psychiatric disorder is not required for these substances to act as instruments of violence. Alcohol is widely known to precipitate violence though sophisticated analysts of the phenomenon accept that there are crucial personal, social and cultural factors also influencing the behaviour when alcohol fuels violence. The disinhibiting effects of alcohol often require some other factor such as the comforting presence of a like-minded mob before appreciable violence is precipitated. The rampaging behaviour of football hooligans is due to both drink and the mob influence. A clear distinction has to be drawn in such cases between public violence and private violence involving individuals who might have been caught up in acts involving the former. Many public exponents of such violence may be peaceable individuals in private. A 35-year-old father, a notorious football hooligan with many convictions and 'away match' bans, wished to have contact with his young child. The public violence he had indulged in had been undertaken under the influence of alcohol and at other times he had also abused cannabis among other illicit substances. Yet, there was no evidence of any violence on his part in private, especially against the child or any other children or, indeed, other individuals. Other cultural factors may also be found operating. In some ethnic minority populations there is perceived to be a greater degree of violence in association with mental disorder. Black patients in high-security psychiatric hospitals are overrepresented by eight times. Unmet needs are more common among black than white patients in these hospitals. Higher prevalence rates of mental illness, particularly schizophrenia, have been found for black Caribbean patients than for white patients. Higher rates of compulsory admission have also been reported and also higher rates of contact with the police and forensic services and with intensive care facilities.

Along with alcohol – a lawful and freely available substance – one must consider the possible role of prescribed drugs in the precipitation of violence. We have already referred to the possibility that the newer antidepressant drugs, the SSRI agents such as fluoxetine (Prozac), could precipitate violence in some predisposed individuals. Diazepam (Valium) is widely known to be and is taken as a sedative and anxiolytic drug. Yet, it could paradoxically release aggression and violence as happened on the facts of *R v Hardie*.[5] The appellant's relationship with his girlfriend had broken down. He became upset and consumed several tablets of Valium which, in fact, had been prescribed for his girlfriend for use as a sedative. Under the influence of this drug he started a fire. On a charge of arson he submitted he had had no mens rea. The trial judge refused him on the ground of voluntary self-administration of the drug. The Court of Appeal allowed his appeal on the grounds of misdirection to the jury, noting that Valium is a drug 'wholly different in kind from drugs which are liable to cause unpredictability or aggressiveness'. This paradoxical disinhibiting effect is, of course, a cause of violence due to alcohol or any other normally sedative or anxiety-relieving agent. In these cases a close study needs to be made of the individual propensities of the patient concerned and the manner in which he has behaved on previous occasions when he has been under the influence of these drugs.

Similar considerations apply to cannabis, usually also taken for its sedative or calming properties but which, in some individuals and in large quantities, is capable of precipitating violence or aggravating aggressive conduct. That cannabis is not entirely innocuous as previously believed – and the focus of campaigners demanding its decriminalisation – is now accepted for there appears to be a significant minority of individuals with a predisposition who may be turned towards violence – and also into suffering psychotic conditions – by the consumption of this drug. The

---

[5]   [1984] 3 All ER 848, [1985] 1 WLR 64, CA.

position with amphetamines, cocaine and many other illicit substances is much clearer for violence is to be expected in certain cases following their use. These stimulant drugs cause an apparent increase in energy along with surging self-confidence and self-esteem which could spill over very easily into aggression especially in the atmosphere and circumstances in which these drugs are usually taken. In the course of illicit use the purity of these substances can also by no means be guaranteed and in those circumstances there is a wholly new dimension to be considered – for the contaminants themselves may be capable of causing aggressive behaviour. Paradoxically, on occasions when there are no contaminants and the drug is taken in pure form, there could also be aggressive behaviour on account of the unwanted effects of the pure substance. It is easy now to see how the analysis of violence attributable to these drugs and their impact on different individuals is a subject fraught with complexity and uncertainty. While the general principles are clear enough it cannot usually be said with any great conviction, as far as any individual is concerned, that any drug or group of drugs, by their actions alone, will cause particular effects or could have been responsible for specific past behaviours.

10.6   VIOLENCE UNASSOCIATED WITH MENTAL DISORDER

When mental disorder is not part of the picture, the analysis of violent behaviour becomes even more difficult. One searches for any available rules that can be applied in these circumstances. Of all the available rules there is one of especial value that has survived the test of time when it comes to predicting the risk of future violent conduct; and that rule involves a history of previous violent conduct which is a strong predictor of future violence. This behaviour has been tested in relation to previous history of offending. One study showed that 14 per cent of those with a previous conviction for violence, 40 per cent of those with two previous convictions, 44 per cent of those with three previous convictions and 55 per cent of those with four previous convictions were likely to have a further conviction for violence. Overall, violence is also still more common in men than in women, although it is said that teenage and adolescent girls are catching up with their male peers in that age group. A man who has behaved violently on one occasion is more likely to behave in such a way on a future occasion than one who has no history of violent behaviour. That is a general truth which is subject to qualification. As we have seen with the football hooligan whose case was mentioned previously, violent behaviour can be situation-specific. The hooligan can be predicted to behave violently at football matches in the future, especially when he is under the influence of alcohol and illicit substances and when he is surrounded by like-minded supporters. But it is by no means certain he could be expected to behave violently in other circumstances. In fact, there was little evidence this particular individual behaved aggressively elsewhere, a point made in child care proceedings in his favour where he had applied to have supervised contact with his young daughter. This illustrates a key point – the precise circumstances of previous episodes of violence need to be studied as well as the situation for which risk is being assessed. The facts required for this analysis include, among other detail, the identity of previous victims, their gender, the particular circumstances (eg whether the individual and victim were previously acquainted and, if so, at what level of intimacy), the role played by alcohol and/or illicit and prescribed drugs and the outcome of the violence including any convictions and the penalties that came to be applied. These are the objective facts. A subjective account should also be obtained from the individual who is being assessed. This is both fair to him and may also help to correct any disputed facts but it may also indicate the attitude he has towards violent behaviour in general and the previous victims in particular. A lack of remorse or regret is taken to be a reliable indicator of future violence and any attitude that is specific (eg hostility to a spouse or partner) or more general (eg against women) is often a dangerous sign.

The role of alcohol and illicit substances has already been touched upon. A rule can be given at a fairly low level of generality that future indulgence in these substances will probably lead to a repetition of acts of violent behaviour but the facts must still need to be analysed with care for even substance-induced violence can be situation-specific (eg domestic violence).

Violent behaviour, if one is to believe what psychologists and anthropologists say, should be commonplace but it is, in fact, an uncommon phenomenon in most civilised societies, though the levels may not be any less worrying for that. Man is supposed to be an inherently aggressive animal. He would not have succeeded in evolutionary terms if he had not been assertive and ruthless in his dealings with the environment. In fact, social and cultural rules that have been developed and are inculcated in children from a young age may be seen to be attempts designed to curtail this aggression so as to enable life to go on in tolerable tranquility among members of a social community. This restraint is meant to apply to all members who are expected to curb their aggressive thoughts and impulses. These are surprisingly common to experience, and are found in the most unlikely of individuals, but are relatively uncommonly acted upon. It follows that anything that interferes with normal impulse control in respect of aggression will conduce to violence. Poor impulse control is a feature of personality disorder and psychopathy, and it is the usual finding in clinical psychiatric practice that a crucial element in future risk assessment is an evaluation of the individual's personality. Impulse control is also associated with the expression of anger and reactions to stressful and provoking stimuli. Anger is well recognised to be a source of violence and anger management is the approach usually suggested to deal with excessive and inappropriate anger. Anger management deals with the problem at the behavioural level and a close analysis is still required of factors such as personality and the misuse of alcohol and illicit substances.

Another factor often suggested to function as a protective influence against habitual violent behaviour is the degree of socialisation achieved by individuals. This phenomenon is related to the successful incorporation of social rules. The thinking here is that a person who has been properly integrated into the requirements of society, and in whom the rules of society have been embedded into those centres of the brain which govern socially appropriate behaviour by suppressing impulses and emotions, achieves proper social integration. Such individuals are less likely to resort to violence either because they can successfully master their impulses or they have otherwise learned to take the co-operative and lawful route to achieving their needs and desires and do not have to resort to the 'coerced transactions' (as the economic philosophers characterise robbery) when individuals have failed to use negotiation and persuasion in the market place for transactions but have turned instead to force to achieve their ends. The lesson to be learned for purposes of risk assessment is that a poorly socialised individual may pose a higher risk of future violence than one who is normally socialised and in whom a solitary act of aggression may be attributed to aberrant behaviour on one occasion. Social isolation with poor social networks, a lonely existence and solitary interests are believed to indicate a lack of proper socialisation.

Violence, of course, occurs against the person or property. The interaction between assailant and his victim has attracted enormous interest in recent years. At one level, it could be said there is always some interaction, however minimal in degree, between attacker and victim even when a victim might only have found himself, as is said, in the 'wrong place at the wrong time'. This book, however, is concerned with more substantial levels of contact and the relationship that has existed between attacker and victim. The features present in the victim must also be studied, wherever possible, with care. The age of the victim is of importance for while most assailants and their victims are young men, the selective and purposeful targeting of victims of a certain age, eg at the extremes of age, the elderly and the very young, may give a clue as to the prospects for future violent conduct. The gender of the victim is an obvious consideration. The personality of the victim, whether it also underlies some mental disorder, may be as important to take account of as that of the assailant. One must seek to find out, especially in situations where recurrent violence has taken place, whether the victim himself is aggressive, unduly anxious or overly dependent on a potential assailant for these features are often associated with individuals who tend to become victims, especially in the domestic context. We shall consider some of the more specific features of this condition when we later take up domestic violence but the attitude of the victim is always important to evaluate. If recurrent violence has taken place, involving one set of assailant and victim, has the victim complained and supported previous proceedings? If not, why not? It is an obvious inference that if an assailant knows he can get away with violence he will be more prone to violence or aggressive conduct for even the most impulsive of persons usually has some idea of self-preservation and normally has little wish to entangle himself unnecessarily with the criminal law. The role of mental disorder and the misuse of alcohol and illicit substances in the victim may also be material considerations. It follows that in the ideal situation the assailant and any identifiable future victim should both be assessed although the absence of resources (and possibly consent) do not usually permit this endeavour.

10.7   SOME CONCLUSIONS FROM FORENSIC PSYCHIATRY

Studies in forensic psychiatric practice have been usefully summarised[6] in terms of risk factors influencing reoffending:

(1)   The mental disorder itself and its lack of recognition by professionals. In a study at the Rampton Hospital of those mentally ill patients who had committed homicide it was found that all these patients had been mentally disordered at the time of committing the offence but only some 25 per cent of them were receiving treatment. Premature discharge from hospital adds to the risk. Repetition of violent acts may be determined by the situation in which a mentally disordered offender finds himself and the emotional demands that are made on him. It is vital before discharge from hospital to ensure that the offender's psychological resources are sufficient to cope with the vagaries of life in the community. More recently, Swinson et al[7] have found that around 50 homicides per year are committed by those in recent contact with mental health services, a figure that represents nine per cent of all homicides. About five per cent of the perpetrators of homicide have a diagnosis of schizophrenia. Perpetrators with mental illness are less likely to kill strangers and the rate of 'stranger homicide' by those with mental illness has not increased with national trends.

(2)   The tendency to engage in impulsive antisocial acts on little or no provocation is another pointer towards increased risk. If aggressive antisocial tendencies co-exist with mental illness or other disorder the risk may increase.

(3)   The nature of the index offence may give clues as to future risk especially if the victim had been specifically targeted, eg as being a

---

6   See D J Power et al 'Dangerous Patients and the Public' in *Criminal Law and Forensic Psychiatry* (Barry Rose, 1996).

7   See N Swinson et al 'National Confidential Inquiry into Suicide and Homicide by People with Mental illness: new directions' (2007) *Psychiatric Bulletin* 31, 161–163.

member of a particular age group (the elderly or children) or of a particular gender. This may indicate a habitual pattern of serious antisocial behaviour. Random killings by individuals suffering from schizophrenia or other psychotic disorders involving strangers may indicate continuing risk to the public. Incidents prior to the index offence, which if they had not involved prosecution might not have revealed the full facts, could be important. In the notorious Zito case, Mr Jonathan Zito had been stabbed to death at a London Underground station by Christopher Clunis who had a history of paranoid schizophrenia and of violence. It transpired at the official inquiry into this case that Clunis had stabbed a fellow resident in a hostel some five months before his attack on Mr Zito but had not been prosecuted, a matter which came to be criticised.

(4)   The uncertainty of the clinical prognosis, especially where there are multiple diagnoses, eg mental illness with learning disabilities, mental illness associated with a personality disorder, may increase the risk or, at any rate, make it even less predictable.

(5)   Persisting lack of remorse or continuing denial in the face of overwhelming evidence may be a sign of high risk. This will be enhanced if the clinical condition associated with previous violence – persecutory symptoms, morbid jealousy – persist. A declared intention of future violence in the midst of an unsettled mental state is obviously of considerable concern.

(6)   The continuing presence of sadistic fantasies even after incarceration and attempts at treatment may be indicative of high risk of reoffending.

(7)   A history of misuse of alcohol and/or illicit substances, even if the behaviour is in abeyance on incarceration, may be a sign of risk if it is believed the patient may resume his patterns of substance abuse, especially on release from custody. Swinson et al have also found that alcohol and drug misuse contribute to homicide in 61 per cent of cases, a figure which has major public health implications.

(8)   A paradoxical situation involves the offender, often a psychopath, who learns to work the system, appears to be most amenable and succeeds in fooling the professionals evaluating his progress. He may pose a serious risk if only because it is never wholly possible to properly assess future risk to be posed in the community by an individual who is being evaluated in an artificial situation of containment. Good behaviour in an institution does not necessarily mean it will be translated to conditions in the world outside.

In recent years there have been attempts to standardise assessment of the risk of violence and the management of that risk. This has included the introduction of structured approaches to risk assessment. The rationale for this is that there is believed to be both clinical and actuarial approaches that can be taken in regard to risk assessment and aspects of both these approaches could be included in a structured approach. Studies have shown there not to be any significant relationship between specific diagnosis and future violence in the community. There is also support for the view that after-care arrangements can offer a degree of protection against future violence on the part of patients. Psychopathy, when diagnosed, was, however, predictive of future violence. While the assessment of future risk of violence remains essentially a clinical procedure at present, a rating scale has been put forward in the form of HCR-20 Violence Risk Assessment Scheme and may come to find more widespread acceptance in the future.[8] It provides an outline of the factors clinicians could use in assessing risk and provides a structured basis for doing so. This instrument contains 20 items organised around three scales:

- historical data (ten items);

- clinical evidence (five items); and

- risk (five items).

The ten historical items include history of violence, age at first violence, relationship history, employment history, history of substance misuse, previous mental illness, psychopathy, early maladjustment, personality disorder and previous conditional release failure. The five clinical evidence items include lack of insight, negative attitudes, symptomatology, lack of behavioural stability and lack of treatability. The five risk items are concerned with forecasting the patient's future social, living and treatment circumstances, as well as anticipating the patient's reactions to those conditions. This includes lack of plan feasibility, access to destabilisers, lack of support, future non-compliance and stress. Reviews have suggested that the HCR-20 was the most robust predictor of subsequent violence in the community and that the clinical and risk management items (referred to as the 'dynamic' element) add significantly to the validity of risk assessment as compared with the more 'static' factors such as the items listed under the historical scale of the HCR-20. The historical data appear to be of limited predictive value in clinical risk assessment. It appears that strategies for risk management could be successful if they are feasible, treat active symptoms of mental illness, address issues of attitude, impulse control and emotional regulation in patients, reduce the likelihood of non-compliance and improve insight. In summary, it appears that while 'static' measures of risk relating to past history and personality may make some limited contribution to

---

8   See C D Webster et al 'Violence risk assessment using structured clinical guidelines professionally' (2002) *International Journal of Mental Health* 1, 185–193.

assessment of risk violence, consideration of current 'dynamic' factors relating to illness and risk management significantly improves predictive accuracy.

10.8   SEXUAL VIOLENCE

This subject, too, may be studied as a subspecies of general violence, though, of course, some special factors also apply. We have already learned that a process of socialisation undertaken beginning in childhood leads, by learning to control primitive instincts, to the development of responsible adult behaviour. Persistent violent behaviour, whether it involves sexual misconduct or not, often shows a failure of this process of socialisation and many of the risk factors involved with aggressive behaviour in general are also applicable here. The social elements involved, including those affecting the victim, are also important to consider.

Formal mental illness is uncommon among sex offenders although a manic illness may involve aggressive sexual conduct and morbid jealousy is a special case further taken up in the next chapter. Brain degenerative processes and the consequences of head injury, as in the *Meah* case, are occasionally present in sex offenders as is dementia in the early stages of that degenerative condition. Where mental disorder is present in an offender, as with violence generally, the condition most often met with is personality disorder. This is commonly associated with misuse of alcohol and illicit drugs, substances which lead to disinhibition in terms of sexual behaviour as well as of violent conduct generally.

Given the diverse circumstances involved with sexual offending, general rules are hard to lay down. It seems the following points could be reasonably made:

(1)   The vast majority of sex offenders do not appear to be suffering from a recognisable psychiatric disorder. In other words, they are not ill in a way that a doctor or lay person would recognise. They may have a psychological disturbance which may, at least in a statistical sense, indicate abnormality.

(2)   As far as we can tell, most sexual offences, and those involving rape in particular, occur between parties who are acquainted with one another, often intimately so. In other words, most sexual offences involve the issue of 'consent', not 'identity'.

(3)   Where mental disorder is found, personality disorder is the most common of the conditions involved.

(4)   Substance misuse is commonly involved. This may involve a situation where the rapist has gone 'too far' in presuming consent

when under the influence of a substance (that is, he might have abused consent which might have been given), those situations involving 'date rape' resulting from administered drugs (likely to be far less common in incidence than is portrayed by the popular media) and the rare 'sprees' which follow the ingestion of substances, most commonly the stimulant drugs such as cocaine and the amphetamines.

(5) Where there has been significant victim complicity substance misuse is usually an important factor.

(6) Many of the studies purporting to study the characteristics of rapists involve 'serial rapists' and their conclusions are as limited in application to the most common type of 'one-off' sexual offender as a study of serial murderers is to the study of the average murderer.

(7) The absence of mental illness and mental disorder in the usual run of cases limits the effectiveness of psychiatric treatment. Medical and surgical treatment involving drugs and/or surgery are also very limited in scope, beneficial perhaps to an occasional offender but not generally.

(8) The risk assessment of sexual offending is probably best approached in the terms employed for the study of violent behaviour generally where, the best predictor of future conduct being deemed past behaviour, those factors that applied at the time of the index offence need to be analysed. It is salutary to remind oneself of the low reliability of most predictive indices. To give but one example, it used to be believed that a lone individual who was poorly socialised was most prone to sexual violence. The number of married and otherwise apparently socially adept men being thrown up by DNA analysis several years after the commission by them of sexual offences, which long lay unsolved, reveals that generalities are just that – with little application to the individual case. There is no alternative, it seems, to a detailed study being made of all the available facts of case, paying attention to all the surrounding circumstances as well as the behaviour of the victim.

10.9 SUMMARY

- Suicidal behaviour is to be distinguished from parasuicidal or self-harming behaviour by the presence of intent in the former and recklessness in the latter. There may be different characteristics associated with each type of behaviour but there is also a relationship between them in that a certain proportion of self-harming individuals will succeed in killing themselves. Risk is to be assessed in each case of suicidal or deliberate self-harming behaviour to ensure the absence of formal mental illness or disorder and also to make an evaluation of possible risk factors.

- Violence associated with mental disorder invariably shows that a relatively high proportion of offenders have not had contact with the treatment services and, also, where there has been contact, that such contact has been lost or that the perpetrator has become non-compliant with treatment. Certain conditions of mental illness are particularly serious for violence. This includes the psychotic condition known as morbid jealousy which puts the spouse or partner at real risk of violence. Contrary to popular belief most forms of violence occur between individuals who are acquainted with one another. Personality disorder may be heavily implicated in cases of violence associated with mental disorder. Rating scales are now becoming more frequently use in the systematic assessment of risk.

- Violence unassociated with mental disorder is often difficult to subject to risk assessment. The most valuable rule still available to clinicians is the maxim that the best predictor of future conduct is past behaviour. The heavy association between violent behaviour and misuse of alcohol and illicit drugs must also be stressed

- As a rule, sexual violence is not associated with formal mental illness. Reliable figures are hard to come by but most forms of sexual violence appear to involve those who are acquainted with one another. Studies of serial perpetrators of sexual violence may not be applicable to the usual kind of offender.

CHAPTER 11

RISK ASSESSMENT IN FAMILY AND CHILD LAW PRACTICE

11.1   INTRODUCTION

Violence plays an important part in family and child law practice and is thus considered here. There is a necessary overlap between what is discussed here and what was considered in the previous chapter but some special factors apply also.

11.2   DOMESTIC VIOLENCE

Domestic violence belongs to a special category of aggressive behaviour and may be deemed to be a subspecies of violent behaviour in its general aspect. Many of the points already made in regard to violence in general are applicable when studying this special case from a psychiatric point of view. However, some preliminary points may be made in respect of this issue. Firstly, while all criminal statistics are far from reliable, domestic violence is probably in a league of its own for unreliability. We have to resort to anecdotal evidence and personal professional experience when writing about this issue but it seems true to say domestic violence is far from uncommon. It is found in the most unlikely of situations, no age and neither sex is preferentially favoured among victims, and it cuts across every social class and every community. Social and, especially, cultural factors play a decisive role in determining the level of domestic violence that is found within any given community. There are some communities now established in Britain where cultural practices inform behaviour that leads to domestic violence which, in fact, may not even be recognised as such. Much bewilderment and even offence may be caused to these individuals by investigating such behaviour which, in some communities, may be seen as the norm. Chastising one's wife or child (the wife also joining in the latter activity) is time-honoured and sanctioned by long-standing cultural practice in some communities. It is one of the challenges faced by the family and child law practitioner to deal with such behaviour which comes into conflict with the much more enlightened attitudes which now find reflection in English law. One of the insights to be gained from studying practices which are habitual in migrant communities is that they also offer an understanding of behaviour which may be found in native subcultures, e g those involving persistent criminal activity especially involving gangs associated with the use also of illicit substances where the constituent populations of those marginal communities may be entirely of native origins. It is a conclusion one draws from studying domestic violence, at any rate from the psychiatric point of view, that aggressive behaviour may stem not only from the actions of individuals but also as a reflection of the dynamics and shared values of a particular family or community.

Whether special cultural factors are present or not, one still needs to study the mental states of the members of the family who are involved as victims of violence. Where illness or disorder is present (depressive illness, an anxiety state, perhaps dementia in spouse or partner, or some behavioural disorder involving a child) the provoking factors for violence may be clear enough. But often there may not be overt mental disorder present but rather the presence of personality difficulties or defects in the spouse or partner which tends to make him or her a readier victim than would have been the case if such an individual had possessed a normal, well adjusted personality. The remarks made concerning the aggressive, anxious or dependent individuals who may become victims of repeated violence apply a fortiori to cases of conflict in the domestic situation. There may also be apparent collusion on the part of the victim, who conceals or denies the acts of violence being perpetrated against him or her and also shows ambivalent behaviour where criminal proceedings are concerned, making and withdrawing complaints and first supporting and then drawing back from prosecutions. A full assessment of incidents of domestic violence involves the examination of both parties. There are obviously other factors besides those of personal emotions operating in families – financial difficulties, debt, housing problems, and physical factors such as disability and age. An individual who is trapped within a domestic setting for whatever reason is at greater risk of continuing violence – physical as well as emotional – than one who has the independence of spirit and body and the means to assert himself and, where necessary, effect an escape. Desperation may make one a victim, or renew one's status as a victim. A 35-year-old woman of uncertain immigration status was trapped in a marriage with a man who was said by her to be a brute and a bully, causing her to flee to a refuge with her son. They separated and the child resided with her. Unfortunately, she suffered a bout (her second) of a stress-related psychotic illness and had to yield the son to his father. She was not entitled to housing or social benefits on account of her unsettled immigration status and was rendered both homeless and penniless. She was reduced to accepting lodgings with a relation of her ex-husband and to accepting money from the ex-husband. In formal child care proceedings she consented to the child living with its father and accepted sessions of contact left to the discretion of the father to arrange. The portents for renewed domestic violence were not good.

As all the studies show, there is high risk of repeated violence in a domestic setting and it has been estimated that there are at least two murders each week involving spouses or partners. Risk involves both parties to different degrees for, in a minority of cases, the abused partner, in a case of the 'worm turning', may kill the abusing partner. This is the extreme case. Far more common is the involvement of both parties in routine acts of violence committed on one another. The term 'battered wives' syndrome' has sometimes been applied to the mental state a chronically abused spouse or partner suffers as a result of repeated beatings. The term is obviously a misnomer for a growing number of husbands or male partners are also found to be victims. Further, it is not as yet a recognised psychiatric syndrome and there must be doubt if a special category is needed for violence occurring in a domestic context as opposed to non-domestic situations. Where murder comes to be charged it could be argued in most instances the facts could satisfy the partial defences of diminished responsibility or provocation, the domestic circumstances merely forming the backdrop to these partial defences.

Mental disorder in the perpetration of domestic violence is relatively uncommon though recognised psychiatric illnesses such as schizophrenia, depressive or bipolar illness may predispose to violence, especially in the acute phase of psychotic illness. Morbid jealousy, as already discussed, is known to produce risk of battery or worse suffered by spouse or partner. By far the most common type of mental disorder involved in these cases is personality disorder where the spouse or partner suffering from this condition acts out his aggressive tendencies in the face of domestic stresses or following no provocation at all. Mental disorder, as said, may also be exhibited by the victim when it takes on a similar presentation. In the absence of obvious mental disorder on the part of the assaulting partner or spouse, one is reduced to looking at a situation of bullying translated to the domestic context, cultural or subcultural factors, and any previous experience the perpetrator has been exposed to, especially childhood physical abuse. Many abused spouses or partners show anxiety (avoidant) or dependent personalities. The inability to escape – for whatever reason, be it emotional or financial – may be a factor in exposing such an individual to further violence. Other factors noted in the literature include immaturity, lack of adaptability, and emotional conflict suffered by the abusing spouse or partner. Some victims, by repeatedly returning to situations of violence, are believed to have masochistic tendencies along with feelings of being needed. Aggression may also be provoked when the assailant spouse or partner finds himself unable to satisfy the needs of a spouse or partner for excessive dependence on the other. Some men have sadistic tendencies with sexual connotations in that they do not feel fully potent unless they can establish their authority over a helpless female, in the absence of which he cannot give or receive affection in a manner which is emotionally satisfying to him. There is also an element of learned behaviour which contributes to situations of domestic violence. Some individuals have learned in childhood that violence had helped them to achieve their desires and this tendency to aggression might have been reinforced by parental example. This learned violence is carried over into his own relationships when domination is sought to be created over his spouse or partner. Cultural constraints such as the stigma attaching to the separating party, especially when female, in some communities also exposes the victim to recurrent acts of violence. In many cases one is left musing upon that notorious phrase – 'he or she does it because he or she can' – when trying to explain why a violent spouse or partner appears to be getting away with repeated acts of violence. Single mothers appear in general to make up a vulnerable group. They are significantly more likely to have psychiatric disorders and poor mental health outcomes, particularly anxiety states and substance misuse. Lone mothers are also more likely to have experienced physical and sexual violence and these severe traumatic experiences are more strongly associated with the presence of psychiatric disorders than either single parent status or other socio-demographic characteristics.

The role alcohol and illicit drugs play in the victim may also be a crucial element in situations of continuing violence. If both spouses or partners engage in the misuse of alcohol or illicit substances, they may together also inhabit a subculture from which neither feels free to withdraw. One partner may well be dependent on the other for the supply of substances, and the craving associated with the need for alcohol or illicit drugs may make them more literally dependent on the other to ease them out of a withdrawal state. There are other explanations proffered for why spouses or partners – usually women victims but an increasing number of men caught up in these situations as well – continue to accept violence and abuse but most of these (eg a perverse desire to improve or 'cure' a violent partner) are beyond the scope of ordinary clinical observation and consideration. Similar considerations apply to situations concerning forced marriage.

An individual's personality is formed in the context of his childhood spent within his family and it is well accepted (though not yet provable in any quantifiable fashion) that formative experiences are vital to the shaping of any personality. What could be positive experiences and which are negative are not all known by any means but there is sufficient evidence that childhood experiences of abuse – physical, emotional or sexual – do come to play an important part in the psychological make up of the adult individual and if such adverse experiences do influence the finished personality in relevant ways the stage may be set for the behaviours determined by such a personality to make an impact on those with whom such an individual comes to have relationships with in adult life. Where children are concerned, such difficulties involving the personality may be transmitted to yet another generation. The saying that the abused become abusers has some truth where, at least, physical violence is concerned.

11.3 DOMESTIC VIOLENCE DIRECTLY INVOLVING CHILDREN

The physical abuse of children which, of course involves violence, has been the subject of several studies. What kind of parent is likely to abuse children in this fashion has been subject to research. Some studies have shown that in cases of physical abuse the parents need not belong exclusively to any particular social class, level of educational attainment or occupational group but are to be found everywhere in the community. But other studies have found an association between physical abuse of children and deprived areas which held parents belonging to lower socio-economic classes and also a higher number of mothers who were of less than average intelligence. These parents also frequently showed personality disorders which involved high levels of emotional conflict and anxiety with difficulty in tolerating frustration and controlling impulsive behaviour. Most, though by no means all, had had a history of unsatisfactory parenting themselves and poor childhood experiences. These individuals were emotionally deprived, felt rejected and their need for a dependent relationship frustrated. Their self-esteem, confidence and capacity for trust were correspondingly low. Many had been punished excessively as children and themselves subjected to physical abuse and they, in turn, tended to repeat the styles of parenting and child control to which they themselves had been subjected. They lacked adequate knowledge of the practicalities involved in child care and failed also to understand or accept the needs and dependence of immature children.

One study has suggested there may be three styles of family relationships associated with the physical abuse of children:

(1) The severely hostile, aggressive parent who appeared to suffer almost continual anger, had uncontrolled outbursts of temper and violence at any irritation or frustration, including those provoked by the child.

(2) The passive, inadequate parent who looked desperately for opportunities to be dependent, and competed with the children for the attention and support of the spouse or partner. These parents were highly anxious and frequently became depressed. They were capable of neglect as well as abuse of the child.

(3) The rigid, compulsively controlled and orderly parent, who lacked warmth and tended to reject the child. Their own need for success and order made it difficult for them to accept the demands and mess created by the child who was expected to show excellence in behaviour and development to assuage the parents' doubts and fears about their parental ability.

Psychiatric disorders are relatively uncommon in cases involving physical violence directed against children. But psychological disturbance of the kind noted above is a commonplace occurrence. The subject has been discussed by Van Rooyen and Mahendra.[1] Among the issues of interest for purposes of this book are some of the risk factors that have been identified. Risk of violence is said to be higher with younger children, where there has been developmental delay in the child, frequent illness in the child and where the child has a difficult temperament and itself is aggressive. Parents who pose a high risk usually also have an unrealistic, even fanciful, expectation of the child, little knowledge of child development and poor mood and anger regulation skills along with deficient skills in showing empathy with a child. An additional area which raises risk involves attachment problems involving the child, marital discord and poor social networks available for the parent.

11.4   DOMESTIC VIOLENCE INVOLVING CHILDREN INDIRECTLY

A child does not need to suffer direct violence to show emotional or behavioural effects due to the harm caused to it. While it is usual to focus attention on the individual parent, occasionally on both, the family as a dynamic system may be causative of harm suffered by the child. Both parents may play a contributory role in causing harm to a child, a situation which indicates bi-parental failure in some cases. In cases where a troubled relationship with one parent is offset sufficiently by a more positive relationship between the child and the second parent, this could serve as a buffer of protection against the development of the consequences of harm. The bi-parental failure occurs where both mothers and fathers show significant impairment and a failure to carry out properly their parental functions. Characteristics of families showing disturbed functioning which could lead to emotional harm to the child include those where there is or are:

(1)   frequent separations and disruptions within the family;

(2)   violent arguments witnessed by the child and serious marital discord;

(3)   an atmosphere in the home of turmoil and impending violence;

(4)   lack of adequate role models to identify with;

(5)   a degree of neglect and parental rejection;

(6)   unstable and inconsistent mothering;

---

[1]   See C L Van Rooyen and B Mahendra *Psychology in Family and Child Law* (Family Law, 2007).

(7)   continuing abuse of the child making it feel helpless and angry;

(8)   psychiatric disorders present in family members.

Children from families in which both parents suffer from psychiatric illness may be at a double disadvantage. Not only could they inherit the illness of one or both parents but they are also made vulnerable by separation, whether physical or emotional, due to the disorder suffered by the parents and in the course of the treatment of these disorders. However, it is by no means the case that whenever there is disorder in one or both parents one finds a child at emotional risk. Many, perhaps most, parents in a situation involving dual pathology on their part are perfectly capable of offering adequate parenting. Every case needs to be studied in respect of the parenting jointly or severally offered to a child and the child itself investigated for signs of emotional harm suffered.

Psychopathology in the parent may also lead to poor attachment between it and the child. Many emotional difficulties faced by a child in its growth and development are said to be due to the poor or even non-existent attachment between it and the parent. We have already stressed in the section on post-partum psychiatric disorders the urgent need to treat the mother in these circumstances and also the need to be mindful of avoiding unnecessary separation between a mother and her new born child. Any psychiatric disorder carries the potential to compromise the processes of attachment. Those where the emotions could be impaired such as the chronic schizophrenic states are commonly found to be a cause of malattachment. But chronic or recurrent depressive illness, an uncorrected anxiety state, personality disorders with emotional distur-bance and, of course, the misuse of substances may all lead to the impairment of the process of attachment. But, as with everything else involving parenting, there can no fixed rules about the effects of mental disorder on any aspect of parenting. Attachment, in particular, appears to be a complex process and what the requirements are for parent and child leading to satisfactory attachment between them are far from completely understood. In other words, there cannot be any assumption that mental disorder on the part of the parent, by that fact alone, will necessarily lead to poor or non-existent attachment. Once again it is a matter for investigation in every case where poor attachment is suspected.

11.5   PARENTAL ALIENATION

This is a subject of current and growing interest as was realised when the issue of greatest excitement to reviewers of *Psychology in Family and Child Law*[2] appeared to be the inclusion of a discussion on this subject. It has to be said straightaway that there is little evidence that in the vast

---

[2]   See C L Van Rooyen and B Mahendra *Psychology in Family and Child Law* (Family Law, 2007).

majority of cases there is mental disorder affecting either parent in this situation although it is not at all uncommon for allegations of mental disorder to be directed against one parent or the other. As such, the real interest from a professional standpoint resides in the manifestations of what could be called nuisance behaviour, akin to those behaviours which are considered later in Chapter 15 of this book.

Put in its simplest form, the phenomenon involves an attempt by one parent to turn the child (or children) against the other. Characteristically, there are accusations and counter-accusations involving the parents. The end result could be a fully alienated child who wishes to have no contact with one parent, refers to such a parent in the most negative of terms and, usually, expresses positive feelings for the other parent, invariably the parent with whom it resides. As so many disputes arise regarding the children in cases of marital or relationship breakdown it is not surprising the subject has caught the imagination.

As already stated, it is uncommon to find true formal mental illness in either of the parents involved in this situation. However, it is usual to make allegations of mental disorder suffered by one parent or both. Another allegation involves that of sexual abuse perpetrated on a child by the parent who is at risk of being alienated. The numbers of these allegations are high enough for the phenomenon to have attracted a name for itself – 'sexual allegations in divorce syndrome' (SAIDS). Other allegations may involve domestic violence against a parent, physical abuse of the child, emotional abuse of the child, mental illness on the part of the non-resident parent, misuse of substances and deviant sexual practices. On investigation, the presence of mental disorder, at any rate, is rarely sustained.

One case involved accusations of mental disorder on the part of one parent and sexual misconduct against a child on the part of the other. The mother alleged that the father had sexually abused their daughter. Extensive investigation revealed no evidence to support such a claim. A finding of fact exonerated the father. The mother refused to accept any of the findings, maintained the father's guilt and developed the 'over valued' idea that is the stock in trade of such individuals as vexatious litigants and others harbouring an *idée fixe*. The father thereupon claimed the mother was mentally unbalanced. A study of the medical records revealed that the mother had indeed suffered from a long-standing anxiety state which was much influenced by her poor personal and social circumstances. The mental disorder was, however, insufficient to explain the fixity of her idea that the father had committed abuse. As time passed and the contact disputes progressed with increasing virulence it became clear that this was closer to the run-of-the-mill contact dispute with little relevant contribution by way of mental disorder. The risk to the child in its relationship with its father as well as for its own development was constantly stressed by the professionals to no avail. The matter had to be decided by judicial intervention.

As with other examples of nuisance behaviour to be discussed in Chapter 15, the conduct relating to parental alienation behaviour is beyond all conventional psychiatric treatment and any recommendation for such 'therapy' is probably valueless. As with its congeners, the maxim that the 'best predictor of future behaviour is past behaviour' is probably the most valid observation to offer in cases such as this.

11.6   DOMESTIC SEXUAL VIOLENCE

This subject, too, may be regarded as another subspecies of general violence, though, of course, some special factors also apply. The subject is vast and controversial and the observations made here are only those which have some relevance to family and child law practice. Marital rape or quasi-marital rape is now to be treated like any other act of rape or sexual assault although evidential problems concerning consent may present difficulties above the usual when trying to get a conviction. Domestic sexual violence is usually present in the context of circumstances where non-sexual violence also takes place. Mental disorder is as uncommon as in any other area of domestic violence although periodic sexual violence against spouse or partner may be a characteristic of manic illness which may feature an increase in levels of libido, energy and aggression. Far more likely are personality factors (involving both parties) and a tendency to bully and intimidate a vulnerable partner. Morbid jealousy, either as a symptom of another psychotic illness or as a paranoid disorder in its own right, may be associated with sexual violence against an allegedly unfaithful spouse or partner along with non-sexual violence. The difference usually observable between domestic and non-domestic sexual violence is that in the latter case personality problems associated with inadequacy and antisocial tendencies may be commoner than in cases involving domestic sexual violence. This is only a general observation but it does appear that persons engaging in domestic sexual violence do so because, in the words of George Bernard Shaw's dictum on marriage: 'there is a maximum of temptation with a maximum of opportunity'. Many individuals, especially men, involved in domestic sexual violence appear to be only too conscious of their rights and, as may readily be appreciated, cultural forces applying in some communities may also especially endow the husband or male partner with rights he feels at liberty to enforce irrespective of the consent of the other party.

11.7   SEXUAL VIOLENCE AGAINST CHILDREN

A distinction needs to be drawn between sexual activity, which is by definition unlawful, carried on with children in a public setting as opposed to such activities in a domestic atmosphere. Family and child law practitioners are naturally concerned with cases involving the latter type, but it is in general true to say that mental pathology is more likely to be found in those cases involving children in a public setting rather than in a domestic context. Formal illness is not common although any form of disinhibition – which tends to loosen social restraints – may also affect sexual conduct. Thus, with the psychoses, in cases of dementia or head injury, inappropriate sexual activity with children may occur. In fact, it is not unknown for dementia, whether senile or pre-senile, to present with uncharacteristic behaviour which may include also sexual misconduct with children. Alcohol and illicit substances also have a tendency to disinhibit normal, socially approved behaviour. Far more likely is a personality problem on the part of the perpetrator which may make normal sexual relationships difficult to achieve. Inadequacy of personality is notoriously common. Paedophilia itself is classified (F.65.4 – ICD-10) as a disorder of sexual preference. In one American study involving child sex offenders it was seen that those who committed new sex offences had previously committed more sex offences, had been admitted to correctional institutions more frequently, were more likely to have been diagnosed as being personality disordered, were more likely to be single and had shown more inappropriate sexual preferences on initial assessment than those who did not reoffend. Behavioural treatment did not seem to affect the rates of recidivism.

Domestic sexual violence against children takes on a different colouring. Mental disorder is still uncommon where parents are concerned as perpetrators although it may exist among acquaintances outside the family committing the abuse. More usually there is a dysfunctional relationship within the family, commonly involving the parents, and the children could be sucked into this maelstrom. There is also the case where the parents are feckless and are also into the abuse of alcohol and illicit substances when the general air of neglect pervading the household is conducive also to sexual abuse of the children. Personality problems are not uncommon and add to the inadequacy most often observed in the dependent personality who (most often the wife or female partner) attracts and sustains the type of partner who may proceed to the abuse of children, hers or perhaps even theirs. It is notorious in the netherworld of paedophiliacs that certain men (and some women) are known to prey on vulnerable individuals so as to gain access to their children. The parent with a dependent or inadequate personality, through psychological weakness brought about by his or her need to be cared for by someone at all costs, however unsatisfactory such an individual may be, sometimes perhaps also through the incapacity brought about as a result of misuse of alcohol or illicit substances, may through the effects of these factors come to leave the child unprotected. In many cases incidents of domestic sexual abuse are traceable to a poor relationship between the parents and the seeking of revenge against spouse or partner, a tendency to bullying and a failure to control impulses, aggravated on occasion by alcohol and illicit substances in the context also of a rather disordered and structureless life.

A 35-year-old man with a long history of personality inadequacy had been convicted of a sexual assault on his five-year-old niece. He fully accepted his guilt and did not dispute the facts, merely proffering the explanation that he 'loved' the child. He had poor adjustment generally and was virtually incapable of forming normal adult relationships. In time he fathered a child. This child came to make equivocal complaint of possible sexual interference. The man strongly denied he had been responsible in any way for inappropriate behaviour with the child. His seriously inadequate and abnormal personality, however, was sufficient to put him in the high risk category of sexual offending in respect of children – for his previous behaviour could be deemed reasonably likely to recur – whether his child's allegations were proved to be true or not. Only supervised contact with the child was deemed to be appropriate.

The assessment of risk in respect of child sexual abuse involves several stages. At a basic level, the assessment concerns historical and factual data such as the individual's age, past convictions for sexual or violent offences and the characteristics of previous victims. These are the 'static' elements referred to previously in the assessment of risk in general. The second stage of assessment involves the intrinsic features of individuals that are relatively stable over time such as psychological characteristics, personality, cognitive processes and behaviour patterns. Although these elements are stable, they do have the potential for change with or without treatment. Characteristics of these second level risk factors include features such as sexual interests and sexual drive. Thinking processes, cognitive patterns, emotional management, ability to regulate impulses and the management of lifestyle are all considered. As stated before, an important area of assessment is victim empathy. Where this is lacking it may suggest that there may be a lack of emotional intimacy, lack of emotional congruence with children (that is, identifying with them and feeling more comfortable in their presence) and thereby could be an indicator of a high risk of re-offending. Cognitive distortions, which are thought patterns, processes and beliefs associated with offending such as, for example, believing that a young child has enticed an adult into a sexual relationship (thereby also revealing a lack of insight) needs to be assessed alongside levels of victim empathy.

The final stage of risk assessment concerns acute factors, that is those behaviours and circumstances that are ongoing. These are liable to change over short periods of time and could be associated with short-term high risk. It could be considered a situation of high risk if the offender's behaviour and interests were to bring him into contact with potential victims, or if such individuals were to engage in hobbies, interests and employment that brought them into contact with potential victims, or if such individuals were to demonstrate a deterioration in their lifestyle such as breakdown of relationships, loss of accommodation, loss of employment, change in mood state and the perception that the individual is suffering from stress. Where supervision and treatment of the offender are involved, missed appointments, lying, deceit and rule-breaking would in general indicate heightened risk.

Van Rooyen and Mahendra[3] reviewed the research that indicated possible prognostic indices in the risk assessment of offenders who had been engaged in the sexual abuse of children. Good prognostic factors included:

- the offender attending treatment sessions;

- not preferring children as sexual partners;

- the index incident being situational (eg occurring while the usual partner was away);

- abuse was relatively minor (eg confined to touching);

- the offender referring himself for treatment rather than being ordered to attend;

- the history of abuse was of recent onset;

- the offender displaying many areas of appropriate parental functioning;

- genuine guilt and remorse being expressed;

- there being empathy with the child; and

- a full acceptance of responsibility for his conduct.

Poor prognostic features included:

- a desire to leave treatment;

- the preference for children as sexual partners;

- the abuse not being limited to specific situations;

- the abuse being serious in itself;

---

[3]   See C L Van Rooyen and B Mahendra *Psychology in Family and Child Law* (Family Law, 2007).

- the offender being ordered to attend treatment in the face of his reluctance;

- there being a long history of abuse involving several children;

- there being a lengthy history of antisocial behaviour with substance abuse;

- the offender's guilt being related rather to apprehension felt about consequences;

- blaming others;

- the use of physical force in the abuse; and

- a history of sexual abuse experienced by the offender himself.

What the long-term effects are on a child suffering sexual abuse remains to be fully established. A recent study clearly demonstrated that childhood sexual abuse is associated with increased rates of a range of mental disorders in childhood and adult life. Male victims of childhood sexual abuse seem as likely as female victims to show subsequent psychopathology. Conduct disorders are significantly more frequently found in both male and female victims of childhood sexual abuse but males have significantly higher rates than females.

11.8   SUMMARY

- Domestic violence is invariably under-recognised in both its frequency and gravity. There are said to be at least two killings each week associated with domestic violence. Social and cultural factors play an important part although no social group seems spared from this form of violence. As a rule, formal mental illness is uncommonly found among perpetrators of domestic violence. The most common disorder met with in these cases is personality disorder which in turn is strongly associated with the misuse of alcohol and illicit drugs. While the characteristics of any victim in a situation of violence are important to study, the issue takes on special importance in cases of domestic violence where there may be an appreciable presence of personality difficulties, if not disorder, in the victims who may also be vulnerable for other reasons of personal or social weakness.

- Violence directed against children is also under-estimated. Many of the factors concerned with domestic violence involving adults also affect children. Personality disorder and the misuse of alcohol and illicit drugs is especially important to consider. Children are also at risk of being adversely affected by the effects of indirect violence when they are witnesses to adult violence. As much social behaviour is learned, the impact on children of situations of violence may be considerable.

- Children may also be at risk from parental behaviour even when violence is not in issue. Disputes between parents, especially concerning residence and contact arrangements, may result in the children's minds being set against one parent or other. The growing importance of the parental alienation syndrome is now better appreciated.

- Domestic sexual violence, whether or not involving children, is not usually associated with mental disorder but appears to have its roots in the personal and social characteristics also linked to domestic violence in general. Misuse of alcohol and illicit drugs is common in these situations and there may also be much domestic turmoil.

CHAPTER 12

RISK ASSESSMENT IN EMPLOYMENT

12.1 PSYCHIATRIC ASPECTS OF EMPLOYMENT

Psychiatric aspects of employment may be considered under two broad headings. The first of these involves the part the circumstances of employment themselves plays in causing or contributing to an employee suffering from mental disorder. Second, it involves the effect mental disorder has on the ability of a patient to retain or return to employment. Both these aspects of employment have important legal implications. For convenience the second of these aspects will be dealt with first.

12.2 INTRODUCTION

Employment is a complex area of human activity influenced by social, cultural and economic forces among other factors. The importance of gainful occupation in the maintenance of good mental health has long been recognised. Figures as diverse as Dr Samuel Johnson and Sir Winston Churchill exemplified the importance of work to stave off depression, including the dreaded 'black dog' feared by the latter. Freud laid as much emphasis on work as on love as being the essential requisites for a reasonably contented existence, although for decades only love seemed to have been recognised as being essential for this purpose. It was only with the recurrence of mass employment that it came to be realised that it was not merely material loss due to unemployment that caused unhappiness in workless individuals but the fact of lack of occupation itself. There appear to be complex factors sustaining an employee's well-being. Apart from the more obvious elements such as money, status and responsibility there are less tangible factors somehow contributing to the feeling of self-worth, self-confidence and self-esteem an employee derives from work. To deny or fail to recognise these factors (which are rarely, if ever, reflected in the damages payable for loss of employment in terms of the present and future prospects for a successful claimant) is to fail to appreciate crucial elements going into the make up of an individual's well-being.

The converse situation is also true. Employment by itself does not guarantee satisfaction, for man does not live by work alone. The stresses and strains associated with modern employment are becoming ever more apparent. The strains due to globalisation with a premium being put on increased efficiency mean many of those in employment invariably feel under pressure at work. Interpersonal tensions may become more pronounced in these circumstances. These matters are of vital importance to appreciate whether in the context of evaluating work place pathology or in the state of apparent incapacity to return to employment claimed by many after illness or injury.

12.3   SECONDARY DISABILITY

The concept of secondary disability can be usefully discussed in this connection. A psychiatric disorder, like any other disorder, can produce primary effects of disability by way of the symptoms it presents. In a depressive illness or an anxiety state one may find symptoms of an adverse mood change and related features which may require a patient to absent himself from work while the treatment he is receiving for the condition begins to take effect. The work disability which follows is an understandable reaction to the patient's mental state and it is in everyone's interest, not least the employer's, for the employee to be restored to reasonable health before he resumes the work he was doing at the time when he fell ill. However, if continuing work incapacity persists despite evidence that treatment has had a positive effect one needs to look deeper into matters. It has already been considered in Part I of this book how a patient's personality, in other words his habitual pattern of looking at the world and operating himself there, which is deemed to be substantially separate from the supervening illness, may nevertheless be influencing his full recovery from illness. This could lead to the phenomenon of secondary disability which may be loosely defined as disability that appears to be of a degree which is over and above that which could reasonably be deemed attributable to the disorder itself that the patient had come to suffer from.

Secondary disability has major implications in both the spheres of employment and in the situation of personal injury sustained in an accident. Indeed, these issues may be related in personal injury litigation. The causes of secondary disability may be several. At the simplest level, there could be delay in treatment being instituted for diverse reasons. As is unhappily the common experience, patients may not receive treatment as promptly as may be required, may indeed find necessary treatment delayed or even inaccessible. Second, there are many patients who are disinclined to accept treatment even when it is offered. They may find the notion of psychiatric treatment uncongenial to themselves. In psychiatry the treatment most often offered is in the form of drugs and psychological treatment of one kind or another. Many patients, influenced by what they see and read in the media, may become deeply suspicious of the adverse effects of drugs and the potential that some of these agents have for causing dependence. Psychological treatment, especially in the form of psychotherapy, makes heavy demands on the patient and may appear to some of them to be personally intrusive. Cultural factors are important to consider in this respect. Unlike, say, in France, where there appears to be a civic right to receive medication in what we would consider to be in staggering quantities, the British experience is altogether more moderate in its belief in the efficacy of therapeutic drugs, although even here the pattern may be changing as more and more of these become available 'over the counter' or 'off-prescription'. As far as psychotherapy is concerned, British attitudes, although also subject to change, remain conservative and considerably removed from North American attitudes. Patients still generally believe in the concept of the 'stiff upper lip' and are in general more inclined to work through their problems by themselves or in the company of their intimates rather than through the medium of a stranger, albeit a professional one. While, in general, this attitude is laudable and, in certain circumstances, may even have therapeutic merit to commend it, there are always dangers associated with delayed or absent treatment where the treatment is clinically indicated. Some symptoms, as noted in Part I of this book, can become entrenched. One well-known example of this involves the acute phobic states. If an individual has been involved – as a passenger in, or driver of, a motor vehicle involved in an accident – a common consequence may be the development of the features of anxiety in relation to future motor travel. Evidence shows that prompt treatment – through the medium of drugs and cognitive behavioural therapy – leads to good results. The longer the treatment is delayed the less satisfactory the results obtained are. In these circumstances a failure, for whatever reason, to embark on corrective measures may not only delay recovery but cause secondary disability and cause, in fact and in addition, a form of invalidism in some cases.

Secondary disability may also result from delayed or inadequate rehabilitation in the context of a resumption of employment. There are studies which show that skilled and intensive work rehabilitation can produce much improved results even when the disorder in question is a serious mental illness such as schizophrenia. All the evidence suggests that a well thought out and carefully implemented programme of work rehabilitation can go a long way to prevent secondary disability arising. This point needs to be appreciated against a report by the Social Exclusion Unit (2004) which showed the national figure for unemployment among people with long-term mental health problems is 76 per cent. Unemployment rates among those with a specific diagnosis such as schizophrenia may be even higher and there is some troubling evidence that the figure may be rising. This is especially disturbing as studies continue to show that the apparent incapacity to work is not due to the primary clinical effects of an illness but due to secondary disabilities caused by a variety of factors – one of which appears to be that the rehabilitation of the patient does not appear in the majority of cases to include vocational rehabilitation. It seems[1] that individual placement and support approach (IPS), based on the available evidence, is effective in enabling a substantial proportion of patients with serious mental health problems to gain and sustain open employment. IPS involves the integration of employment specialists into community mental health teams and the rehabilitation approach that is being taken as part of their overall ongoing care. It has been seen that with the employment of these specialists within the clinical teams superior results could be obtained in comparison to those whose expertise lay within the field of occupational therapy alone. This indicates the importance of specialist employment expertise. It has also been shown that there is no relationship between diagnosis and the outcomes of supported employment. There is also an indication that an IPS approach could be as fruitful in enabling those who are already in employment to retain this employment where it had been jeopardised by mental health difficulties as in assisting patients to gain employment after a period of time taken from work while recovering from illness.

Even where treatment is prompt and rehabilitation adequate, there could be secondary disability arising on account of factors which are personal to the individual patient concerned. In most cases this reluctance to return to work may be associated with the personality of the individual. However, there may also be present elements which may not be attributable to the ordinary manifestation of the patient's personality; rather, it may concern issues more specifically associated with the work situation. A 40-year-old man working in one of the public services suffered relatively minor head injuries in an accident unrelated to his work place and had relatively minor psychiatric symptoms. Despite a carefully planned and phased return to work it happened that he could not successfully resume his occupation. It transpired that at the time of the accident and for some months before he was having interpersonal difficulties at work and had made complaints about the attitudes of colleagues and superiors at work. At the time of his proposed return to work he was also due to face a disciplinary inquiry into some extra-curricular work he had been undertaking in possible defiance of the terms of his employment. There seemed no reason to believe his symptoms were not genuine but it is easy enough to understand that there could have been factors operating in his work place which might have caused or exacerbated his disability.

As is also apparent, there may be factors present in general social life that could also encourage secondary disability. It has been reported that the government is proposing to investigate the workings of the social security system, especially in respect of incapacity benefit, to see how, and to what extent, it could be standing in the way of a successful return to work on the part of the individual who, if not for their eligibility for benefits,

---

[1]   See M Rinaldi and R Perkins 'Implementing evidence-based supported employment' (2007) *Psychiatric Bulletin* 31, 244–249.

might well have returned to work. Earlier there was the introduction of a jobseeker's allowance for unemployed individuals where the benefits received were linked to a requirement to register for work and accept suitable work when it became available. The benefits system is hardly generous, let alone munificent, but there is clear evidence that in a substantial number of cases it does reinforce the belief that some individuals have that they are incapable of working. The explanations proffered for this phenomenon are complex, not to say controversial, but a reasonable reading of the evidence suggests that a system of unemployment benefits, first introduced to prevent hardship, may now be, in a sizeable number of cases, actually acting as a disincentive to work.

12.4   SECONDARY DISABILITY ASSOCIATED WITH LITIGATION

This brings us to the even more complex and controversial subject of secondary disability in relation to litigation. The issue of malingering or the deliberate exaggeration of symptoms for gain of one kind or another will not be considered in this section. Instead attention will be drawn to the phenomenon which has been variously described as 'accident neurosis' or 'litigation neurosis'. Clearly, in a legal system which offers compensation in money terms – and sees its duty of compensation in those terms – there is positive incentive for a claimant to exaggerate his injuries and disabilities in the hope of maximising his award. It will not come as a surprise to learn that the 40-year-old individual referred to in the previous section was engaged in litigation against those who had caused his injuries (who were not his employers). If one adds to this situation the often very great difficulty inherent in reliably establishing the presence and extent of psychiatric symptoms and conditions – for there are virtually no reliable or valid objective measures of psychiatric illness – one can see that the incentive to exaggerate disability may become pronounced. It has already been noted that when describing the post-concussional state due to minor head injury there is evidence to suggest that the notoriously vague and ill-defined symptoms associated with that condition may be dependent to some extent on the processes involving relevant ligation. In orthopaedic practice there is a controversial entity called 'whiplash injury' which follows road traffic accidents and is very commonly pleaded in the litigation that follows. It has been shown, in some studies, that chronic whiplash injury of the kind that founds claims in personal injury cases following road traffic accidents are rare or non-existent in countries such as Lithuania and Greece where the legal system does not operate to offer compensation for such injuries. And, yet, there is also evidence in these cases that even after settlement the disabilities could persist. They appear then to have taken on a life of their own. What could have started as conscious exaggeration of minor injury and disability has thereafter become chronic and persistent. The suspicion is that there are subtle forces working, perhaps unconsciously, in some of these cases. The phenomenon is further complicated by the interaction between so-called physical and mental injuries. It is a common phenomenon to observe that chronic pain and disability following physical injury can lead to or exacerbate a depressive illness and that the depressive mood itself can lead to heightened perception of physical pain and disability. A vicious circle of the effects of physical injury and an adverse mental state can thereby come into being and feed each other. This conclusion should come as no surprise when one realises that all phenomena are traceable to the brain but that our understanding of these mechanisms involved are too meagre at present to permit any worthwhile explanation of these phenomena.

12.5   WORK-RELATED PSYCHIATRIC INJURY

The cart was somewhat put before the horse in considering the second of the themes of this chapter first. Attention must now be drawn to how the stresses of work could induce psychiatric injury. That psychiatric illness can arise in, and as a result of, the work place is now not only a commonplace truth but one acknowledged by the law. The law appeared to be put on a sure footing in this respect by the Court of Appeal in a composite judgment in *Hatton v Sutherland*[2] . The judgment – and those that have followed it – confirmed that the modern work place is often to be deemed a pathogenic one. The causation of psychiatric illness and its maintenance by and in the work place is, however, a subject that is fraught with difficulty and one that must be studied with great care. The factual matrix, as the courts have repeatedly held, is everything. An employee claiming liability must be treated in his individual aspect; his fellows might not have reacted to any potential hazard in the way he did. Foreseeability of psychiatric injury is now longer sufficient to establish a claim. Also, what is in point is clinically recognisable psychiatric disorder – mere 'stress' is insufficient to found a claim. What 'stress' might be is both problematical and ambiguous. Stress may refer to both the experience and the reaction to that experience, the difficulty compounded by the use by many doctors (with the collusion of their patients) of the term as a euphemism. This reflects the stigma still attaching to mental illness in virtually all walks of life. Despite the laudable if somewhat idealistic aim of diverse campaigners to rid society of this stigma, it still prevails. A generation ago a US politician aspiring to the highest office in his land had to renounce his candidature when it was discovered he had once suffered a depressive illness and had received treatment for it. Wags asked if the American people did not prefer as their president someone who had received treatment for a mental illness to someone who had not been treated. It is hard to see, even with all these sentiments expressed and with the bite of anti-discrimination measures, any employer, given a choice, preferring some employee with a history of mental disorder over one who claims he has suffered no such illness. Not many parents will

---

2   [2002] EWCA Civ 76.

appoint a nanny who has a background of mental disorder. That is the harsh reality. An employee is expected to alert his employer to the fact that he has suffered, or is suffering, mental illness so as to warn the latter to the possibility of taking measures so as to minimise the risk of aggravating the condition. Alerting an employer to the fact of mental ill health is not easy to do when such information will inevitably become widespread and be used in certain cases to that employee's detriment. Several countries still deny entry to would-be migrants with a history of mental disorder.

The law can also be seen at work when the case of *Barber v Somerset County Council*[3] is considered. This was one of the cases concerned in *Hatton* which made its way to the House of Lords on further appeal. Mr Barber had been a schoolmaster who had taken early retirement at the age of 52 after suffering a mental breakdown at his school. Since that time he had been unable to work as a teacher or do any work other than undemanding part-time work. He sued his employers for damages for serious personal injuries (depressive illness) and won in the county court, being awarded damages. In the Court of Appeal the appeal of his employers was one of those allowed, the court holding that the employers had not been in breach of their duty of care. The House of Lords by a 4:1 majority allowed Mr Barber's appeal. Their Lordships preferred the trial judge's evaluation of the facts and assessment of the demeanour and credibility of the witnesses to the Court of Appeal's consideration of these matters. The trial judge had not found Mr Barber's headmistress an impartial or convincing witness. Among other matters she appeared to be suggesting Mr Barber was a malingerer out to 'work the system' in order to gain early retirement. The House of Lords drew attention to the relevant facts – such as Mr Barber's absences from work (in a man with a previous good record of attendance), his depressive illness, which should have been the trigger for further enquiries on the part of his employer, and the unsympathetic responses of the senior staff at the school. In *Hatton*, Hale LJ said there is a threshold which had to be crossed before liability could be found. The employer had to ask himself:

> 'whether this kind of harm to this particular employee was reasonably foreseeable. This has two components:
> (a)   an injury to health (as distinct from occupational stress), which
> (b)   is attributable to stress at work (as distinct from other factors).'

Unless an employee tells his employer that he is suffering from stress at work an employer was entitled to assume that an employee could cope. Employers must take notice of unusual absences, poor performance and other factors that might point to psychiatric illness. The employer who provides a confidential counselling service will usually have discharged his duty of care. This will be practical only for the larger employer and the size and resources of the employer are factors in deciding if the employer

---

3   [2004] UKHL 13.

has breached or discharged the duty of care. There is no employment that is inherently likely to psychiatric injury. All jobs are equal in this respect. An employer is not obliged to dismiss an employee who is prepared to take the risk of injury by continuing in a job that exposes him to hazard of which he is aware. However, there is a duty on the part of the employer to minimise the risk as much as possible.

In *Hartman v South Essex Mental Health and Community Care NHS Trust*[4] the appeals involved six test cases concerning claims for damages for psychiatric injury arising out of stress at work. The Court of Appeal held that caring for children with serious learning difficulties was not an unduly high risk employment in this context. In another case a bank was found liable for an employee's psychiatric illness for failing to act on its own medical advice. Bullying can lead potentially to psychiatric injury and is to be treated like any other cause of work-related psychiatric illness.

There is an understandable overlap between employment cases and personal injury cases where work incapacity is pleaded and there are illustrated examples which will be taken up in the next chapter.

12.6 DISABILITY DISCRIMINATION

The law now offers a measure of protection to an employee who suffers disability – whether or not it is derived from factors at work – and comes to face discrimination as a result of that disability

Section 1 of the Disability Discrimination Act 1995 (as amended in 2005) (DDA 1995) provides:

> '... a person has a disability for purposes of this Act ... if he has a physical or mental impairment which has a substantial and long-term adverse effect on his ability to carry out normal day-to-day activities.'

The provision appears on the face of it to be straightforward although one could express surprise at the somewhat archaic term employed, namely mental impairment. There is, however, a reason for the use of this term. It is that in the original DDA 1995 – amended in 2005 – there was a requirement that where a mental impairment arose from, or consisted of, a mental illness, that illness had to be a clinically well recognised in order for it to be regarded as mental impairment for the purposes of the DDA 1995. That requirement has been removed as a result of the 2005 amendment. Thus, where previously the requirement was for the presence of psychiatric disorder as it would be diagnosed in a clinical setting, now 'mental impairment', according to the guidelines accompanying the DDA 1995, 'should be given its ordinary meaning'.[5] In para A6 of the

---

[4]   [2005] EWCA Civ 6.
[5]   A3 – Guidelines issues by the Secretary of State.

Guidelines examples are given of 'mental impairments' which could lead to disability. For psychiatric purposes these include 'mental health conditions and mental illnesses such as depression, schizophrenia, eating disorders, bipolar affective disorders, obsessive compulsive disorders, as well as personality disorders and some self-harming behaviour'. Therefore, it appears that, self-harming behaviour apart, the examples still amount to what are, in practice, clinically well recognised disorders.

Greater confusion may arise in the interpretation of para 2 of Sch 1 to the DDA 1995 which provides:

2 Long-term effects

(1) The effect of an impairment is a long-term effect if—

    (a)   it has lasted at least 12 months;

    (b)   the period for which it lasts is likely to be at least 12 months; or

    (c)   it is likely to last for the rest of the life of the person affected.

(2) Where an impairment ceases to have a substantial adverse effect on a person's ability to carry out normal day-to-day activities, it is to be treated as continuing to have that effect if that effect is likely to recur.

(3) For the purposes of sub-paragraph (2), the likelihood of an effect recurring shall be disregarded in prescribed circumstances.

(4) Regulations may prescribe circumstances in which, for the purposes of this Act—

    (a)   an effect which would not otherwise be a long-term effect is to be treated as such an effect; or

    (b)   an effect which would otherwise be a long-term effect is to be treated as not being such an effect.

At first sight, two interpretations of Sch 1, para 2(2) of the DDA 1995 seem possible when the condition concerns some mental disorder. The first of these is that the provision refers to the recurrence of the condition leading to mental impairment. The second of these interpretations is that it is not so much the recurrence of the condition that is in point but the recurrence of a 'substantial adverse effect' that is being referred to as the recurrence of the condition does not in all cases necessarily lead to a recurrence of 'substantial adverse effect'. The matter is of some importance for psychiatric conditions commonly recur. The guidance offers a couple of examples.

The first of these involves a patient with bipolar affective disorder. The first episode of illness occurred in months 1 and 2 of a 13-month period. The second episode took place in month 13. This man will satisfy the requirements of the definition in respect of the meaning of long-term because the adverse effects have recurred beyond 12 months after the first occurrence and are therefore treated as having continued for the whole period (in this case, a period of 13 months).

The second example concerns a woman who has two discrete episodes of depression within a 10-month period. In month 1 she loses her job and has a period of depression lasting six weeks. In month 9 she suffers a bereavement and has a further episode of depression lasting eight weeks. Even though she has experienced two episodes of depression she will not be covered by the DDA 1995. This is because, as at this stage, the effects of her impairment have not yet lasted more than 12 months after the first occurrence, and there is no evidence that these episodes are part of an underlying condition of depression which is likely to recur beyond the 12-month period.

12.7   SUMMARY

- There is a complex relationship between mental disorder and employment and also an overlap between this situation and that involving post-traumatic states involving personal injury. That the work environment can lead to psychiatric illness and disorder is now well recognised. However, there must be clinically recognised disorder present, mere stress being insufficient for the law. There must usually also be some form of disclosure from an employee or a warning given to the employer that the employee is ill or at risk of becoming ill so that the employer can take corrective measures as far as is reasonably practicable for him, considering the resources available.

- Although few mental disorders need permanently incapacitate any patient from work, there is still a considerable degree of incapacity which cannot all be explained in terms of the clinical condition of the patient. There is now accepted to be substantial secondary disability in such patients standing in the way of their overall functioning, including employment. This is attributable to the want of adequate rehabilitation following illness. It has been shown that even with serious mental illness, adequate rehabilitation including the use of specialist vocational staff can lead to a significant increase in the prospects for employment and re-employment.

CHAPTER 13

RISK ASSESSMENT IN POST-TRAUMATIC STATES

13.1 INTRODUCTION

Although there is an overlap between this chapter and the previous chapter, the importance of post-traumatic states in litigation is such that the subject merits some words of its own. As seen in Part I of this book, trauma can lead to diverse manifestations of psychiatric disorder. The presentation of post-traumatic states could be in the form of a depressive illness, an anxiety state and in the combination of the two conditions as are found with adjustment disorders and the post-traumatic stress disorder.

13.2 INTERACTIONS CAUSING POST-TRAUMATIC INJURY

The traumatic incident by itself, even though it might have attained dangerously life-threatening proportions, may reveal little about the likely mental reaction of any individual. This is due to those factors that were discussed previously in relation to reactions to stressful life experiences, namely that a stress or trauma-related condition is invariably due to an interplay between an individual's personality, his existing mental make-up and the perception he has of the stressful or traumatic event. This means the examiner has to make a close study not only of such an individual's personality but also of his experiences of life. The former task is never easy for an individual's personality (much like his reputation) is a matter for the judgment on the part of those who are acquainted with him. It is possible to make broad assumptions about an individual's pre-existing personality though the value of doing this in clinical practice is limited. An individual's previous life experiences, insofar as they concern medical matters, may be recorded in his medical records but the limitations of this record should be appreciated. Where psychiatric matters are concerned, a doctor, by and large, can only record what he is told by his patient unless the latter has some disorder which is sufficiently serious for him to have had in-patient hospital care when the hospital, having made its own observations, sends a summary of these to the patient's doctor on discharge. Thus, say, where a patient suffers from a mental disorder due to the misuse of alcohol or illicit drugs but prefers not to confide in his doctor, the latter may remain ignorant of these details. Even convictions due to an offence caused by some behaviour relating to substance abuse need not reach the ears of a GP. Even a term of imprisonment on the part of his patient may remain unknown to a doctor. Less serious conditions, not involving prescriptions of drugs, may also not feature in the medical record. Even when the GP becomes aware of some mental disorder suffered by his patient, collusion between doctor and patient may lead to the recording of bland entries couched in euphemistic language which may reveal little. As discussed, this is due both to the stigma still attaching to mental illness generally as well as the fear the patient has that his medical records could be requisitioned for a variety of purposes and he understandably wishes to retain his privacy on matters of intimate detail. The recent scares involving loss of data in various situations concerning the public authorities might also have compounded many a patient's fears and persuaded him to keep his counsel on matters medical and personal. Thus the limitations inherent in the medical records, especially in regard to psychiatric disorder, must be recognised. Greater reliability of information may be obtained through a study of the occupational record in addition to a perusal of the medical record for the former can be extensive especially if the employer is a large concern. Absences, ostensibly for reasons of self-certified sickness, notes on interpersonal relationships and the disciplinary record often yield far more useful information about an individual's personality than his medical record might do. A record of criminal convictions is also, in the appropriate case, a useful additional source of information. By using all these sources the examiner may be able to derive a fairly complete and reasonably reliable picture of the individual as he could have been at the time he was involved in some traumatic event.

The clinical features after a traumatic event could be various. There is no necessary relationship between the severity of the traumatic event, as objectively measured, and the subjective reaction on the part of the individual concerned with the trauma. Neither the gravity of the trauma nor the extent of any physical injuries sustained need bear any relation to the psychiatric features that may come to be displayed. This result may be due to the functions of the individual's pre-existing personality. A well adjusted individual with a robust personality may be able to withstand trauma better than one with a fragile personality and perhaps a marginal personal and social adjustment. However, even where prior frailty can be established, how any particular individual might have reacted to trauma is hard to predict with any accuracy as the experience of any trauma is intensely personal and may have special significance to the individual. Trauma due to sexual assaults is especially conducive to the experiencing of significant adverse emotion. A road traffic accident which appears at first sight not to have been unduly serious may in an individual's mind attain a greater gravity if his children were in a motor vehicle with him. An industrial accident involving the limbs may lead to major psychiatric trauma on account of the implications of such an injury for future work capacity and, hence, for earning potential. On the other hand, the mechanisms involved in some traumatic situations, eg the post-concussional state following minor or trivial head injury remain unclear and insufficiently known to explain the complaint of symptoms made by a victim. As has been noted, the influence of litigation may also come to bedevil the process of assessment and evaluation.

13.3 PRE-EXISTING AND CONCURRENT PSYCHIATRIC DISORDER

Tort law has long accepted that a tortfeasor must take his victim as he finds him. Some victims of trauma may display a pre-existing psychological vulnerability to trauma on account of a previously experienced psychiatric disorder or may have a condition such as a personality disorder which could colour the reaction to the trauma suffered. Other victims could even have been suffering, at the time of the trauma, with some psychiatric disorder. The challenge in the latter case is to attempt to apportion the respective contributions made to the current clinical picture by the pre-existing condition as well as the post-traumatic reaction. This can only be an approximate measurement but help may be forthcoming if one compares the previous symptoms and features with the symptoms that have developed after the trauma. A 60-year-old woman with a long history of depressive illness with symptoms of anxiety due to her personal circumstances (including an unhappy marriage) was involved in an accident in the course of which she suffered serious spinal injuries. She had been depressed at the time of the accident and in the weeks before it. In the immediate aftermath of the accident she feared (with some justification) paralysis below the waist and although that eventuality did not supervene she was left with what was probably permanent damage to her spine. Her depressive illness continued but the symptoms now included a fear of increasing invalidism due to the spinal injuries. A demarcation was therefore possible between the features of pre-traumatic and post-traumatic depressive illness. Some patients who have suffered depressive illness previously may go on to develop phobic or situational anxiety features, especially in relation to driving or travelling by car, features they did not have before the accident even though they might have carried a long history of depressive illness which might even have reached chronic proportions.

As is well recognised, psychiatric disorder is associated with, and may be related to, personal and social factors. A traumatic incident may be a new event in such a patient's life. If there is a relapse or prolongation of the pre-existing condition one must pay attention to the possibility that it was those personal and social factors rather than the consequences of the traumatic event that are the real causative elements in the illness now arising. This evaluation may not be easy to carry out. If an individual becomes depressed as a result of marital difficulties, is then involved in an accident, in consequence of which he suffers an anxiety state in which is featured irritability, there could be an exacerbation in his interpersonal difficulties leading him to suffer a renewed bout of depressive illness or a more serious version of the illness he had already been suffering from. The possibility of interaction between pre-existing elements causing or contributing to a psychiatric disorder and those arising for the first time in the post-traumatic state needs to be borne in mind.

13.4   EXAGGERATED RESPONSES TO POST-TRAUMATIC INJURY

The emergence of symptoms after a traumatic event may be easily comprehended. However, their severity and persistence may not be capable of easy explanation. Two factors need to be considered which have already been touched upon in the previous chapter when considering matters in relation to employment and mental health. The first of these involves the great difficulties inherent in the assessment in any objectively reliable way of psychiatric pathology. There are no laboratory tests. Rating scales and questionnaires are of questionable value, and, in any event, do not reveal underlying disease mechanisms. Minor trauma may lead to genuinely severe psychiatric complications. These difficulties are always present in any case of psychiatric evaluation of an individual who has been involved in a traumatic incident. The second difficulty lies in, what may be called for convenience, the interaction between physical and mental injuries that have been caused by the same accident. This book has already considered the possible interplay between physical injuries resulting in pain and disability and the exacerbation of these by a depressive illness which also resulted from the circumstances of that accident. Clinicians are sometimes nonplussed by the seeming intractability of, say, soft tissue injuries which appear not to be responding to treatment. Conversely, psychiatric symptoms may not show amelioration despite substantial improvement in the concurrent physical symptoms. The situation may threaten to bedevil the processes of litigation and the question naturally arises as to what extent conscious exaggeration of symptomatology is the cause of the puzzling clinical presentation. It is not always easy to answer this question on conscious exaggeration, although it is a perfectly sensible one to ask in a legal system which compensates in terms of money and where the more severe and longer lasting the symptoms the greater the potential reward is to any victim. To allege malingering on the part of the victim in these circumstances is to engage the nuclear option. It is an accusation of fraud and, in the absence of cogent evidence to support it, serious questions of professional ethics may arise on the part of the accuser. In any event, in psychiatric practice, in the absence of direct evidence such as those due to surveillance recordings, observation, and reports which attest the seeming well-being of a patient previously believed to have been incapacitated, a claim of malingering cannot usually be upheld. One has to consider more subtle forces that may also be at work – one being the hysterical mechanisms outlined in Part I of this book. The result of these hysterical mechanisms may be an unconscious exaggeration of disability. An individual may appear to be, and complain of being, severely disabled after an accident. There may be no objective findings offering support for the presence of such a state. No litigation in relation to the accident is pending or, if the law had been involved, matters have been settled or concluded, perhaps even to the advantage of the victim who continues to remain apparently seriously ill and disabled. In these cases one needs to look further and deeper. The individual's serious disability could well have been born out of mechanisms which might have been triggered by the trauma involved in an accident but the maintenance of the symptoms and disability could possibly be due to conflicts in the personal sphere which were unrelated to the accident – conflicts associated, perhaps, with the spouse, or an unhappy work situation. The reaction of the patient may illustrate the kinds of gain that could occur in hysterical reactions. There is said to be relief from anxiety which results in the primary gain. Being able to avoid spouse or employer leads to the situation of secondary gain.

13.5 SECONDARY DISABILITY FOLLOWING TRAUMA

The phenomenon of secondary disability is as applicable here as it was in cases concerning employment. For the reasons already discussed – lack of treatment, delayed treatment, disinclination to accept treatment, the influence of the social benefits system, the effects of litigation – an individual suffering from some psychiatric disorder as a result of the trauma may become more disabled than he would have been expected to on account of the trauma itself. This is the result of failed rehabilitation and the end result could be pernicious. An individual who should have made an uneventful recovery from his psychiatric injuries is now at risk of ending up as a chronic invalid. It is perhaps fair to say that for every case of genuine psychiatric disability following trauma there is probably another in which inadequate or failed rehabilitation has led to protracted disorder and disability.

The overlap between post-traumatic injury and employment is also seen in cases involving work incapacity. In personal injury cases involving post-traumatic psychiatric injury the issue becomes one of considerable importance. If one takes, say, a 40-year-old individual, he has probably a quarter of a century of work before him. If he claims he is unable to work as a result of trauma, is deemed not able to work again, and had been earning an average national wage at the time of the trauma, his likely award is about £500,000 before a discount is applied. It is a large prize for a claimant to aim for and defendant lawyers are astute to ask searching questions regarding the basis for the injury that may lead to such an award.

The analysis of the relationship between objective indices of injury and the subjective perception and report of its consequences can sometimes be a complicated one. At one end of the spectrum lie the features of illness far transcending what is found on objective examination. The example given above illustrates this. At the other end of the spectrum there is reduced emphasis on illness or injury, sometimes approaching complete denial of obvious pathology. In this state a loss of insight on the part of the patient may be suspected, a common feature of some forms of mental disorder. These cases rarely, however, trouble the law.

13.6   MALINGERING

A cardinal feature of malingering, or the conscious exaggeration of illness or injury, is that some readily observable gain accrues to the subject. In personal injury cases, the gain through conscious exaggeration of injury is obvious – the claimant is after more money. A case may help illustrate this issue. This involved a 37-year-old builder whose car had been struck by another. He suffered what appeared to the surgical experts to be minor soft tissue injuries in the region of the back and neck. However, he persisted in complaining of severe incapacitating pain and disability which, he said, had prevented him from returning to work. As a result he had also become depressed. Repeated orthopaedic examination could not match the disability to the minor injuries that could be shown objectively to exist. The depression, though no doubt playing some part in the patient coming to take a darker view of his injuries, could by no means explain this degree of physical disability. The defendants, faced with a large claim by a relatively young man insisting he was unable to resume employment, hired investigators. Video footage surreptitiously gathered showed the man to be leading as normal an existence as was imaginable.

In the criminal law a convenient loss of memory may be beneficial to a defendant. Conscious gain must be distinguished from unconscious gain, a matter we have discussed previously. The test of conscious gain benefiting the subject may, however, also be used to rule out malingering. A 35-year-old man of unstable mental health and long-standing heroin dependence was involved in a couple of incidents that took place in curious circumstances. One day, for some unexplained reason, he was alleged to have stabbed another man. The very next day, while still at large, he himself was set upon by this victim of the day before and was seriously injured by stabbing, losing several pints of blood. He had to undergo emergency chest and abdominal surgery and spent several days in intensive care. There was no obvious head injury reported but general anaesthesia had been given and sedation in liberal quantities had been employed in the post-operative period. Upon regaining consciousness he was left with a period of amnesia for a few days, from before the assault on himself to the time he woke up from post-operative sedation. At the trial at which he was the defendant (the first incident) the Crown challenged the genuineness of his loss of memory. It was far from apparent to the defence team and its experts what benefit the man could hope to derive by simulating amnesia in these circumstances. The memory loss denied him the chance of running, for instance, the legal defence of self-defence and, indeed, to make any useful contribution to the discussion of his defence. Moreover, in the trial following the second incident (where the man himself had been the victim) his testimony against his assailant had been compromised. The absence of gain was a powerful argument against his amnesia being due to malingering.

It can be said straightaway that there are no definitive tests – whether they be medical, psychiatric or psychological – to prove or refute the suggestion that a subject could be malingering. On the contrary, a great deal of painstaking investigation needs to be undertaken to find out the truth where that is feasible. From time to time someone complaining of a more or less complete loss of memory, including personal identity, may turn up in the accident and emergency department of hospitals. Apart from routine medical investigation being undertaken, the matter is quickly raised with the local police force who – in collaboration with their colleagues in this country as well as, on occasion, Interpol – try to trace the individual's identity and what might have befallen him.

It has long been known that malingerers, whether or not believing themselves to be under surveillance, are unable to carry on with their pretence for any length of time. But it is by no means practical to undertake repeated or multiple examination of a patient in the context of ordinary legal proceedings. Recourse, therefore, is increasingly being had by defendants to covert surveillance through the use of investigating agents.

There is, however, a third category of case which has considerable legal interest. While, as discussed, an exaggerated response to injury may be a conscious phenomenon, as happens with malingering, there may also be subconscious, unconscious or other as yet undetermined mechanisms at work in some cases. These appear to involve almost always genuinely pathological responses to injury, and the real mystery lies in the fact that most processes of the brain determining these matters are as yet not fully understood.

13.7 SUMMARY

- Psychiatric injury that follows trauma is best understood in terms of the pre-existing personality of an individual and its interaction with the circumstances of the traumatic event. Delays in recovery may be due to prior psychiatric vulnerability which may be due to deficiencies in the personality or pre-existing illness. Apportionment may become necessary as to what part is due to pre-existing or concurrent illness and what part may be reasonably attributed to the trauma itself.

- Secondary disability is as important a feature in post-traumatic states as it is with issues concerning employment. Delayed or inadequate treatment and rehabilitation may lead to handicaps being suffered which may be even more serious than the disability due to the injury itself. There may be major implications for the resumption of employment.

- Malingering or the simulation of illness or injury is not uncommon in post-traumatic states as tort law compensates for injury according to the severity of injury and the ensuing disability, and this may encourage the conscious exaggeration of illness or injury. Only prolonged observation will elicit reliable evidence of malingering and, in practice, covert surveillance has disclosed many instances of malingering.

CHAPTER 14

RISK ASSESSMENT OF CHANGING MENTAL STATES

14.1   INTRODUCTION

As the philosopher Heraclitus remarked 'one does not step into the same river twice'. Things are always in a state of flux. It is self-evident that a medical examination undertaken at different times will yield different results, however small these differences might be. However, what is more important to realise is that changes in mental states may have implications in various branches of the law because the law expects individuals concerned with various acts and procedures with legal consequences to be in a position to understand what is required of them and to give effect to that understanding. In other areas of the law disposal by way of sentencing may depend on the diagnosis given to a defendant at the time the matter is to be disposed of. Both the civil law and the criminal law may thus be concerned with changes in mental state. The subject is large one and this chapter will consider a selection of the issues so as to give a flavour of the subject as a whole.

14.2   CAPACITY

The issue of capacity is a consideration in virtually every branch of the law. The coming into force of the Mental Capacity Act 2005 (MCA 2005) has helped to focus attention on the issue of capacity, perhaps the least well understood concept in the whole of medico-legal practice. One reason for befuddlement appears to be the tendency to equate illness and disorder – especially where mental illness or disorder are involved – with possible loss of capacity. Conversely, it is not always appreciated that sound physical and mental health does not preclude a loss of capacity. Capacity is a function of the exercise of autonomy on the part of an individual. In its essence the law requires a party to proceedings (or, as in the case of testamentary capacity, an individual dealing with a matter with legal implications) to demonstrate his understanding of the issues and be able to give proper instructions to his legal advisers and to take sensible and effective part in the proceedings. Capacity also involves behaviour that needs to be evaluated, often in the presence of mental disorder. In family and child law, capacity rears its head in several situations. Capacity to marry may be in issue and the question of capacity to litigate may arise in the course of divorce proceedings, as well as in child care and adoption proceedings. Essentially, capacity means to have the ability to understand certain relevant ideas – have the capability to grasp them, retain them, weigh them up and come to an informed decision on a basis of such understanding – and be able to communicate in some way that understanding. This ability may be impaired in cases of mental disorder whether that involves mental illness, learning disabilities, personality disorders or substance-related disorders. However, it is by no means the case that mental disorder need necessarily and in all cases lead to impaired understanding, a not uncommon belief among lay persons. In fact, the common law long held that an individual's capacity was to be presumed and that legal rule could only be rebutted through sufficient evidence to the contrary. This rule is now given statutory force by s 1(2) of the MCA 2005, which states:

> 'A person must be assumed to have capacity unless it is established that he lacks capacity'.

There is a further injunction against undue prejudice in the form of s 2(3) of the MCA 2005, which states:

> 'A lack of capacity cannot be established merely by reference to (a) a person's age or appearance or, (b) a condition of his, or an aspect of his behaviour, which might lead others to make unjustified assumptions about his capacity.'

Thus, an aged, bedraggled or eccentric appearance must not lead to assumptions being made about an individual's capacity to decide on some matter. The behaviour relevant to some issue must be evaluated in every case with an open mind.

The second misconception arises in believing that in the absence of mental disorder there is no scope for capacity to be impaired. Section 2(1) of the MCA 2005 now provides that:

> 'For the purposes of this Act, a person lacks capacity in relation to a matter if at the material time he is unable to make a decision for himself in relation to the matter because of an impairment of or disturbance in the functioning of the mind or brain.'

It will be noted that the issue of the cause of impairment is widely drawn and is not restricted to any narrow question of mental disorder. This reflects the complexity of the process of capacity, whose underlying mechanisms are far from fully understood today. All manner of factors may influence whether and to what extent an individual is capable of achieving the necessary understanding, of which mental disorder is but one. Personal, social and cultural beliefs may have obvious influences on the way an individual comes to have an understanding of some matter. The situation not uncommonly arises which leads one to ask why it is that an individual who is apparently competent in running other areas of his life is seemingly unable to grasp the essentials in validly giving or refusing consent to, say, medical treatment?

In some individuals, otherwise normal in medical terms, there appears to be a kind of 'blind spot' present in that individual's functioning in some very circumscribed area of activity. A parallel could be drawn with the cases of individuals who are very able – may indeed be outstandingly successful in their own fields of endeavour – who appear to be deficient in some mundane skill, for example, the ability to drive a motor vehicle or operate a personal computer or some other commonly utilised household machine. It is plain that in these cases the individual concerned is in general perfectly competent; his competence only falls down in relation to one subject or issue on which the law requires that he demonstrate his understanding. This is reflected in the common law rules that have long held that capacity is both subject-specific and issue-specific. Paragraph 4.4 of the MCA 2005 Code of Practice now states:

> 'An assessment of a person's capacity must be based on their [sic] ability to make a specific decision at the time it needs to be made and not their ability to make decisions in general.'

This is well illustrated in practice by the cases in which an individual may have capacity in child care proceedings, but fails to show an understanding of the issues involved in the placement and adoption of a child. It is also well accepted in personal injury law that an individual may have capacity to litigate, but may lack competence to deal with his property and affairs upon the award of damages, especially when these have been large and need to be managed with some skill and discretion.

It is the tendency of mental states, the phrase used in its widest meaning, to fluctuate that creates an element of risk in this situation, and it is this risk that requires assessment. It is an example of the need to focus attention not on any diagnosis but on the behaviour displayed by any individual in these situations.[1]

14.3   CAPACITY IN CIVIL CASES

Any psychiatric condition can lead to fluctuation in terms of the mental state that is subject to examination and, hence, the capacity to consent to or participate in some activity becomes an issue in every case although competence on the part of the individual is self-evident in most cases. The case of dementing patients is of special importance in issues involving testamentary capacity and will be taken up later. The tests of capacity to be applied in other civil matters are, broadly speaking, similar and are

---

[1]   See B Mahendra 'Behaviour, not diagnosis, the key: some misconceptions in the psychiatry of family and child law' [Feb 2008] Fam Law 159.

reflected in a handful of leading cases. Many of the cases in which the concept of capacity has been investigated have involved consent to medical treatment although the principles derived are generally applicable to any situation where capacity becomes an issue. The classic formulation of the policy lying behind capacity are the words of Cardozo J in *Schloendorff v Society of New York Hospital*:[2]

> 'Every person of adult years and sound mind has a right to determine what shall be done with his own body.'

The implications of this view go well beyond issues of consent to medical treatment and affect every aspect of a person's existence in a free modern society. There is acknowledged a right to be wrong, absurd, bizarre, eccentric or capricious as long as one has capacity. The state can impose its paternalistic view only if one is incapable. English law has jealously guarded this right, as evidenced by the wide discretion given to testators to dispose of their property after their death and has even now extended the principle to mature children on matters involving contraceptive advice, abortion and sexual health.

A useful summary of what the law requires comes from this passage of a judgment by Boreham J in *White v Fell*:[3]

> 'To have capacity (the party) requires first insight and understanding of the fact that she has a problem in respect of which she needs advice. Secondly, having identified the problem, it will be necessary for her to seek an appropriate adviser and to instruct him with sufficient clarity to enable him to understand the problem and to advise her appropriately. Finally, she needs sufficient mental capacity to understand and to make decisions based upon, or otherwise give effect to, such advice as she may receive.'

A leading case on capacity is *Masterman-Lister v Brutton & Co*[4] which involved personal injury litigation. The following points, taken from the judgment, will help to set out the essence of the issue of capacity:

(1)   The mental abilities required include the ability to recognise a problem, obtain and receive, understand and retain relevant information including advice, the ability to weigh the information(including that derived from advice) in the balance in reaching a decision.

(2)   Capacity is an important issue because it determines whether an individual will in law have autonomy over decision-making in relation to himself and his affairs. If he does not have capacity, the law proceeds on the basis that he needs to be protected from harm. Accordingly, in determining an issue as to an individual's capacity,

---

2   (1914) 105 N.E.92.
3   (unreported) 12 November 1987.
4   [2003] EWCA Civ 70, [2003] 1 WLR 1511, CA.

the court must bear in mind that a decision that an individual is incapable of managing his affairs has the effect of removing decision-making from him.

(3)   Capacity must be approached in a common sense way, not by reference to each step in the process of litigation but bearing in mind the basic right of any person to manage his property and affairs for himself, a right with which no lawyer and no court should rush to interfere.

(4)   What, however, does seem ... of some importance is the issue-specific nature of the test, that is to say the requirement to consider the question of capacity in relation to the particular transaction (its nature and complexity) in respect of which the decisions as to capacity fall to be made. It is not difficult to envisage claimants in personal injury actions with capacity to deal with all matters and take all 'lay client' decisions related to their actions up to and including a decision whether or not to settle but lacking capacity to decide (even with advice) how to administer a large award.

(5)   It is not the task of the courts to prevent those who have the mental capacity to make rational decisions from making decisions which others may regard as rash or irresponsible.

(6)   The court is concerned with the quality of the decision-making and not the wisdom of a decision.

The other leading case on capacity is *Re: MB (an adult: medical treatment)*[5] in which Butler-Sloss LJ set out the requirements for capacity. The facts of that case involved a caesarean section operation but the decision in the case has had a profound influence on other areas of the law concerning capacity. It was stressed that a decision in any individual case had to be based on the particular facts of that case:

(1)   Every person is presumed to have capacity unless and until that presumption is rebutted.

(2)   A competent woman, who has the capacity to decide may, for religious reasons, other reasons, for rational or irrational reasons or for no reason at all, choose not to have medical intervention even though the consequence may be the death or serious handicap of the child she bears, or her own death. In that event the courts do not have the jurisdiction to declare medical intervention to be lawful and the question of her best interests does not arise.

---

5   [1997] 2 FLR 426, [1997] Fam Law 542, CA.

(3)   Irrationality is here used to connote a decision which is so outrageous in its defiance of logic or of accepted moral standards that no sane person who has applied his mind to the question to be decided could have arrived at it. It might be otherwise if the decision is based on a misperception of reality (eg the blood is poisoned because it is red). Such a misperception will be more readily accepted to be a disorder of the mind. Although it might be thought that irrationality sits uneasily with competence to decide, panic, indecisiveness and irrationality in themselves do not as such amount to incompetence but they may be symptoms or evidence of incompetence. The graver the consequences of the decision the commensurately greater the level of competence is required to take the decision.

(4)   A person lacks capacity if some impairment or disturbance of mental functioning renders the person unable to make a decision whether to consent or refuse treatment. That inability to make a decision will occur when:
     (a)   the patient is unable to comprehend and retain the information which is material to the decision, especially as to the likely consequences of having or not having the treatment in question;
     (b)   the patient is unable to use the information and weigh it in the balance as part of the process of arriving at the decision. If a compulsive disorder or phobia from which the patient suffers stifles belief in the information presented to her, then the decision may not be a true one. As was said in *Banks v Goodfellow*[6] 'one object may be so forced upon the attention of the invalid as to shut out all others that might require consideration.'

(5)   Temporary factors (confusion, shock, fatigue, pain or drugs) may completely erode capacity but those concerned must be satisfied that such factors are operating to such a degree that the ability to decide is absent.

(6)   Another such influence may be panic induced by fear. Again, careful scrutiny of the evidence is necessary because fear of an operation may be a rational reason for refusing to undergo it. Fear may also, however, paralyse the will and thus destroy the capacity to make a decision.

A simpler form of test used by the courts in assessing a patient's capacity is the three-stage test outlined by Thorpe J in *Re C*.[7] The patient must be able to:

---

6   (1870) L.R. 5 QB 549.
7   [1994] 1 All ER 891.

(1)   comprehend and retain the relevant information;

(2)   believe it;

(3)   weigh it in the balance so as to arrive at a choice.

14.4   TESTAMENTARY CAPACITY

A special case in the civil law involves testamentary capacity. Although individuals of all ages of adult life are encouraged to make wills, virtually all problems concerning testamentary capacity involve those of an advanced age. That is usually the age at which dementia comes to ravage the population. The salient characteristics of dementia, especially of the senile variety, have been discussed in Part I of this book. One must here consider the risks involved in the changing mental states due to this condition. In most cases, senile dementia does not lead to decline in any gradual fashion. In many cases deterioration in the mental state in this condition occurs by fits and starts. A patient who may appear to have reached a plateau in his mental decline could suffer a crisis – say, due to some intercurrent medical or surgical condition – and may be seen to be less capable in terms of his mental processes after that crisis has passed. Or, as commonly happens, the patient with senile dementia may suffer an episode of confusion brought about through an infection. The end result in either case may be to produce adverse change in his abilities to deal with his affairs. A testator deemed capable of making a valid will one day may become incapable of doing so a few days later. The effects due to a confusional state brought about through an infection are usually reversible but in a demented patient a full recovery to previous mental levels may not be forthcoming. As in all cases where capacity is in issue, competence is not merely subject-specific and issue-specific but is also time-specific, something the testator's advisers will do well to bear in mind.

A testator is required to possess 'a sound and disposing mind and memory'.[8] This requirement is usually broken down into three parts:

(1)   The testator must understand the nature of the act of will making and its effects. Here the testator is required to demonstrate a broad understanding of the process of will making and its consequences, not a precise knowledge of the legal technicalities.

(2)   The testator must be aware of the extent of the property he is disposing of. Once again the testator need not demonstrate awareness of every detail of the property he owns, a broad recollection being sufficient.

---

[8]   See *Banks v Goodfellow* LR 5 QB 549.

(3)   He must show an understanding of the claims to which he ought to give effect. Despite the wide discretion allowed to the testator under English law, he must be able to show that he has considered the moral claims of those who have been intimate with him or, as was put in *Boughton v Knight*,[9] considered the persons 'who are fitting objects of the testator's bounty'. All he has to do is show he is capable of considering these moral claims; it is unnecessary, of course, to leave any property to these persons. As was said in *Bird v Luckie*,[10] the testator need not act 'in such a manner as to deserve approbation from the prudent, the wise and the good.' However, in *Battan Singh v Amirchand*[11] the testator had left his property to creditors claiming he had no living relations. In fact, he had had three nephews with whom he had been on good terms. The lapse was taken to show loss of capacity as the moral claims of the nephews had not been taken into account.

A little regarded gloss in *Banks v Goodfellow* was considered recently in *Sharp v Adam*.[12] This is that:

> 'no disorder of the mind shall poison (the testator's) affections, pervert his sense of right, or prevent the exercise of his natural faculties.'

The testator had suffered progressive multiple sclerosis and was severely physically disabled. The issue was whether there had been mental impairment in the terminal stages of his life. He had made a will the consequences of which would have been the exclusion of two daughters of his with whom he had been on good terms and who were expected by those who knew him to have been beneficiaries. This impressed the judge who ruled the will in question invalid. Thus, matters other than the purely cognitive, such as intelligence and memory, may be in point when assessing testamentary capacity.

As is well known, individuals appear to be reluctant to make their wills. Inevitably, there are delays caused perhaps by the vacillations that follow the unwelcome intimations of mortality, the genuine uncertainties of mundane life and what the Bard referred to as the 'law's delays'. This may mean there occur many a slip between intention to make a will and its execution. As has already been noted, capacity is time-specific. One may have capacity, then lose it within days or weeks, and, then, occasionally, even regain it. In *Clancy v Clancy*,[13] it was held, applying *Parker v Felgate*[14] that lack of testamentary capacity at the time of executing a will did not invalidate that will, provided the testator had had capacity when giving instructions on its making, the will had been prepared in

---

9   (1873) LR 3 P and D 64 (1861–73) All ER Rep 40.
10   (1850) 8 Hare 301.
11   (1948) AC 161.
12   [2006] EWCA Civ 449.
13   (2003) WTLR 1097.
14   (1883) 8 PD 171.

accordance with those instructions and, when executing the will, the testator had been aware he was signing a will and believed it gave effect to those instructions. As for revocation of a will – presumably in order for a new one to be made – the test of capacity remains the same as for the making of a will.[15]

Given an ageing population, we should also be prepared to deal with the curious situation where, in an action in probate, it is not the testator's capacity that is in question but that of a witness in proceedings. In *Phillips and others v Symes and others*,[16] the court had to consider the matter – involving a party's fitness to follow the proceedings, give instructions and endure cross-examination – and came to re-iterate the points applicable that accord with the accepted tests for capacity in other civil situations.

Mental illness or disorder is, of course, the commonest cause for the loss of capacity. However, the diagnosis of an illness or a symptom, per se, for example, a delusion may not vitiate the whole will. In *Dew v Clark and Clark*,[17] the testator was deluded about his daughter and left her nothing. This made the will invalid. It might have been valid if the delusion had not influenced the dispositions. Also, if the delusion affects only a section of the will, only that section will be declared invalid.[18]

14.5 WITNESS COMPETENCE

The possible effects mental frailty could have on an elderly witness in cases of proceedings in probate have already been noted. Other situations may also arise where the capacity of a witness is brought into question. In *R v Sed*,[19] the appellant had been convicted of the attempted rape of an 81-year-old woman suffering from senile dementia. The complainant's evidence had been put in the form of a videotaped statement under ss 23 and 26 of the Criminal Justice Act 1988. The ground of appeal was that the trial judge should have considered the competence of the complainant as a witness when dealing with the issue of admissibility of the videotaped evidence. The statutory provisions in question offer an exception to the hearsay rule. The common law on capacity in this respect is now modified by s 53 of the Youth Justice and Criminal Evidence Act 1999. The court held that this provision requires of a potential witness that he only be intelligible – that is, he is able to understand questions and to give answers to these that are understandable. As to what weight is to be given to the evidence that remains a matter for the jury.

---

[15] See *Sabatini* (1970) 114 SJ 35.
[16] [2004] EWHC 1887 (Ch).
[17] (1826) 3 Add 79.
[18] See *Bohrmann's estate, Re Caesar v Watmough v Bohrmann* (1938) 1 All ER 271.
[19] [2004] EWCA Crim 1294.

In *Phillips and others v Symes*[20] Mr Symes and a partner (since dead) had
built up a successful business trading in antiquities. Mr Symes had later
developed strokes which had rendered him unconscious. Although
disabled on recovery he was able to carry on with his business. A dispute
arose between him and the administrators of his late partner's estate. It
involved very complex litigation. Mr Symes' general practitioner raised
the matter of his stroke. The medical and lay evidence was virtually of the
view that notwithstanding the strokes of two decades before Mr Symes
was possessed of capacity in matters involving the proceedings. The trial
judge remarked that the only difficulty he appeared to have in dealing
with questions was 'because answering them truthfully was inconvenient'.

14.6   SUGGESTIBLE DEFENDANT

In the criminal law a situation not uncommonly arises in the context of a
defendant's undue suggestibility with or without the presence of low
intelligence which renders him vulnerable to exploitation by a mentally
stronger individual. In *R v Antor*,[21] the appellant had been convicted of
conspiracy to rob. On appeal he relied on a psychological report in respect
of his low IQ and his level of suggestibility, and submitted that his
statement taken at police interview should have been excluded at trial. The
trial judge had declined to admit the psychological evidence. The
psychological report had shown that when the appellant had been tested
on the Gudjonsson Suggestibility Scale he had tended to acquiesce to
leading questions and change his responses under pressure at a higher
level than that of the general population. The Court of Appeal allowed
the appeal saying that was an important feature of the psychological
opinion and should have been put before the jury.

In *R v Blackburn*[22] the Court of Appeal recognised the reliability of a
confession could be impaired by several factors. There is the possibility of
undue susceptibility which is related to the personality of an individual.
There is also the phenomenon of the 'coerced compliant confession'
which may be related to fatigue which, together with an inability to
control what was happening, could induce an individual to give up
resisting suggestions put to him. Youth contributes further vulnerability.
Normal persons not suffering from any personality disorders or
abnormality could be rendered compliant by prolonged interrogation.

14.7   CHANGING DIAGNOSIS

It is a popular misconception that any diagnosis given is fixed and for all
time. As is plain from some of the examples already given, this is not so. A
change in diagnosis can have serious legal implications and lead in the

---

[20]   [2004] EWHC 1887 (Ch).
[21]   (2004) *The Times*, 4 November.
[22]   (2005) *The Times*, 10 June.

criminal law to changes being made in the sentencing of a convicted defendant and also to other options for disposal becoming available. In *R (AL) v Home Secretary*[23] the appellant had killed his girlfriend. A jury returned a verdict of not guilty by reason of insanity whereupon he was committed to hospital. Upon his release he formed another relationship which gave cause for concern. He was recalled to hospital by the Home Secretary when he was diagnosed to have an untreatable psychopathic disorder. He disputed this diagnosis. It was held that the statutory provision which had determined his initial incarceration – namely, s 5(1)(a) of the Criminal Procedure (Insanity) Act 1964 (unamended at that time) – did not specify the particular form of mental disorder and incarceration, rather than a medical disposal for a treatable condition, was therefore justified.

In *R v Beatty*[24] the appellant had been convicted of serious offences. He appeared to suffer a mental disorder which at the time of trial appeared to be untreatable. However, as time passed, he was found also to be suffering from a depressive illness and disclosed also a history of childhood sexual abuse. His condition now was deemed treatable, at least in part. His life sentence was quashed and a hospital order with restriction under the Mental Health Act 1983 was substituted.

14.8 SUMMARY

- Changing mental states may lead to situations of risk involving diverse forms. The elderly testator's capacity may be adversely affected not only by an underlying dementing illness but also due to a supervening confusional state usually a result of an intercurrent infection. This confusional state is usually liable to successful treatment with a result that there may be further change in the cognitive functioning of the patient.

- Issues of capacity may also concern witnesses to proceedings especially if they are elderly or have serious illness affecting the brain.

- The suggestible defendant is a matter for concern in criminal proceedings. Vulnerability may be due to mental disorder such as learning disabilities or personality disorder but normal individuals may also be rendered unduly suggestible in certain circumstances such as fatigue induced by prolonged interrogation or by emotional pressure put on them through aggressive interrogation. Changing diagnoses in respect of mental disorder may also have implications for the disposal of cases upon conviction.

---

[23] [2005] EWCA Civ 2.
[24] [2006] EWCA Crim 2349.

CHAPTER 15

RISK ASSESSMENT OF NUISANCE BEHAVIOUR

15.1   INTRODUCTION

One of the more complex areas of human behaviour that comes up for psychiatric assessment from time to time is behaviour that may be called, in one sense, antisocial behaviour. The psychiatrist is at once at a disadvantage for it is unusual to find evidence of formal mental illness or disorder in the individuals alleged to take part in these antisocial behaviours. He is usually reduced to describing the behaviour and its antecedents and coming to the conclusion that, as the best predictor of future behaviour is past conduct, that the nuisance behaviour will, in all probability, continue. Conventional treatment is of little avail in these circumstances but the description of the behaviours alleged, their possible roots, some comment on the individual's known previous personality, and even the humdrum prediction that the behaviours are bound to continue as they are beyond the reach of standard treatment measures seems to give comfort and assurance to bodies and professionals who commission assessment such as the courts, probation officers, the police, housing managers and social workers who are then able to cite the opinion as being the underlying authority for any sanction they wish to impose or recommend.

Nuisance behaviour forms a motley collection and in this chapter the kind of case that may come to the attention of a psychiatrist will be considered. There are significant socio-demographic and personal characteristics distinguishing between the individuals perpetrating these activities but there are also exceptions to whatever rule is stated.

15.2   ANTISOCIAL BEHAVIOUR

This compendious term includes those kinds of behaviours that have come to public attention since the introduction of antisocial behaviour orders (ASBO). The typical case involving antisocial behaviour concerns a youth – nowadays of either sex and increasingly of a younger age – whose activities are virtually indistinguishable from the conduct and behavioural problems seen in childhood and adolescence and, which at those ages and to that extent, may merit a diagnosis of mental disorder. There appear to be a preponderance of youths from the lower socio-economic classes and much social, economic and emotional deprivation is observable in their backgrounds. Parents of these youths are absent or ineffectual and seem mostly to seek comfort in such diagnoses in their children as attention deficit hyperactivity disorder and the autistic syndrome. There is almost certainly an overdiagnosis of pathology in cases of antisocial behaviour and much unnecessary medication may be given, especially to the younger offender, in respect of this behaviour. Social factors, the term used in its widest meaning, are almost always, if not the cause, the major contributory factor to behaviour of this kind.

As one sees from the ASBOs occasionally imposed on older individuals, antisocial behaviour is not unknown to adults who may be of varying ages. Some of these have been in trouble of some kind from a young age such as the 30-year-old woman who was incarcerated for persistent breaches of her ASBO. She had engaged in aggressive acts of begging, soliciting and general misbehaviour and underlying these behaviours was a strong dependence on heroin. Detoxification in prison was the first step towards her possible eventual rehabilitation. Other individuals take to antisocial behaviour later in life and one can often see an overlap between the behaviour of these individuals and those who inhabit the remaining categories of this chapter. Apart from being of adult age, the social status of these individuals may often be higher than that of young delinquents and, on examination, one unmistakably feels that these older individuals are, to an appreciable extent, also being influenced by changes in legislation and in society itself. Many of these older individuals are reasonably well informed and, more tellingly, are increasingly conscious of their rights. A rights-based assertion of their claims is a common thread that runs through the behaviour of this subcategory of persons persisting in forms of antisocial behaviour. The consciousness of their entitlement, especially since the coming into force of the Human Rights Act 1998, fuels the impression that there could have been an increase in antisocial behaviour on the part of individuals who are older, better educated and altogether more privileged than the adult whose provenance was that of a youthful tearaway.

While the average case of antisocial behaviour may be deemed a tiresome inconvenience, there may be occasional others with graver repercussions especially for the professionals involved. In *R v Jan*[1] the appellant had been convicted of causing a public nuisance and arson with intent to endanger life. He was sentenced to life imprisonment. In 1996, following concern expressed by his mother, a mental health assessment had been undertaken on him and he had been diagnosed to be suffering from a psychopathic disorder. He was not detained. However, he felt his personal liberty had been violated, he was greatly upset by the diagnosis given and he warned that he would be contemplating various actions in protest. Complaints by him followed against the assessing mental health team and

---

[1]   [2006] EWCA Crim 2314.

those who were associated with them. The list of his victims was vast. Over the next few years 6,000 pages of documents of complaint were compiled by him and there were floods of threatening telephone calls. Individuals were followed to their home address, their cars were damaged and there were numerous acts of harassment and vandalism committed. A car belonging to a social worker was set alight twice and another social worker was repeatedly assaulted, occasioning hospital treatment and her taking refuge. Acts of arson followed, with a petrol bomb thrown at a hospital manager, and a councillor's home was set on fire. On his arrest and following a search of his property numerous writings of a deranged and disturbing kind alleging conspiracy were found. There was no doubt a complex and cunning campaign was afoot, all arising out of dissatisfaction following one routine mental health assessment.

15.3   NEIGHBOUR DISPUTES

These involve a special category of the kind of problems involving neighbours that may follow common-or-garden disputes between neighbours. If mental disorder is to be found associated with nuisance this is probably the place to seek it although one hastens to add that the vast majority of neighbours engaged in intractable conflict between themselves demonstrate no readily diagnosable mental disorder. The reason for the apparently higher presence of mental disorder in these cases rather than other cases involving nuisance is that in a small minority of cases involving disputes between (or among) neighbours is probably the fact that some inhabitants of dwellings are to begin with already disordered in personality, are solitary and suspicious and in some cases given to suffering from frank mental illness and therefore quick to take offence. Not much discrimination – if that is feasible in the current climate – appears to have been shown in these cases in housing such individuals, without support, among others whose outlook on life could be wholly different. Rights associated with tenancy appear to compound the problem. The growing unaffordability and shortage of housing may make moving out – probably the only effective device available to settle these disputes, if only in the short-term (for there will be new neighbours to fall out with in due course) – difficult, if not impossible. The increased consciousness of personal rights may help to entrench the problem as also the fact that to the majority of individuals their most valued possession is their home, whether they be owners or tenants. This cocktail made up of these diverse ingredients fuels the many neighbour disputes that appear to move from bitterness through rancour and acrimony to occasional murderous violence.

There also appears to be a connection between neighbour disputes and the attitudes and behaviours essayed by vexatious litigants (see below). Behaviours seen with those engaged in the usual kind of neighbour disputes (like that involving vexatious litigants) rarely, if ever, emerge in a vacuum. In the vast majority of cases there has been some mundane dispute at the outset – which could have involved the overhanging branch of a tree, the right to car parking, perhaps a straying cat or dog or child or the disposal of rubbish – which sets off the conflagration. Investigation suggests that one of the parties to the later dispute could have been slow to respond to a complaint or had been insensitive in his dealings with the other, and matters escalate from that point. When the law intervenes, positions become entrenched and, as a rule, the opportunities for amicable mediation are then lost, perhaps for ever. There usually have been wrongs involved on both sides (or on all when other residents also become involved with the parties). A 30-year-old woman moved into rural premises in an attempt to get away from the difficulties she had previously had with urban neighbours. Her personality was a difficult and litigious one (she was also attempting to sue her general practitioner on account of his alleged tardiness in referring her for some specialist treatment). Within a matter of weeks in this location she had fallen out with her new neighbours. She claimed that they were 'putting it about' that she practised as a prostitute and was also an illicit drug user. She herself created some melodrama for, in an attempt to avert the gaze of prying neighbours, she took to entertaining her policeman boyfriend surreptitiously and got him to scale the fence at the back of her house at the dead of night, and thereby drew even more attention to herself. Relations between her and her new neighbours became so strained she eventually attracted a custodial sentence for a breach of an injunction.

That may seem an extreme case but violence between neighbours in dispute, even including homicide, is not unknown. The lesson to learn is that the behaviours that come to the attention of any assessing psychiatrist are usually far removed from the original circumstances of the dispute. It is this fact, and the absence of any diagnosable mental disorder, that makes worthwhile intervention difficult and often impossible; there is little to get one's teeth into.

15.4   PARENTAL DISPUTES

Disputes between parents concerning contact or residence in respect of a child or children are commonplace. We have already discussed the issue of parental alienation, or the attempts that could lead to it, in the chapter considering risk assessment in family and child proceedings. Three kinds of behaviours are usually seen in these circumstances. The first of these is due to formal mental illness or mental disorder suffered by a parent whose actions are dictated to a significant extent by the presence in him or her of illness or disorder. At the other extreme, wilful obstructive behaviour due to a cold-blooded attempt to thwart, obstruct or manipulate the processes of the law and also the other parent who, in most instances, has now become ex-spouse or partner. In between these two extremes lies behaviour which may, in part, be due to mental disorder but also has a measure of bloody-mindedness thrown in. The chronicity, persistence and single-mindedness of the resulting behaviour can come to cause alarm and despondency in those charged with ensuring the welfare of the child or children is put first.

A couple of examples will help illustrate the problem. A 35-year-old woman had become estranged from her husband. As the marriage was breaking up, as a result of the dissent caused within the marriage and for other reasons as well, the husband suffered a depressive illness. As his illness progressed he became preoccupied with sex in various forms – on the internet, pornographic magazines and massage parlours. These interests subsided as he recovered fully from the depressive illness with treatment. As contact arrangements came to be discussed, the wife persistently brought up the husband's behaviour during the course of his depressive illness in an attempt to deny him contact with his children even though his depressive illness had by now receded to the remote past and her own behaviour had in part been responsible for the way he had first reacted. What was striking was the lack of logic in her subsequent actions. Having after a struggle yielded unsupervised contact to him she began to quibble about every advance he sought – from increasing the time at contact to how many hours the children should spend with him at the weekends. No one who had investigated the husband's behaviour or had observed him with his children believed he posed any form of threat to his children, yet the mother persisted, even insisting that all his medical records be recovered and studied. In the event the court had to intercede. This was a case of a combination of a mother's natural anxiety, wilful obstructiveness and possibly some pathology in relation to sexual matters (she refused psychiatric assessment of herself).

A second case involved a 38-year-old mother who became convinced that her estranged partner had sexually assaulted their four-year-old daughter. As she consented to psychiatric assessment her condition could be studied in greater depth. What was striking in this case was the nature of her belief – which was to be characterised as an 'overvalued idea', a belief which lies somewhere in the spectrum between a true belief and a delusion – which led her to reject all the evidence (or the lack of it) concerning the matter including a finding of facts by a court. She went to extreme lengths to collect the 'disclosures' she claimed had been made by the child even when no one else had observed these. A system of belief was being created before one's eyes. There was a long history of anxiety states afflicting her and which were only partially treated, and she was also beset by numerous personal and social difficulties. It was against this background that a chance remark, perhaps, by the child that had probably inserted the germ of an idea into her mind and this appears to have grown into the structure that she held onto to defy every professional who was involved in the matter and continued to blacken the father's name.

The psychopathology underlying this behaviour is not fully understood but, in contrast to the cases of vexatious litigants to be taken up below, there often appears to be a greater incidence of psychological vulnerability demonstrated by those parents who come to show the behaviours that may lead to parental alienation. This predisposition may be due to the fact that a child of theirs is involved, thereby raising the emotional temperature, and it could also owe something to the fact that the parents involved once had a good deal of emotion of a positive kind invested in their relationship whose break up had released a great deal of emotional energy some of which at any rate had been transformed into a negative force.

True nuisance behaviour involving a parent in relation to another usually takes the form of making allegations – concerning sex, alcohol or illicit drug abuse, mental disorder, criminal tendencies, suicidal behaviour – which may not be true at all or are matters from so long in the past that it has become irrelevant to any current consideration of his or her mental health. Although some of the concerns may be due to ignorance – say, about the long-term effects of some disorder suffered by the other parent previously – the sheer persistence in the allegations even in the face of information received and reassurance supplied is an indicator in these cases that the behaviour engaged in approaches the form of a nuisance. Unless there is clear evidence of mental disorder present, and the parent accepts the treatment offered and is motivated to come half-way to seek improvement, there is hardly any intervention that is feasible in these cases. It is for the court to crack the whip and put a halt to the nonsense but, even then, there are parents prepared to defy the orders and directions of the court and risk its sanctions.

15.5   STALKING NUISANCE

The paranoid psychotic illness that occasionally underlies this condition has been discussed in the chapter on unusual psychiatric illnesses. It involves the condition of erotomania or De Clerambault's syndrome. This usually affects single women in middle age, and a psychological vulnerability is often discernible in these isolated, solitary and withdrawn individuals who come to crave attention. The descent into psychosis – in the imagined securement of a lover – could be seen, if somewhat heartlessly, as the last throw of the emotional dice for them.

The average case of 'stalking', as now understood, only rarely involves any formal mental illness. Even then, those who are the victims of these individuals could be relative strangers, sometimes celebrities. Probably the most common form of stalking involves a former spouse or partner as the victim, the individual concerned attempting to make contact, occasionally violently, with the other ex-spouse or partner, one with whom any children arising from their union usually reside. In some cases it appears to be simple curiosity that first drives these individuals, to see where the ex-partner may be living. In these cases all emotion appears to have been expended. In most other cases the attention paid to the ex-partner and the children may take on the features of harassment and even menace. It is then a potentially dangerous situation and the victim could be at real risk, a state of affairs now well appreciated by the courts and the police. Barriers placed by way of injunctions and non-molestation orders are of little avail in some cases. As a rule, no diagnosable mental disorder is found in the perpetrator in these cases who is unable to 'let go', his emotions which are not quite readjusted to the new situation concerning him as well as the ex-partner. Disputes about financial arrangements and residence of and contact with the children may add fuel to this situation, a strong argument for the speedy resolution of outstanding matters on the ending of a marriage or a relationship. If matters drag on – when the proceedings sometimes appear to be lasting longer than the relationship did – there is incentive for further bad behaviour which only rarely has any basis in pathology. A recent case illustrates the escalation possible when the parties to a relationship cannot be reconciled with its ending – the wife sold off an expensive and much-prized number plate belonging to the husband and he retaliated by purloining one shoe from each pair of shoes belonging to the wife and also burned her clothes thereby earning a conviction for criminal damage. In the average case there is little or nothing by way of psychiatric intervention to offer.

15.6 VEXATIOUS LITIGANTS

Nuisance behaviour *par excellence* is seen in this category of individuals. It is in many ways easier to study the full details of this condition, as compared to the others referred to in this chapter, as the ultimate sanction is for these individuals to be branded as vexatious litigants by the High Court on an application brought by the Attorney General and full judgments are given in these cases and published. As a rule, these individuals do not have any significant history of mental disorder in their past and also do not display any psychological vulnerability or predisposition to stressful life experiences. The provoking event – or the 'germ' – is some disappointment sustained in the course of some past proceedings. It is quite possible that some miscarriage of justice had taken place in their case. If the civil standard of proof can be converted into mathematical terms, 51 per cent proof conveys success, 49 per cent only failure. The judgment in any case – as lawyers know to their cost – can go either way and an unsuccessful litigant is entitled to feel cheated much as when his favourite cricket team lose a match by two runs, rather than winning it by one wicket, as a result of a dubious umpiring decision. But most individuals in these circumstances take a philosophical view of their failure and move on. The vexatious litigant does not and perhaps cannot do so. There is a burning sense of injustice lit within him and he resolves to fight with all the powers he has got in order to seek redress for this injustice. When questioned, he will often say it is his right to have justice rendered to him. Once again one sees the rights-based justification for excessive behaviour among these individuals. The steps taken by the individual to secure his rights can lead to such individuals sacrificing everything else – health, money, marriage and relationships, even their liberty – in this pursuit of some personal holy grail. A 55-year-old woman was referred by her general practitioner on account of her poor sleep and generally declining health, both physical and mental. It transpired that her son had been convicted of murder, a verdict upheld on appeal. She was adamant that he was innocent (of murder at any rate: 'The knife just fell out of his pocket, doctor') and came to spend her waking hours, and most of those which should have been dedicated to sleep, writing endless letters to the Prime Minister, the Lord Chancellor and the Lord Chief Justice among others. She was not quite a vexatious litigant but her obsessive behaviour had much in common with those individuals.

The spectrum of those dissatisfied with the processes of the law runs from the 'barrack room lawyer' inveighing in saloon bars against judges and lawyers through to the person preoccupied by one irksome decision – involving himself or someone close to him – to those who are truly successful in getting into the hair of the law, namely, the vexatious litigant. These are persons who usually come to have a staggering knowledge of some area of the law, enough to put many specialist lawyers to shame, not to mention the law firms where they soon become persona non grata. In *Attorney General v Chitolie*[2] Mr Chitolie had been involved in extensive litigation. One case involved repossession proceedings. He responded by suing the bank responsible in fraud. A second action involved rent arrears, conversion of chattels, an action for possession and bankruptcy proceedings involving, on the way, a dispute with Railtrack over a parcel of land and another against the Law Society claiming compensation for the alleged illegality of the solicitors who had represented him. A third group of litigation involved a disputed will of his late sister. A fourth group involved his being a litigation friend of a woman who was herself involved in extensive litigation. He had also compared the Patent Office to the Third Reich. The upshot was he was declared a vexatious litigant.

In the case of *Attorney General v Benton*[3] Mr Benton had instituted 32 separate proceedings over 25 months. There were claims against the highest in the land. Unusually, he was said to be suffering from a mental illness for which he was receiving treatment. He was said on the medical advice to be suffering from a fixed delusional system which was considered to be resistant to treatment. He was also declared a vexatious litigant.

In *Attorney General v Perotti*,[4] Mr Perotti's crusade for justice for himself began over a disputed will contested in 1984. He sought to have the

---

2   [2002] EWHC 1943 (Admin).
3   [2004] EWHC 1952 (Admin).
4   [2006] EWHC 1002 (Admin).

administrators removed. He then went on to sue various solicitors and counsel, two local authorities, a building society and a bank. He was also declared to be a vexatious litigant.

In these cases the law itself provides the remedy for these vexatious litigants cannot henceforth bring proceedings without first applying for leave. This works infinitely better than any attempt at medical treatment.

15.7 SUMMARY

* Nuisance behaviour takes diverse forms. Antisocial behaviour apart, there is usually some initial cause or justification for the behaviour which later goes on to become a nuisance. Mental disorder, at any rate of a significant degree, is usually absent in those perpetrating these behaviours.

* Antisocial behaviour is normally to be studied in terms of social and cultural factors involved, mental disorder being rare except in those cases of misbehaviour due to the psychopathic states or in chronic schizophrenia. The misuse of alcohol and illicit drugs has a considerable influence on the manifestation of antisocial behaviour. There is no reliably established form of treatment for these individuals especially when they are adult.

* Other nuisance behaviours in several instances are due to the presence in the mind of perpetrators of what is referred to as an 'over valued' idea, namely an idea which is not quite normal but does not amount to a delusion. This is well seen in neighbour disputes, the discord in parental relations concerning children and, most especially, among vexatious litigants where the actions of these individuals are driven by some perceived injustice. These behaviours are usually beyond any reliable treatment.

APPENDIX 1

PRACTICE DIRECTION:
EXPERTS IN FAMILY PROCEEDINGS
RELATING TO CHILDREN

[April 2008]

The Practice Direction below is made by the President of the Family Division under the powers delegated to him by the Lord Chief Justice under Schedule 2, Part 1, paragraph 2(2) of the Constitutional Reform Act 2005, and is approved by the Lord Chancellor

1. INTRODUCTION

1.1 This Practice Direction deals with the use of expert evidence and the instruction of experts in family proceedings relating to children, and comes into force on 1st April 2008. The guidance supersedes, for such proceedings, that contained in Appendix C (the *Code of Guidance for Expert Witnesses in Family Proceedings*) to the Protocol of June 2003 (*Judicial Case Management in Public Law Children Act Cases*) and in the Practice Direction to Part 17 (*Experts*) of the Family Procedure (Adoption) Rules 2005[1] ('FP(AR) 2005') with effect on and from 1st April 2008.

Where the guidance refers to 'an expert' or 'the expert', this includes a reference to an expert team.

1.2 For the purposes of this guidance, the phrase 'family proceedings relating to children' is a convenient description. It is not a legal term of art and has no statutory force. In this guidance it means[2] –

- placement and adoption proceedings, or
- family proceedings held in private which
  - relate to the exercise of the inherent jurisdiction of the High Court with respect to children,
  - are brought under the Children Act 1989 in any family court, or

---

[1]   SI 2005/2795.

[2]   Following r 10.20A(1) of the Family Proceedings Rules 1991, SI 1991/1247 ('FPR 1991') which defines the application of r 10.20A (*Communication of information relating to proceedings*). Compare the definition of 'relevant proceedings' in s 93(3) of the Children Act 1989 (*Rules of court*), applied in the equivalent r 23A (*Confidentiality of documents*) of the Family Proceedings Courts (Children Act 1989) Rules 1991, SI 1991/1395 ('FPC(ChA)R 1991').

    –   are brought in the High Court and county courts and 'otherwise relate wholly or mainly to the maintenance or upbringing of a minor'.

Aims of the guidance

1.3 The guidance aims to provide the court in family proceedings relating to children with early information to determine whether an expert or expert evidence will assist the court to:

- identify, narrow and where possible agree the issues between the parties;
- provide an opinion about a question that is not within the skill and experience of the court;
- encourage the early identification of questions that need to be answered by an expert; and
- encourage disclosure of full and frank information between the parties, the court and any expert instructed.

1.4 The guidance does not aim to cover all possible eventualities. Thus it should be complied with so far as consistent in all the circumstances with the just disposal of the matter in accordance with the rules and guidance applying to the procedure in question.

Permission to instruct an expert or to use expert evidence

1.5 In family proceedings relating to children, the court's permission is required to instruct an expert. Such proceedings are confidential and, in the absence of the court's permission, disclosure of information and documents relating to such proceedings risks contravening the law of contempt of court or the various statutory provisions protecting this confidentiality. Thus, for the purposes of the law of contempt of court, information relating to such proceedings (whether or not contained in a document filed with the court or recorded in any form) may be communicated only to an expert whose instruction by a party has been permitted by the court.[3] Additionally, in proceedings under the Children Act 1989, the court's permission is required to cause the child to be medically or psychiatrically examined or otherwise assessed for the purpose of the preparation of expert evidence for use in the proceedings; and, where the court's permission has not been given, no evidence arising out of such an examination or assessment may be adduced without the court's permission.[4]

1.6 In practice, the need to have the court's permission to disclose information or documents to an expert – and, in Children Act 1989 proceedings, to have the child examined or assessed – means that in

---

[3]   FPR 1991, r 10.20A(2)(vii); FPC(ChA)R 1991, r 23A(1)(c)(vii); FP(A)R 2005, r 78(1)(c)(vii).

[4]   FPR 1991, r 4.18(1) and (3); FPC(ChA)R 1991, r 18(1) and (3).

proceedings relating to children the court strictly controls the number, fields of expertise and identity of the experts who may be first instructed and then called.

1.7   Before permission is obtained from the court to instruct an expert in family proceedings relating to children, it will be necessary for the party wishing to instruct an expert to make enquiries designed so as to provide the court with information about that expert which will enable the court to decide whether or not to give permission. In practice, enquiries may need to be made of more than one expert for this purpose. This will in turn require each expert to be given sufficient information about the case to enable that expert to decide whether or not he or she is in a position to accept instructions. Such preliminary enquiries, and the disclosure of anonymised information about the case which is a necessary part of such enquiries, will not require the court's permission and will not amount to a contempt of court: see sections 4.1 and 4.2 (*Preliminary Enquiries of the Expert* and *Expert's Response to Preliminary Enquiries*).

1.8   Section 4 (*Preparation for the relevant hearing*) gives guidance on applying for the court's permission to instruct an expert, and on instructing the expert, in family proceedings relating to children. The court, when granting permission to instruct an expert, will also give directions for the expert to be called to give evidence, or for the expert's report to be put in evidence: see section 4.4 (*Draft Order for the relevant hearing*).

When should the court be asked for permission?

1.9   The key event is 'the relevant hearing', which is any hearing at which the court's permission is sought to instruct an expert or to use expert evidence. Both expert issues should be raised with the court – and, where appropriate, with the other parties – as early as possible. This means:

–   in public law proceedings under the Children Act 1989, by or at the Case Management Conference: see the *Practice Direction: Guide to Case Management in Public Law Proceedings*, paragraphs 13.7, 14.3 and 25(29) which contains the definition of public law proceedings for the purposes of that practice direction;

–   in private law proceedings under the Children Act 1989, by or at the First Hearing Dispute Resolution Appointment: see the *Private Law Programme* (9th November 2004), section 4 (*Process*);

–   in placement and adoption proceedings, by or at the First Directions Hearing: see FP(A)R 2005 rule 26 and the *President's Guidance: Adoption: the New Law and Procedure* (March 2006), paragraph 23.

2. GENERAL MATTERS

Scope of the Guidance

2.1 This guidance does not apply to cases issued before 1ˢᵗ April 2008, but in such a case the court may direct that this guidance will apply either wholly or partly. This is subject to the overriding objective for the type of proceedings, and to the proviso that such a direction will neither cause further delay nor involve repetition of steps already taken or of decisions already made in the case.

2.2 This guidance applies to all experts who are or have been instructed to give or prepare evidence for the purpose of family proceedings relating to children in a court in England and Wales.

Pre-application instruction of experts

2.3 When experts' reports are commissioned before the commencement of proceedings, it should be made clear to the expert that he or she may in due course be reporting to the court and should therefore consider himself or herself bound by this guidance. A prospective party to family proceedings relating to children (for example, a local authority) should always write a letter of instruction when asking a potential witness for a report or an opinion, whether that request is within proceedings or pre-proceedings (for example, when commissioning specialist assessment materials, reports from a treating expert or other evidential materials); and the letter of instruction should conform to the principles set out in this guidance.

Emergency and urgent cases

2.4 In emergency or urgent cases – for example, where, before formal issue of proceedings, a without-notice application is made to the court during or out of business hours; or where, after proceedings have been issued, a previously unforeseen need for (further) expert evidence arises at short notice – a party may wish to call expert evidence without having complied with all or any part of this guidance. In such circumstances, the party wishing to call the expert evidence must apply forthwith to the court – where possible or appropriate, on notice to the other parties – for directions as to the future steps to be taken in respect of the expert evidence in question.

Orders

2.5 Where an order or direction requires an act to be done by an expert, or otherwise affects an expert, the party instructing that expert – or, in the case of a jointly instructed expert, the lead solicitor – must serve a copy of the order or direction on the expert forthwith upon receiving it.

Adults who may be protected parties

2.6   The court will investigate as soon as possible any issue as to whether an adult party or intended party to family proceedings relating to children lacks capacity (within the meaning of the Mental Capacity Act 2005) to conduct the proceedings. An adult who lacks capacity to act as a party to the proceedings is a protected party and must have a representative (a litigation friend, next friend or guardian ad litem) to conduct the proceedings on his or her behalf.

2.7   Any issue as to the capacity of an adult to conduct the proceedings must be determined before the court gives any directions relevant to that adult's role in the proceedings.

2.8   Where the adult is a protected party, his or her representative should be involved in any instruction of an expert, including the instruction of an expert to assess whether the adult, although a protected party, is competent to give evidence. The instruction of an expert is a significant step in the proceedings. The representative will wish to consider (and ask the expert to consider), if the protected party is competent to give evidence, their best interests in this regard. The representative may wish to seek advice about 'special measures'. The representative may put forward an argument on behalf of the protected party that the protected party should not give evidence.

2.9   If at any time during the proceedings there is reason to believe that a party may lack capacity to conduct the proceedings, then the court must be notified and directions sought to ensure that this issue is investigated without delay.

Child likely to lack capacity to conduct the proceedings on when he or she reaches 18

2.10   Where it appears that a child is:

- – a party to the proceedings and not the subject of them;
- – nearing his or her 18th birthday, and
- – considered likely to lack capacity to conduct the proceedings when he or she attains the age of 18,

the court will consider giving directions for the child's capacity in this respect to be investigated.

3. THE DUTIES OF EXPERTS

Overriding Duty

3.1 An expert in family proceedings relating to children has an overriding duty to the court that takes precedence over any obligation to the person from whom the expert has received instructions or by whom the expert is paid.

Particular Duties

3.2   Among any other duties an expert may have, an expert shall have regard to the following duties:

(1)   to assist the court in accordance with the overriding duty;

(2)   to provide advice to the court that conforms to the best practice of the expert's profession;

(3)   to provide an opinion that is independent of the party or parties instructing the expert;

(4)   to confine the opinion to matters material to the issues between the parties and in relation only to questions that are within the expert's expertise (skill and experience);

(5)   where a question has been put which falls outside the expert's expertise, to state this at the earliest opportunity and to volunteer an opinion as to whether another expert is required to bring expertise not possessed by those already involved or, in the rare case, as to whether a second opinion is required on a key issue and, if possible, what questions should be asked of the second expert;

(6)   in expressing an opinion, to take into consideration all of the material facts including any relevant factors arising from ethnic, cultural, religious or linguistic contexts at the time the opinion is expressed;

(7)   to inform those instructing the expert without delay of any change in the opinion and of the reason for the change.

Content of the Expert's Report

3.3   The expert's report shall be addressed to the court and prepared and filed **in accordance with the court's timetable** and shall:

(1)   give details of the expert's qualifications and experience;

(2)   contain a statement setting out the substance of all material instructions (whether written or oral) summarising the facts stated and instructions given to the expert which are material to the conclusions and opinions expressed in the report;

(3)   identify materials that have not been produced either as original medical or other professional records or in response to an instruction from a party, as such materials may contain an assumption as to the standard of proof, the admissibility or otherwise of hearsay evidence, and other important procedural and substantive questions relating to the different purposes of other enquiries (for example, criminal or disciplinary proceedings);

(4)   identify all requests to third parties for disclosure and their responses in order to avoid partial disclosure which tends only to prove a case rather than give full and frank information;

(5)   make clear which of the facts stated in the report are within the expert's own knowledge;

(6) state who carried out any test, examination or interview which the expert has used for the report and whether or not the test, examination or interview has been carried out under the expert's supervision;

(7) give details of the qualifications of any person who carried out the test, examination or interview;

(8) in expressing an opinion to the court:

    (a) take into consideration all of the material facts including any relevant factors arising from ethnic, cultural, religious or linguistic contexts at the time the opinion is expressed, identifying the facts, literature and any other material including research material that the expert has relied upon in forming an opinion;

    (b) describe their own professional risk assessment process and process of differential diagnosis, highlighting factual assumptions, deductions from the factual assumptions, and any unusual, contradictory or inconsistent features of the case;

    (c) highlight whether a proposition is an hypothesis (in particular a controversial hypothesis), or an opinion deduced in accordance with peer-reviewed and –tested technique, research and experience accepted as a consensus in the scientific community;

    (d) indicate whether the opinion is provisional (or qualified, as the case may be), stating the qualification and the reason for it, and identifying what further information is required to give an opinion without qualification;

(9) where there is a range of opinion on any question to be answered by the expert:

    (a) summarise the range of opinion;

    (b) highlight and analyse within the range of opinion an 'unknown cause', whether on the facts of the case (for example, there is too little information to form a scientific opinion) or because of limited experience, lack of research, peer review or support in the field of expertise which the expert professes;

    (c) give reasons for any opinion expressed: the use of a balance sheet approach to the factors that support or undermine an opinion can be of great assistance to the court;

(10) contain a summary of the expert's conclusions and opinions;

(11) contain a statement that the expert understands his or her duty to the court and has complied and will continue to comply with that duty;

(12) contain a statement that the expert:

    (a) has no conflict of interest of any kind, other than any conflict disclosed in his or her report;

    (b)   does not consider that any interest disclosed affects his or her suitability as an expert witness on any issue on which he or she has given evidence;

    (c)   will advise the instructing party if, between the date of the expert's report and the final hearing, there is any change in circumstances which affects the expert's answers to (a) or (b) above;

(13) be verified by a statement of truth in the following form:

> 'I confirm that insofar as the facts stated in my report are within my own knowledge I have made clear which they are and I believe them to be true, and that the opinions I have expressed represent my true and complete professional opinion.'

4. PREPARATION FOR THE RELEVANT HEARING

Preliminary Enquiries of the Expert

4.1   In good time for the information requested to be available for the relevant hearing or for the advocates' meeting or discussion where one takes place before the relevant hearing, the solicitor for the party proposing to instruct the expert (or lead solicitor or solicitor for the child if the instruction proposed is joint) shall approach the expert with the following information:

(1)   the nature of the proceedings and the issues likely to require determination by the court;

(2)   the questions about which the expert is to be asked to give an opinion (including any ethnic, cultural, religious or linguistic contexts);

(3)   the date when the court is to be asked to give permission for the instruction (or if – unusually – permission has already been given, the date and details of that permission);

(4)   whether permission is to be asked of the court for the instruction of another expert in the same or any related field (that is, to give an opinion on the same or related questions);

(5)   the volume of reading which the expert will need to undertake;

(6)   whether or not permission has been applied for or given for the expert to examine the child;

(7)   whether or not it will be necessary for the expert to conduct interviews – and, if so, with whom;

(8)   the likely timetable of legal and social work steps;

(9)   when the expert's report is likely to be required;

(10) whether and, if so, what date has been fixed by the court for any hearing at which the expert may be required to give evidence (in particular the Final Hearing).

It is essential that there should be proper co-ordination between the court and the expert when drawing up the case management timetable: the needs of the court should be balanced with the needs of the expert whose forensic work is undertaken as an adjunct to his or her main professional duties, whether in the National Health Service or elsewhere.

The expert should be informed at this stage of the possibility of making, through his or her instructing solicitor, representations to the court about being named or otherwise identified in any public judgment given by the court.

Expert's Response to Preliminary Enquiries

4.2   In good time for the relevant hearing or for the advocates' meeting or discussion where one takes place before the relevant hearing, the solicitors intending to instruct the expert shall obtain confirmation from the expert:

(1)   that acceptance of the proposed instructions will not involve the expert in any conflict of interest;

(2)   that the work required is within the expert's expertise;

(3)   that the expert is available to do the relevant work within the suggested time scale;

(4)   when the expert is available to give evidence, of the dates and times to avoid and, where a hearing date has not been fixed, of the amount of notice the expert will require to make arrangements to come to court (or to give evidence by video link) without undue disruption to his or her normal professional routines;

(5)   of the cost, including hourly or other charging rates, and likely hours to be spent, attending experts' meetings, attending court and writing the report (to include any examinations and interviews);

(6)   of any representations which the expert wishes to make to the court about being named or otherwise identified in any public judgment given by the court.

Where parties have not agreed on the appointment of a single joint expert before the relevant hearing, they should obtain the above confirmations in respect of all experts whom they intend to put to the court as candidates for the appointment.

The proposal to instruct an expert

4.3   Any party who proposes to ask the court for permission to instruct an expert shall, **by 11 a.m. on the business day before the relevant hearing,** file and serve a written proposal to instruct the expert in the following detail:

(1)   the name, discipline, qualifications and expertise of the expert (by way of C.V. where possible);

(2)   the expert's availability to undertake the work;

(3)   the relevance of the expert evidence sought to be adduced to the issues in the proceedings and the specific questions upon which it is proposed that the expert should give an opinion (including the relevance of any ethnic, cultural, religious or linguistic contexts);

(4)   the timetable for the report;

(5)   the responsibility for instruction;

(6)   whether or not the expert evidence can properly be obtained by the joint instruction of the expert by two or more of the parties;

(7)   whether the expert evidence can properly be obtained by only one party (for example, on behalf of the child);

(8)   why the expert evidence proposed cannot be given by social services undertaking a core assessment or by the Children's Guardian in accordance with their respective statutory duties;

(9)   the likely cost of the report on an hourly or other charging basis: where possible, the expert's terms of instruction should be made available to the court;

(10) the proposed apportionment (at least in the first instance) of any jointly instructed expert's fee; when it is to be paid; and, if applicable, whether public funding has been approved.

Draft Order for the relevant hearing

4.4   Any party proposing to instruct an expert shall, **by 11 a.m. on the business day before the relevant hearing**, submit to the court a draft order for directions dealing in particular with:

(1)   the party who is to be responsible for drafting the letter of instruction and providing the documents to the expert;

(2)   the issues identified by the court and the questions about which the expert is to give an opinion;

(3)   the timetable within which the report is to be prepared, filed and served;

(4)   the disclosure of the report to the parties and to any other expert;

(5)   the organisation of, preparation for and conduct of an experts' discussion;

(6)   the preparation of a statement of agreement and disagreement by the experts following an experts' discussion;

(7)   making available to the court at an early opportunity the expert reports in electronic form;

(8)   the attendance of the expert at court to give oral evidence (alternatively, the expert giving his or her evidence in writing or remotely by video link), whether at or for the Final Hearing or another hearing; unless agreement about the opinions given by the expert is reached at or before the Issues Resolution Hearing ('IRH') or, if no IRH is to be held, by a specified date prior to the hearing at which the expert is to give oral evidence ('the specified date').

5. LETTER OF INSTRUCTION

5.1   The solicitor instructing the expert shall, **within 5 business days after the relevant hearing**, prepare (in agreement with the other parties where appropriate), file and serve a letter of instruction to the expert which shall:

(1)   set out the context in which the expert's opinion is sought (including any ethnic, cultural, religious or linguistic contexts);

(2)   set out the specific questions which the expert is required to answer, ensuring that they:

    (a)   are within the ambit of the expert's area of expertise;

    (b)   do not contain unnecessary or irrelevant detail;

    (c)   are kept to a manageable number and are clear, focused and direct; and

    (d)   reflect what the expert has been requested to do by the court.

The Annex to this guidance sets out suggested questions in letters of instruction to (1) child mental health professionals or paediatricians, and (2) adult psychiatrists and applied psychologists, in Children Act 1989 proceedings;

(3)   list the documentation provided, or provide for the expert an indexed and paginated bundle which shall include:

    (a)   a copy of the order (or those parts of the order) which gives permission for the instruction of the expert, immediately the order becomes available;

    (b)   an agreed list of essential reading; and

    (c)   a copy of this guidance;

(4)   identify materials that have not been produced either as original medical (or other professional) records or in response to an instruction from a party, as such materials may contain an assumption as to the standard of proof, the admissibility or otherwise of hearsay evidence, and other important procedural and substantive questions relating to the different purposes of other enquiries (for example, criminal or disciplinary proceedings);

(5)   identify all requests to third parties for disclosure and their responses, to avoid partial disclosure, which tends only to prove a case rather than give full and frank information;

(6)   identify the relevant people concerned with the proceedings (for example, the treating clinicians) and inform the expert of his or her right to talk to them provided that an accurate record is made of the discussions;

(7)   identify any other expert instructed in the proceedings and advise the expert of his or her right to talk to the other experts provided that an accurate record is made of the discussions;

(8)   subject to any public funding requirement for prior authority, define the contractual basis upon which the expert is retained and

in particular the funding mechanism including how much the expert will be paid (an hourly rate and overall estimate should already have been obtained), when the expert will be paid, and what limitation there might be on the amount the expert can charge for the work which he or she will have to do. In cases where the parties are publicly funded, there should also be a brief explanation of the costs and expenses excluded from public funding by Funding Code criterion 1.3 and the detailed assessment process.

Asking the court to settle the letter of instruction to a joint expert

5.2 Where the court has directed that the instructions to the expert are to be contained in a jointly agreed letter and the terms of the letter cannot be agreed, any instructing party may submit to the court a written request, which must be copied to the other instructing parties, that the court settle the letter of instruction. Where possible, the written request should be set out in an e-mail to the court, preferably sent directly to the judge dealing with the proceedings (or, in the Family Proceedings Court, to the legal adviser who will forward it to the appropriate judge or justices), and be copied by e-mail to the other instructing parties. The court will settle the letter of instruction, usually without a hearing to avoid delay; and will send (where practicable, by e-mail) the settled letter to the lead solicitor for transmission forthwith to the expert, and copy it to the other instructing parties for information.

Keeping the expert up to date with new documents

5.3 As often as may be necessary, the expert should be provided promptly with a copy of any new document filed at court, together with an updated document list or bundle index.

6. THE COURT'S CONTROL OF EXPERT EVIDENCE: CONSEQUENTIAL ISSUES

Written Questions

6.1 Any party wishing to put written questions to an expert for the purpose of clarifying the expert's report must put the questions to the expert **not later than 10 business days after receipt of the report**.

The court will specify the timetable according to which the expert is to answer the written questions.

Experts' Discussion or Meeting: Purpose

6.2 **By the specified date**, the court may – if it has not already given such a direction – direct that the experts are to meet or communicate:

(1) to identify and narrow the issues in the case;

(2)   where possible, to reach agreement on the expert issues;

(3)   to identify the reasons for disagreement on any expert question and what, if any, action needs to be taken to resolve any outstanding disagreement or question;

(4)   to explain or add to the evidence in order to assist the court to determine the issues;

(5)   to limit, wherever possible, the need for the experts to attend court to give oral evidence.

Experts' Discussion or Meeting: Arrangements

6.3   In accordance with the directions given by the court, the solicitor or other professional who is given the responsibility by the court ('the nominated professional') shall – **within 15 business days after the experts' reports have been filed and copied to the other parties** – make arrangements for the experts to meet or communicate. Where applicable, the following matters should be considered:

(1)   where permission has been given for the instruction of experts from different disciplines, a global discussion may be held relating to those questions that concern all or most of them;

(2)   separate discussions may have to be held among experts from the same or related disciplines, but care should be taken to ensure that the discussions complement each other so that related questions are discussed by all relevant experts;

(3)   **5 business days prior to a discussion or meeting**, the nominated professional should formulate an agenda including a list of questions for consideration. The agenda should contain only those questions which are intended to clarify areas of agreement or disagreement. Questions which repeat questions asked in the letter of instruction or which seek to rehearse cross-examination in advance of the hearing should be rejected as likely to defeat the purpose of the meeting.

The agenda may usefully take the form of a list of questions to be circulated among the other parties in advance. The agenda should comprise all questions that each party wishes the experts to consider. The agenda and list of questions should be sent to each of the experts **not later than 2 clear business days before the discussion;**

(4)   the nominated professional may exercise his or her discretion to accept further questions after the agenda with list of questions has been circulated to the parties. **Only in exceptional circumstances should questions be added to the agenda within the 2-day period before the meeting. Under no circumstances should any question received on the day of or during the meeting be accepted.** Strictness in this regard is vital, for adequate notice of the questions enables the parties to identify and isolate the issues in the case before the meeting so that the experts' discussion at the meeting can concentrate on those issues;

(5)   the discussion should be chaired by the nominated professional. A minute must be taken of the questions answered by the experts, and a Statement of Agreement and Disagreement must be prepared which should be agreed and signed by each of the experts who participated in the discussion. The statement should be served and filed **not later than 5 business days after the discussion has taken place;**

(6)   in each case, whether some or all of the experts participate by telephone conference or video link to ensure that minimum disruption is caused to professional schedules and that costs are minimised.

Meetings or conferences attended by a jointly instructed expert

6.4   Jointly instructed experts should not attend any meeting or conference which is not a joint one, unless all the parties have agreed in writing or the court has directed that such a meeting may be held, and it is agreed or directed who is to pay the expert's fees for the meeting or conference. Any meeting or conference attended by a jointly instructed expert should be proportionate to the case.

Court-directed meetings involving experts in public law Children Act cases

6.5   In public law Children Act proceedings, where the court gives a direction that a meeting shall take place between the local authority and any relevant named experts for the purpose of providing assistance to the local authority in the formulation of plans and proposals for the child, the meeting shall be arranged, chaired and minuted in accordance with the directions given by the court.

7. POSITIONS OF THE PARTIES

7.1   Where a party refuses to be bound by an agreement that has been reached at an experts' discussion or meeting, that party must inform the court and the other parties in writing, **within 10 business days after the discussion or meeting or, where an IRH is to be held, not less than 5 business days before the IRH,** of his reasons for refusing to accept the agreement.

8. ARRANGEMENTS FOR EXPERTS TO GIVE EVIDENCE

Preparation

8.1   Where the court has directed the attendance of an expert witness, the party who is responsible for the instruction of the expert shall, **by the specified date or, where an IRH is to be held, by the IRH,** ensure that:

(1) a date and time (if possible, convenient to the expert) are fixed for the court to hear the expert's evidence, substantially in advance of the hearing at which the expert is to give oral evidence and no later than a specified date prior to that hearing or, where an IRH is to be held, than the IRH;

(2) if the expert's oral evidence is not required, the expert is notified as soon as possible;

(3) the witness template accurately indicates how long the expert is likely to be giving evidence, in order to avoid the inconvenience of the expert being delayed at court;

(4) consideration is given in each case to whether some or all of the experts participate by telephone conference or video link, or submit their evidence in writing, to ensure that minimum disruption is caused to professional schedules and that costs are minimised.

Experts attending Court

8.2 Where expert witnesses are to be called, all parties shall, **by the specified date or, where an IRH is to be held, by the IRH**, ensure that:

(1) the parties' advocates have identified (whether at an advocates' meeting or by other means) the issues which the experts are to address;

(2) wherever possible, a logical sequence to the evidence is arranged, with experts of the same discipline giving evidence on the same day;

(3) the court is informed of any circumstance where all experts agree but a party nevertheless does not accept the agreed opinion, so that directions can be given for the proper consideration of the experts' evidence and of the party's reasons for not accepting the agreed opinion;

(4) in the exceptional case the court is informed of the need for a witness summons.

9. ACTION AFTER THE FINAL HEARING

9.1 Within 10 business days after the Final Hearing, the solicitor instructing the expert shall inform the expert in writing of the outcome of the case, and of the use made by the court of the expert's opinion.

9.2 Where the court directs preparation of a transcript, it may also direct that the solicitor instructing the expert shall send a copy to the **expert within 10 business days after receiving the transcript.**

9.3 After a Final Hearing in the Family Proceedings Court, the (lead) solicitor instructing the expert shall send the expert a copy of the court's written reasons for its decision **within 10 business days after receiving the written reasons**.

ANNEX[5]

Questions in letters of instruction to child mental health professional or paediatrician in Children Act 1989 proceedings

A: THE CHILD(REN)

1. Please describe the child(ren)'s current health, development and functioning (according to your area of expertise), and identify the nature of any significant changes which have occurred

- Behavioural
- Emotional
- Attachment organisation
- Social / peer / sibling relationships
- Cognitive / educational
- Physical
    - Growth, eating, sleep
    - Non-organic physical problems (including wetting and soiling)
    - Injuries
    - Paediatric conditions

2. Please comment on the likely explanation for / aetiology of the child(ren)'s problems / difficulties / injuries

- History / experiences (including intrauterine influences, and abuse and neglect)
- Genetic / innate / developmental difficulties
- Paediatric / psychiatric disorders

3. Please provide a prognosis and risk if difficulties not addressed above.

4. Please describe the child(ren)'s needs in the light of the above

- Nature of care-giving
- Education
- Treatment

in the short and long term (subject, where appropriate, to further assessment later).

B: THE PARENTS / PRIMARY CARE-GIVERS

5. Please describe the factors and mechanisms which would explain the parents' (or primary care-givers') harmful or neglectful interactions with the child(ren) (if relevant)

6. What interventions have been tried and what has been the result?

7. Please assess the ability of the parents or primary care-givers to fulfil the child(ren)'s identified needs now.

---

[5]   Drafted by the Family Justice Council.

8. What other assessments of the parents or primary care-givers are indicated

- Adult mental health assessment
- Forensic risk assessment
- Physical assessment
- Cognitive assessment

9. What, if anything, is needed to assist the parents or primary care-givers now, within the child(ren)'s time scales and what is the prognosis for change

- Parenting work
- Support
- Treatment / therapy

C: ALTERNATIVES

10. Please consider the alternative possibilities for the fulfilment of the child(ren)'s needs.

- What sort of placement
- Contact arrangements

Please consider the advantages, disadvantages and implications of each for the child(ren).

Questions in letters of instruction to adult psychiatrists and applied psychologists in Children Act 1989 proceedings

1. Does the parent / adult have – whether in his / her history or presentation – a mental illness / disorder (including substance abuse) or other psychological / emotional difficulty and, if so, what is the diagnosis?

2. How do any / all of the above (and their current treatment if applicable) affect his / her functioning, including interpersonal relationships?

3. If the answer to Q1 is yes, are there any features of either the mental illness or psychological / emotional difficulty or personality disorder which could be associated with risk to others, based on the available evidence base (whether published studies or evidence from clinical experience)?

4. What are the experiences / antecedents / aetiology which would explain his / her difficulties, if any, (taking into account any available evidence base or other clinical experience)?

5. What treatment is indicated, what is its nature and the likely duration?

6. What is his / her capacity to engage in / partake of the treatment / therapy?

7. Are you able to indicate the prognosis for, time scales for achieving, and likely durability of, change?

8. What other factors might indicate positive change?

(It is assumed that this opinion will be based on collateral information as well as interviewing the adult).

APPENDIX 2

DISABILITY DISCRIMINATION ACT 1995, PT 1

DISABILITY

1   Meaning of 'disability' and 'disabled person'

(1) Subject to the provisions of Schedule 1, a person has a disability for the purposes of this Act if he has a physical or mental impairment which has a substantial and long-term adverse effect on his ability to carry out normal day-to-day activities.

(2) In this Act 'disabled person' means a person who has a disability.

2   Past disabilities

(1) The provisions of this Part and Parts II to 4 and 5A apply in relation to a person who has had a disability as they apply in relation to a person who has that disability.

(2) Those provisions are subject to the modifications made by Schedule 2.

(3) Any regulations or order made under this Act by the Secretary of State, the Scottish Ministers or the Welsh Ministers may include provision with respect to persons who have had a disability.

(4) In any proceedings under Part 2, 3 , 4 or 5A of this Act, the question whether a person had a disability at a particular time ('the relevant time') shall be determined, for the purposes of this section, as if the provisions of, or made under, this Act in force when the act complained of was done had been in force at the relevant time.

(5) The relevant time may be a time before the passing of this Act.

Amendment—Amended by Special Educational Needs and Disability Act 2001, s 38(1), (2); iDisability Discrimination Act 2005, s 19(1), Sch 1, Pt 1, paras 1, 2(1), (2); 2007/1388, art 3, Sch 1, Paras 47, 48.

3   Guidance

(A1) The Secretary of State may issue guidance about matters to be taken into account in determining whether a person is a disabled person.

(1) Without prejudice to the generality of subsection (A1) the Secretary of State may in particular, issue guidance about the matters to be taken into account in determining—

    (a)   whether an impairment has a substantial adverse effect on a person's ability to carry out normal day-to-day activities; or

    (b)   whether such an impairment has a long-term effect.

(2) Without prejudice to the generality of subsection (A1), guidance about the matters mentioned in subsection 1 may, among other things, give examples of—

    (a)   effects which it would be reasonable, in relation to particular activities, to regard for purposes of this Act as substantial adverse effects;

    (b)   effects which it would not be reasonable, in relation to particular activities, to regard for such purposes as substantial adverse effects;

    (c)   substantial adverse effects which it would be reasonable to regard, for such purposes, as long-term;

    (d)   substantial adverse effects which it would not be reasonable to regard, for such purposes, as long-term.

(3) An adjudicating body determining, for any purpose of this Act, whether a person is a disabled person, shall take into account any guidance which appears to it to be relevant.

(3A) 'Adjudicating body' means —

    (a)   a court;

    (b)   a tribunal; and

    (c)   any other person who, or body which, may decide a claim under Part 4.

(4) In preparing a draft of any guidance , the Secretary of State shall consult such persons as he considers appropriate.

(5) Where the Secretary of State proposes to issue any guidance, he shall publish a draft of it, consider any representations that are made to him about the draft and, if he thinks it appropriate, modify his proposals in the light of any of those representations.

(6) If the Secretary of State decides to proceed with any proposed guidance, he shall lay a draft of it before each House of Parliament.

(7) If, within the 40-day period, either House resolves not to approve the draft, the Secretary of State shall take no further steps in relation to the proposed guidance.

(8) If no such resolution is made within the 40-day period, the Secretary of State shall issue the guidance in the form of his draft.

(9) The guidance shall come into force on such date as the Secretary of State may appoint by order.

(10) Subsection (7) does not prevent a new draft of the proposed guidance from being laid before Parliament.

(11) The Secretary of State may—

(a) from time to time revise the whole or part of any guidance and re-issue it;
(b) by order revoke any guidance.

(12) In this section—

'40-day period', in relation to the draft of any proposed guidance, means—
    (a) if the draft is laid before one House on a day later than the day on which it is laid before the other House, the period of 40 days beginning with the later of the two days, and
    (b) in any other case, the period of 40 days beginning with the day on which the draft is laid before each House,
no account being taken of any period during which Parliament is dissolved or prorogued or during which both Houses are adjourned for more than 4 days; and

'guidance' means guidance issued by the Secretary of State under this section and includes guidance which has been revised and re-issued.

Amendment—Amended by Special Educational Needs and Disability Act 2001, s 38(1), (3), (4); Disability Discrimination Act 2005, s 19(1), Sch 1, Pt 1, paras 1, s 3(1), (2), (3) (a), (b), (4), (5).

****

APPENDIX 3

HATTON V SUTHERLAND; BARBER V SOMERSET COUNTY COUNCIL; JONES V SANDWELL METROPOLITAN BOROUGH COUNCIL; BISHOP V BAKER REFRACTORIES LTD

[2002] EWCA Civ 76

Court of Appeal

Hale LJ

1. Introduction

[1]   These four appeals are related only by their subject matter. In each a defendant employer appeals against a finding of liability for an employee's psychiatric illness caused by stress at work. Two of the claimants were teachers in public sector comprehensive schools; another was an administrative assistant at a local authority training centre; the fourth was a raw materials operative in a factory. There is broad agreement as to the applicable principles of law. But there are difficulties in applying the principles developed in the context of industrial accidents to these very different circumstances. Hearing four very different cases together has also cast valuable light upon how those difficulties might be resolved in individual cases.

[2]   This judgment of the court, to which we have all contributed, is arranged as follows. First we consider some relevant background considerations; then the legal principles and how these are to be applied in this class of case; and we conclude with a summary of the questions to be asked in determining individual cases. Then we summarise the facts and our conclusions in each of the four cases under appeal. The details of each of these cases are contained in the appendix, which also contains an analysis of issues relating to damages which arose in two of the appeals.

2. Background considerations

[3]   This type of case has been described as the 'next growth area' in claims for psychiatric illness: see an essay by Nicholas J Mullany in 'Fear for the Future: Liability for the Infliction of Psychiatric Disorder' in *Torts in the Nineties* (1997) (ed Nicholas J Mullany), p 107. This growth is due to developing understanding in two distinct but inter-related areas of knowledge.

Psychiatric ill-health

[4] The first is of psychiatric illness generally. The Law Commission, in their Consultation Paper on Liability for Psychiatric Illness (1995) (Consultation Paper No 137), para 1.9, commented:

> 'We are aware from our preliminary consultations that there are strongly held views on this topic. On the one hand, there are those who are sceptical about the award of damages for psychiatric illness. They argue that such illness can easily be faked; that, in any event, those who are suffering should be able to 'pull themselves together'; and that, even if they cannot do so, there is no good reason why defendants and, through them, those who pay insurance premiums should pay for their inability to do so ... On the other hand, medical and legal experts working in the field, who are the people who most commonly encounter those complaining of psychiatric illness, have impressed upon us how life-shattering psychiatric illness can be and how, in many instances, it can be more debilitating than physical injuries.'

[5] The latter we entirely accept. But, although there have been great advances in understanding of the nature and causes of psychiatric ill-health, there are still important differences between physical and mental disorders:

(1) The dividing line between a normal but unpleasant state of mind or emotion and a recognised psychiatric illness or disorder is not easy to draw. Psychiatric textbooks tell us that with a physical disease or disability, the doctor can presuppose a perfect or 'normal' state of bodily health and then point to the ways in which his patient's condition falls short of this. There is probably no such thing as a state of perfect mental health. The doctor has instead to presuppose some average standard of functioning and then assess whether his patient's condition falls far enough short of that to be considered a disorder. However, there is now a considerable degree of international agreement on the classification of mental disorders and their diagnostic criteria, the two most commonly used tools being the most recent American Diagnostic and Statistical Manual of Mental Disorders, the DSM-IV (1994) and the World Health Organisation's ICD-10 Classification of Mental and Behavioural Disorders (1992).

(2) While some of the major mental illnesses have a known or strongly suspected organic origin, this is not the case with many of the most common disorders. Their causes will often be complex and depend upon the interaction between the patient's personality and a number of factors in the patient's life. It is not easy to predict who will fall victim, how, why or when.

(3) For the same reason, treatment is often not straightforward or its outcome predictable: while some conditions may respond comparatively quickly and easily to appropriate medication others may only respond, if at all, to prolonged and complicated 'talking treatments' or behavioural therapy. There are strong divergences of views amongst psychiatrists on these issues.

[6] In their report on Liability for Psychiatric Illness (1998) (Law Com No 249) at para 1.2, the Law Commission referred to the divergence of academic views on the approach the law should take:

'At one end of the scale are those who argue that the same principles that apply to liability for physical injury should be applied to liability for psychiatric illness, and that there is no legitimate reason to impose special restrictions in respect of claims for the latter [most forcefully by N J Mullany and P R Handford in *Tort Liability for Psychiatric Damage* (1993)]. At the other extreme are those who argue that liability for psychiatric illness should be abandoned altogether. They say that the arbitrary rules which are required to control potential liability are so artificial that they bring the law into disrepute [cogently expressed by Dr J Stapleton, 'In Restraint of Tort', in P Birks (ed), *The Frontiers of Liability* (1994), vol 2, pp 94–96].'

Both the law and the Law Commission have followed a middle course, in some cases treating a recognised psychiatric illness as no different in principle from a physical injury or illness, while in others imposing additional 'control mechanisms' so that liability does not extend too far.

Occupational stress

[7] The second area of developing understanding is of the nature and extent of occupational stress. We have been referred to three particularly helpful documents. The first is the report of a working party of the Health Education Authority, *Stress in the public sector – Nurses, police, social workers and teachers* (1988). This discusses the 'Meaning of Stress' in appendix 1:

'as with many words in a living language, the word 'stress' has acquired a vague, catch-all meaning, used by different people to mean different things. It is used to describe both physical and mental conditions, and the pressures which cause those conditions. It is also used to describe stress which is beneficial and harmful both in its sources and in its effects.'

Hence the definition of stress adopted in that report was 'an excess of demands upon an individual in excess of their ability to cope'. The report confirmed that the four occupations discussed had much in common in this respect.

[8] Second is the report of the Education Service Advisory Committee of the Health and Safety Commission, Managing occupational stress: a guide for managers and teachers in the schools sector (1990). This adopted a similar definition: 'stress is a process that can occur when there is an unresolved mismatch between the perceived pressures of the work situation and an individual's ability to cope.' It confirmed, if confirmation were needed, that teaching can be a stressful profession. It is also a profession which has undergone profound changes in recent years.

[9] The third is a general booklet of guidance from the Health and Safety Executive, *Stress at work* (1995). This is particularly helpful in distinguishing clearly between *pressure*, *stress*, and *the physical or psychiatric consequences* (p 2):

'There is no such thing as a pressure free job. Every job brings its own set of tasks, responsibilities and day-to-day problems, and the pressures and demands these place on us are an unavoidable part of working life. We are, after all, paid to work and to work hard, and to accept the reasonable pressures which go with that.

Some pressures can, in fact, be a good thing. It is often the tasks and challenges we face at work that provide the structure to our working days, keep us motivated and are the key to a sense of achievement and job satisfaction.

But people's ability to deal with pressure is not limitless. Excessive workplace pressure and the stress to which it can lead can be harmful. They can damage your business's performance and undermine the health of your workforce.'

Stress is defined, at p 4, as:

'the reaction people have to excessive pressures or other types of demand placed upon them. It arises when they worry that they can't cope. It can involve both physical and behavioural effects, but these 'are usually short-lived and cause no lasting harm. When the pressures recede, there is a quick return to normal.

Stress is not therefore the same as ill-health. But in some cases, particularly where pressures are intense and continue for some time, the effect of stress can be more sustained and far more damaging, leading to longer-term psychological problems and physical ill-health.'

[10] Two other important messages emerge from these documents. First, and perhaps contrary to popular belief, harmful levels of stress are most likely to occur in situations where people feel powerless or trapped. These are more likely to affect people on the shop floor or at the more junior levels than those who are in a position to shape what they do. Second, stress – in the sense of a perceived mismatch between the pressures of the job and the individual's ability to meet them – is a psychological phenomenon but it can lead to either physical or mental ill-health or both. When considering the issues raised by these four cases, in which the claimants all suffered psychiatric illnesses, it may therefore be important to bear in mind that the same issues might arise had they instead suffered some stress-related physical disorder, such as ulcers, heart disease or hypertension.

Differences from other work-related harm

[11] Mr Hogarth, on behalf of the employer in Mr Barber's case, has pointed to several differences between this and other kinds of work-related harm, such as injuries suffered in accidents at work or illnesses caused by exposure to deleterious physical conditions at work. These are in addition to the general differences between physical and psychiatric disorders discussed earlier:

(1)   The most significant relates to who knows what. The employer is or should be aware of what is going on in his own factory, school or office. He is much less aware of what is going on in his employees' minds or in their lives outside work. There are many other people, such as family, friends and

colleagues, who are likely to know far more about this than the employer. Indeed, the employee may very well wish to minimise or conceal the true state of affairs from his employer: no one wants to be thought unable to cope.

(2)   The employer is or should be largely in control of the workplace, equipment and physical conditions in which the work is done. He is much less in control of the way in which many of his employees, especially professionals or those who are expected to prioritise their own tasks, choose to do their work and balance the demands of their work and life outside the workplace.

(3)   The employer can be expected to take responsibility for keeping the physical risks presented by the workplace to a minimum. But responsibility both for causing and for doing something about its psychological risks may be shared between many people, family, friends and the individual himself, as well as the employer. An individual who recognises that he is experiencing levels of stress which may be harmful to him has to make some decisions about how to respond to this. The employer's room for manoeuvre may in some cases be limited. At the extreme, his only option may be to dismiss the employee who cannot cope with the job.

[12]   There are some jobs which are intrinsically physically dangerous: the most obvious examples are the armed forces, fire-fighting and the police. The employee agrees to run the inevitable risks of the job, although not those which are the result of his employers' negligence. Psychological *pressures* are inevitable in all jobs, although greater in some than in others. But it is, as the documents quoted show, rather more difficult to identify which jobs are intrinsically so *stressful* that physical or psychological *harm* is to be expected more often than in other jobs. Some people thrive on pressure and are so confident of their abilities to cope that they rarely if ever experience stress even in jobs which many would find extremely stressful. Others experience harmful levels of stress in jobs which many would not regard as stressful at all.

[13]   When imposing duties and setting standards, the law tries to strike a balance which is reasonable to both sides. Here there are weighty considerations on each side. It is in everyone's interests that management should be encouraged to recognise the existence and causes of occupational stress and take sensible steps to minimise it within their organisation. It is in the interest of the individual employees who may suffer harm if their employers do not. It is in the interest of the particular enterprise which may lose efficiency and workers if it does not. It is in the public interest that public services should not suffer or public money be wasted. Concern about this issue arose during a period of great upheaval in the workforce, and in many large organisations, bringing changes in management ethos, instability and insecurity. The documents we have seen all aim to encourage management to take the issue of occupational stress seriously.

[14]   The law of tort has an important function in setting standards for employers as well as for drivers, manufacturers, health care professionals and many others whose carelessness may cause harm. But if the standard of care expected of employers is set too high, or the threshold of liability too low, there may also be unforeseen and unwelcome effects upon the employment market. In particular, employers may be even more reluctant than they already are to take on people with a significant psychiatric history or an acknowledged vulnerability to stress-related disorders. If employers are expected to make searching inquiries of

employees who have been off sick, then more employees may be vulnerable to dismissal or demotion on ill-health grounds. If particular employments are singled out as ones in which special care is needed, then other benefits which are available to everyone in those employments, such as longer holidays, better pensions or earlier retirement, may be under threat.

[15]   Some things are no one's fault. No one can blame an employee who tries to soldier on despite his own desperate fears that he cannot cope, perhaps especially where those fears are groundless. No one can blame an employee for being reluctant to give clear warnings to his employer of the stress he is feeling. His very job, let alone his credibility or hopes of promotion, may be at risk. Few would blame an employee for continuing or returning to work despite the warnings of his doctor that he should give it up. There are many reasons why the job may be precious to him. On the other hand it may be difficult in those circumstances to blame the employer for failing to recognise the problem and what might be done to solve it.

[16]   There is an argument that stress is so prevalent in some employments, of which teaching is one, and employees so reluctant to disclose it, that all employers should have in place systems to detect it and prevent its developing into actual harm. As the above discussion shows, this raises some difficult issues of policy and practice which are unsuitable for resolution in individual cases before the courts. If knowledge advances to such an extent as to justify the imposition of obligations upon some or all employers to take particular steps to protect their employees from stress-related harm, this is better done by way of regulations imposing specific statutory duties. In the meantime the ordinary law of negligence governs the matter.

[17]   However, we do know of schemes now being developed and encouraged which recognise and respond to the peculiar problems presented both to employees and employers. The key is to offer help on a completely confidential basis. The employee can then be encouraged to recognise the signs and seek that help without fearing its effects upon his job or prospects; the employer need not make intrusive inquiries or over-react to such problems as he does detect; responsibility for accessing the service can be left with the people who are best equipped to know what the problems are, the employee, his family and friends; and if reasonable help is offered either directly or through referral to other services, then all that reasonably could be done has been done. Obviously, not all employers have the resources to put such systems in place, but an employer who does have a system along those lines is unlikely to be found in breach of his duty of care towards his employees.

3.   The law

[18]   Several times while hearing these appeals we were invited to go back to first principles. Liability in negligence depends upon three inter-related requirements: the existence of a duty to take care; a failure to take the care which can reasonably be expected in the circumstances; and damage suffered as a result of that failure. These elements do not exist in separate compartments: the existence of the duty, for example, depends upon the type of harm suffered. Foreseeability of what

might happen if care is not taken is relevant at each stage of the inquiry. Nevertheless, the traditional elements are always a useful tool of analysis, both in general and in particular cases.

Duty

[19] The existence of a duty of care can be taken for granted. All employers have a duty to take reasonable care for the safety of their employees to see that reasonable care is taken to provide them with a safe place of work, safe tools and equipment, and a safe system of working: see *Wilsons & Clyde Coal Co Ltd v English* [1938] AC 57. However, where psychiatric harm is suffered, the law distinguishes between 'primary' and 'secondary' victims. A primary victim is usually someone within the zone of foreseeable physical harm should the defendant fail to take reasonable care: see *Page v Smith* [1996] AC 155. A secondary victim is usually someone outside that zone: typically such a victim foreseeably suffers psychiatric harm through seeing, hearing or learning of physical harm tortiously inflicted upon others. There are additional control mechanisms to keep liability towards such people strictly within bounds: see *Alcock v Chief Constable of South Yorkshire Police* [1992] 1 AC 310. In *Frost v Chief Constable of South Yorkshire Police* [1999] ICR 216 the House of Lords applied that distinction to police officers (and others) who were not themselves within the zone of physical danger caused by the defendant's negligence, but had to deal with the consequences of catastrophic harm to others in the course of their duties. Lord Steyn observed, at p 255:

> 'The rules to be applied when an employee brings an action against his employer for harm suffered at his workplace are the rules of tort. One is therefore thrown back to the ordinary rules of the law of tort which contain restrictions on the recovery of compensation for psychiatric harm ... The duty of an employer to safeguard his employees from harm could also be formulated in contract ... But such a term could not be wider in scope than the duty imposed by the law of tort.'

Taken to its logical conclusion this would apply the same distinction between those inside and those outside the zone of foreseeable risk of physical harm to the employer's general duty of care to his employees.

[20] We have not been invited to go down that road, no doubt because it is not open to us. In *Petch v Customs and Excise Comrs* [1993] ICR 789 it was accepted that the ordinary principles of employers' liability applied to a claim for psychiatric illness arising from employment, although the claim failed. In the landmark case of *Walker v Northumberland County Council* [1995] ICR 702 Colman J applied those same principles in upholding the claim. Both have recently been cited with approval in this court in *Garrett v Camden London Borough Council* [2001] EWCA Civ 395. Also in the *Frost* case [1999] ICR 216, 262, Lord Hoffman stated:

> 'The control mechanisms were plainly never intended to apply to all cases of psychiatric injury. They contemplate that the injury has been caused in consequence of death or injury suffered (or apprehended to have been suffered or as likely to be suffered) by someone else.'

As to *Walker's* case, he commented, at p 263:

> 'The employee ... was in no sense a secondary victim. His mental
> breakdown was caused by the strain of doing the work which his employer
> had required him to do.'

[21]   In summary, therefore, claims for psychiatric injury fall into four different
categories: (1) tortious claims by primary victims: usually those within the
foreseeable scope of physical injury, for example, the road accident victim in *Page
v Smith* [1996] AC 155; some primary victims may not be at risk of physical harm,
but at risk of foreseeable psychiatric harm because the circumstances are akin to
those of primary victims in contract (see (3) below); (2) tortious claims by
secondary victims: those outside that zone who suffer as a result of harm to
others, for example, the witnesses of the Hillsborough disaster in *Alcock v Chief
Constable of South Yorkshire Police* [1992] 1 AC 310; (3) contractual claims by
primary victims: where the harm is the reasonably foreseeable product of specific
breaches of a contractual duty of care towards a victim whose identity is known
in advance, for example, the solicitors' clients in *Cook v Swinfen* [1967] 1 WLR
457, *McLoughlin v Jones* [2002] 2 WLR 1279 or the employees in *Petch v Customs
and Excise Comrs* [1993] ICR 789, *Walker v Northumberland County Council*
[1995] ICR 702, *Garrett v Camden London Borough Council* [2001] EWCA Civ
395, and in all the cases before us; (4) contractual claims by secondary victims:
where the harm is suffered as a result of harm to others, in the same way as
secondary victims in tort, but there is also a contractual relationship with the
defendant, as with the police officers in the *Frost* case [1999] ICR 216.

[22]   There are, therefore, no special control mechanisms applying to claims for
psychiatric (or physical) injury or illness arising from the stress of doing the work
which the employee is required to do. But these claims do require particular care
in determination, because they give rise to some difficult issues of foreseeability
and causation and, we would add, identifying a relevant breach of duty. As Simon
Brown LJ pithily put it in *Garrett's* case, at para 63:

> 'Many, alas, suffer breakdowns and depressive illnesses and a significant
> proportion could doubtless ascribe some at least of their problems to the
> strains and stresses of their work situation: be it simply overworking, the
> tensions of difficult relationships, career prospect worries, fears or feelings
> of discrimination or harassment, to take just some examples. *Unless,
> however, there was a real risk of breakdown which the claimant's employers
> ought reasonably to have foreseen and which they ought properly to have
> averted, there can be no liability.*' (Emphasis supplied.)

Foreseeability

[23]   To say that the employer has a duty of care to his employee does not tell us
what he has to do (or refrain from doing) in any particular case. The issue in most
if not all of these cases is whether the employer should have taken positive steps to
safeguard the employee from harm: his sins are those of omission rather than
commission. Mr Owen, for the employer in Mr Bishop's case, saw this as a
question of defining the duty; Mr Lewis, for the employer in Mrs Jones's case, saw
it as a question of setting the standard of care in order to decide whether it had

been broken. Whichever is the correct analysis, *the threshold question is whether this kind of harm to this particular employee was reasonably foreseeable*. The question is not whether psychiatric injury is foreseeable in a person of 'ordinary fortitude'. The employer's duty is owed to each individual employee, not to some as yet unidentified outsider: see *Paris v Stepney Borough Council* [1951] AC 367. The employer knows who his employee is. It may be that he knows, as in *Paris's* case, or ought to know, of a particular vulnerability; but he may not. *Because of the very nature of psychiatric disorder, as a sufficiently serious departure from normal or average psychological functioning to be labelled a disorder, it is bound to be harder to foresee than is physical injury.* Shylock could not say of a mental disorder, 'If you prick us, do we not bleed?' *But it may be easier to foresee in a known individual than it is in the population at large.* The principle is the same as in other cases where there is a contractual duty of care, such as solicitors' negligence: see *Cook v Swinfen* [1967] 1 WLR 457 and *McLoughlin v Jones* [2002] 2 WLR 1279.

[24] However, are there some occupations which are so intrinsically stressful that resulting physical or psychological harm is always foreseeable? Mr Lewis appeared to accept that this was so: he gave the examples of traffic police officers who regularly deal with gruesome accidents or child protection officers who regularly investigate unthinkable allegations of child abuse. Some warrant for this might be drawn from the way in which Dillon LJ formulated the foreseeability test in the *Petch* case [1993] ICR 789, 796–797:

> 'unless senior management in the defendants' department were aware or ought to have been aware that the plaintiff was showing signs of impending breakdown, or were aware or ought to have been aware that his workload carried a real risk that he would have a breakdown, then the defendants were not negligent in failing to avert the breakdown ...'

Later, at p 798B, he referred to the same two-pronged test:

> 'but Mr Bamfield had no knowledge of any sign whatever of impending danger, nor was he bound to regard the plaintiff's workload, so eagerly accepted, as per se dangerous.'

These observations were made in the context of a particular employee in a particular high grade Civil Service post. They were not made in the context of such posts as a whole. The notion that some occupations are in themselves dangerous to mental health is not borne out by the literature to which we have already referred: it is not the job but the interaction between the individual and the job which causes the harm. Stress is a subjective concept: the individual's perception that the pressures placed upon him are greater than he may be able to meet. Adverse reactions to stress are equally individual, ranging from minor physical symptoms to major mental illness.

[25] All of this points to there being a single test: *whether a harmful reaction to the pressures of the workplace is reasonably foreseeable in the individual employee concerned. Such a reaction will have two components: (1) an injury to health; which (2) is attributable to stress at work*. The answer to the foreseeability question will therefore depend upon the inter-relationship between the particular characteristics of the employee concerned and the particular demands which the employer casts upon him. As was said in *McLoughlin v Jones* [2002] 2 WLR 1279, expert evidence may be helpful although it can never be determinative of what a reasonable employer should have foreseen. A number of factors are likely to be relevant.

[26] These include the *nature and extent of the work being done by the employee*. Employers should be more alert to picking up signs from an employee who is being overworked in an intellectually or emotionally demanding job than from an employee whose workload is no more than normal for the job or whose job is not particularly demanding for him or her. It will be easier to conclude that harm is foreseeable if the employer is putting pressure upon the individual employee which is in all the circumstances of the case unreasonable. Also relevant is whether there are signs that others doing the same work are under harmful levels of stress. There may be others who have already suffered injury to their health arising from their work. Or there may be an abnormal level of sickness and absence amongst others at the same grade or in the same department. But if there is no evidence of this, then the focus must turn to the individual, as Colman J put it in the *Walker* case [1995] ICR 702, 713:

> 'Accordingly, the question is whether it ought to have been foreseen that Mr Walker was exposed to a risk of mental illness materially higher than that which would ordinarily affect a social services middle manager in his position with a really heavy workload.'

[27] More important are the *signs from the employee himself*. Here again, it is important to distinguish between signs of stress and signs of impending harm to health. Stress is merely the mechanism which may but usually does not lead to damage to health. The *Walker* case is an obvious illustration: Mr Walker was a highly conscientious and seriously overworked manager of a social work area office with a heavy and emotionally demanding case load of child abuse cases. Yet although he complained and asked for help and for extra leave, the judge held that his first mental breakdown was not foreseeable. There was, however, liability when he returned to work with a promise of extra help which did not materialise and experienced a second breakdown only a few months later. If the employee or his doctor makes it plain that unless something is done to help there is a clear risk of a breakdown in mental or physical health, then the employer will have to think what can be done about it.

[28] Harm to health may sometimes be foreseeable without such an express warning. Factors to take into account would be frequent or prolonged absences from work which are uncharacteristic for the person concerned; these could be for physical or psychological complaints; but there must also be good reason to think that the underlying cause is occupational stress rather than other factors; this could arise from the nature of the employee's work or from complaints made about it by the employee or from warnings given by the employee or others around him.

[29] But when considering what the reasonable employer should make of the information which is available to him, from whatever source, what assumptions is he entitled to make about his employee and to what extent is he bound to probe further into what he is told? *Unless he knows of some particular problem or vulnerability, an employer is usually entitled to assume that his employee is up to the normal pressures of the job.* It is only if there is something specific about the job or the employee or the combination of the two that he has to think harder. But thinking harder does not necessarily mean that he has to make searching or intrusive inquiries. *Generally he is entitled to take what he is told by or on behalf of the employee at face value.* If he is concerned he may suggest that the employee consults his own doctor or an occupational health service. But he should not without a very good reason seek the employee's permission to obtain further information from his medical advisers. Otherwise he would risk unacceptable invasions of his employee's privacy.

[30]   It was argued that the employer is entitled to take the expiry of a general practitioner's certificate as implicitly suggesting that the employee is now fit to return to work and even that he is no longer at risk of suffering the same sort of problem again. This cannot be right. A general practitioner's certificate is limited in time but many disorders are not self-limiting and may linger on for some considerable time. Yet an employee who is anxious to return to work, for whatever reason, may not go back to his general practitioner for a further certificate when the current one runs out. Even if the employee is currently fit for work, the earlier time-limited certificate carries no implication that the same or a similar condition will not recur. The point is a rather different one: *an employee who returns to work after a period of sickness without making further disclosure or explanation to his employer is usually implying that he believes himself fit to return to the work which he was doing before.* The employer is usually entitled to take that at face value unless he has other good reasons to think to the contrary: see *McIntyre v Filtrona Ltd* (unreported) 12 March 1996; Court of Appeal Transcript No 1310 of 1996.

[31]   These then are the questions and the possible indications that harm was foreseeable in a particular case. But how strong should those indications be before the employer has a duty to act? Mr Hogarth argued that only 'clear and unequivocal' signs of an impending breakdown should suffice. That may be putting it too high. But *in view of the many difficulties of knowing when and why a particular person will go over the edge from pressure to stress and from stress to injury to health, the indications must be plain enough for any reasonable employer to realise that he should do something about it.*

Breach of duty

[32]   What then is it reasonable to expect the employer to do? His duty is to take reasonable care. What is reasonable depends, as we all know, upon the foreseeability of harm, the magnitude of the risk of that harm occurring, the gravity of the harm which may take place, the cost and practicability of preventing it, and the justifications for running the risk: see the oft-quoted summary of Swanwick J in *Stokes v Guest, Keen Nettlefold (Nuts and Bolts) Ltd* [1968] 1 WLR 1776, 1783D–E.

[33]   It is essential, therefore, once the risk of harm to health from stresses in the workplace is foreseeable, to consider whether and in what respect the employer has broken that duty. There may be a temptation, having concluded that some harm was foreseeable and that harm of that kind has taken place, to go on to conclude that the employer was in breach of his duty of care in failing to prevent that harm (and that that breach of duty caused the harm). But *in every case it is necessary to consider what the employer not only could but should have done.* We are not here

concerned with such comparatively simple things as gloves, goggles, earmuffs or non-slip flooring. Many steps might be suggested: giving the employee a sabbatical; transferring him to other work; redistributing the work; giving him some extra help for a while; arranging treatment or counselling; providing buddying or mentoring schemes to encourage confidence; and much more. But in all of these suggestions it will be necessary to consider how reasonable it is to expect the employer to do this, either in general or in particular: *the size and scope of its operation will be relevant to this, as will its resources, whether in the public or private sector, and the other demands placed upon it. Among those other demands are the interests of other employees in the workplace.* It may not be reasonable to expect the employer to rearrange the work for the sake of one employee in a way which prejudices the others. As we have already said, an employer who tries to balance all these interests by offering confidential help to employees who fear that they may be suffering harmful levels of stress is unlikely to be found in breach of duty: except where he has been placing totally unreasonable demands upon an individual in circumstances where the risk of harm was clear.

[34] Moreover, *the employer can only reasonably be expected to take steps which are likely to do some good.* This is a matter on which the court is likely to require expert evidence. In many of these cases it will be very hard to know what would have done some let alone enough good. In some cases the only effective way of safeguarding the employee would be to dismiss or demote him. There may be no other work at the same level of pay which it is reasonable to expect the employer to offer him. *In principle the law should not be saying to an employer that it is his duty to sack an employee who wants to go on working for him for the employer's own good.* As Devlin LJ put it in *Withers v Perry Chain Co Ltd* [1961] 1 WLR 1314, 1320:

> 'The relationship between employer and employee is not that of a schoolmaster and pupil ... The employee is free to decide for herself what risks she will run ... if the common law were to be otherwise it would be oppressive to the employee, by limiting his ability to find work, rather than beneficial to him.'

Taken to its logical conclusion, of course, this would justify employers in perpetuating the most unsafe practices (not alleged in that case) on the basis that the employee can always leave. But we are not here concerned with physical dangers: we have already rejected the concept of an unsafe occupation for this purpose. If there is no alternative solution, it has to be for the employee to decide whether or not to carry on in the same employment and take the risk of a breakdown in his health or whether to leave that employment and look for work elsewhere before he becomes unemployable.

Causation

[35] Having shown a breach of duty, *it is still necessary to show that the particular breach of duty found caused the harm.* It is not enough to show that occupational stress caused the harm. Where there are several different possible causes, as will often be the case with stress related illness of any kind, the claimant may have difficulty proving that the employer's fault was one of them: see *Wilsher v Essex Area Health Authority* [1988] AC 1074. This will be a particular problem if, as in *Garrett v Camden London Borough Council* [2001] EWCA Civ 395, the main cause

was a vulnerable personality which the employer knew nothing about. However, *the employee does not have to show that the breach of duty was the whole cause of his ill-health: it is enough to show that it made a material contribution*: see *Bonnington Castings Ltd v Wardlaw* [1956] AC 613.

Apportionment and quantification

[36] Many stress-related illnesses are likely to have a complex aetiology with several different causes. In principle a wrongdoer should pay only for that proportion of the harm suffered for which he by his wrongdoing is responsible: see e g *Thompson v Smiths Shiprepairers (North Shields) Ltd* [1984] ICR 236, *Holtby v Brigham & Cowan (Hull) Ltd* [2000] ICR 1086 and *Rahman v Arearose Ltd* [2001] QB 351. The *Thompson* and *Holtby* cases concerned respectively deafness and asbestosis developed over a long period of exposure; not only were different employers involved but in *Thompson* some of the exposure by the same employer was tortious and some was not. Apportionment was possible because the deterioration over particular periods of time could be measured, albeit in a somewhat rough and ready fashion.

[37] *It is different if the harm is truly indivisible*: a tortfeasor who has made a material contribution is liable for the whole, although he may be able to seek contribution from other joint or concurrent tortfeasors who have also contributed to the injury. In the *Rahman* case [2001] QB 351, 361, para 17, Laws LJ quoted the following illuminating discussion from *Prosser & Keeton on Torts*, 5th ed (1984), pp 345–346:

> 'If two defendants, struggling for a single gun, succeed in shooting the plaintiff, there is no reasonable basis for dividing the injury between them, and each will be liable for all of it. If they shoot the plaintiff independently, with separate guns, and the plaintiff dies from the effect of both wounds, there can still be no division, for death cannot be divided or apportioned except by an arbitrary rule ... If they merely inflict separate wounds, and the plaintiff survives, a basis for division exists, because it is possible to regard the two wounds as separate injuries ... There will be obvious difficulties of proof as to the apportionment of certain elements of damages, such as physical and mental suffering and medical expenses, but such difficulties are not insuperable, and it is better to attempt some rough division than to hold one defendant [liable] for the wound inflicted by the other. Upon the same basis, if two defendants each pollute a stream with oil, in some instances it may be possible to say that each has interfered to a separate extent with the plaintiff's rights in the water, and to make some division of the damages. It is not possible if the oil is ignited, and burns the plaintiff's barn.'

[38] In *Bonnington Castings Ltd v Wardlaw* [1956] AC 613 the employee was exposed to harmful dust, all of it at work, but some of it in breach of duty and some not: the employer was held liable for the whole of the damage caused by the combination of the 'guilty' and 'innocent' dust. The question of apportionment was not argued. The problem there, as in *McGhee v National Coal Board* [1973] 1 WLR 1, was whether the claimant could prove causation at all, given the possible contribution of both 'guilty' and 'innocent' dust to his illness.

[39] As Stuart Smith LJ commented in the *Holtby* case [2000] ICR 1086, 1094, para 20:

> '[The claimant] will be entitled to succeed if he can prove that the defendant's tortious conduct made a material contribution to his disability. But strictly speaking the defendant is liable only to the extent of that contribution. However, if the point is never raised or argued by the defendant, the claimant will succeed in full as in *Bonnington* and *McGhee*.'

Clarke LJ went further and placed at least the evidential burden of establishing the case for apportionment upon the defendant, at p 1099, para 35:

> 'It seems to me that once the claimant has shown that the defendant's breach of duty has made a material contribution to his disease, justice requires that he should be entitled to recover in full from those defendants unless they show the extent to which some other factor, whether it be 'innocent' dust or tortious dust caused by others, also contributed.'

But he acknowledged that these cases should not be determined by the burden of proof: assessments of this kind are 'essentially a jury question which has to be determined on a broad basis' (p 1100, para 37).

[40] Hence the learned editors of *Clerk & Lindsell on Torts*, 18th edn (2000), para 2–21, state: 'Where it is possible to identify the extent of the contribution that the defendant's wrong made to the claimant's damage then the defendant is liable only to that extent, and no more.' This may raise some difficult factual questions. *Calascione v Dixon* (1993) 19 BMLR 97 is an example of apportionment between different causes, one the fault of the defendant, the other not: the claimant suffered post traumatic stress disorder as a result of seeing the aftermath of the accident in which her son was killed, but her normal grief reaction had become abnormal as a result of later events. In *Vernon v Bosley (No 1)* [1997] 1 All ER 577 the majority in this court held that the whole of the claimant's psychiatric injury was the result of the accident in which his two daughters died, although Stuart Smith LJ dissented on the ground that it had not been shown that it was caused by his witnessing the unsuccessful attempts to rescue them, that is by the breach of the defendant's duty towards him. These were both, of course, secondary victims. The *Rahman* case [2001] QB 351 is an example of apportionment of the psychiatric injury suffered by a primary victim between different tortfeasors. Neither tort caused the whole injury, some was caused mainly by one, some mainly by the other, and some by their combined effect. Neither tortfeasor would have been held liable for the whole.

[41] Hence if it is established that the constellation of symptoms suffered by the claimant stems from a number of different extrinsic causes then in our view a sensible attempt should be made to apportion liability accordingly. There is no reason to distinguish these conditions from the chronological development of industrial diseases or disabilities. The analogy with the polluted stream is closer than the analogy with the single fire. Nor is there anything in *Bonnington Castings Ltd v Wardlaw* [1956] AC 613 or *McGhee v National Coal Board* [1973] 1 WLR 1 requiring a different approach.

[42] Where the tortfeasor's breach of duty has exacerbated a pre-existing disorder or accelerated the effect of pre-existing vulnerability, the award of general damages for pain, suffering and loss of amenity will reflect only the exacerbation or acceleration. Further, the quantification of damages for financial losses must take some account of contingencies. In this context, one of those contingencies may well be the chance that the claimant would have succumbed to a stress-related disorder in any event. As it happens, all of these principles are exemplified by the decision of Otton J at first instance in *Page v Smith* [1993] PIQR Q55 (and not appealed by the claimant: see *Page v Smith (No 2)* [1996] 1 WLR 855). He reduced the multiplier for future loss of earnings (as it happens as a teacher) from 10 to 6 to reflect the many factors making it probable that the claimant would not have had a full and unbroken period of employment in any event and the real possibility that his employers would have terminated his employment because of his absences from work.

4. Summary

[43] From the above discussion, the following practical propositions emerge:

(1) There are no special control mechanisms applying to claims for psychiatric (or physical) illness or injury arising from the stress of doing the work the employee is required to do (para 22). The ordinary principles of employer's liability apply (para 20).

(2) The threshold question is whether this kind of harm to this particular employee was reasonably foreseeable (para 23): this has two components (a) an injury to health (as distinct from occupational stress) which (b) is attributable to stress at work (as distinct from other factors) (para 25).

(3) Foreseeability depends upon what the employer knows (or ought reasonably to know) about the individual employee. Because of the nature of mental disorder, it is harder to foresee than physical injury, but may be easier to foresee in a known individual than in the population at large (para 23). An employer is usually entitled to assume that the employee can withstand the normal pressures of the job unless he knows of some particular problem or vulnerability (para 29).

(4) The test is the same whatever the employment: there are no occupations which should be regarded as intrinsically dangerous to mental health (para 24).

(5) Factors likely to be relevant in answering the threshold question include: (a) the nature and extent of the work done by the employee (para 26). Is the workload much more than is normal for the particular job? Is the work particularly intellectually or emotionally demanding for this employee? Are demands being made of this employee unreasonable when compared with the demands made of others in the same or comparable jobs? Or are there signs that others doing this job are suffering harmful levels of stress? Is there an abnormal level of sickness or absenteeism in the same job or the same department? (b) Signs from the employee of impending harm to health (paras 27 and 28). Has he a particular problem or vulnerability? Has he already suffered from illness attributable to stress at work? Have there recently been frequent or prolonged absences which are uncharacteristic of him? Is there reason to think that these are attributable to stress at work, for example because of complaints or warnings from him or others?

(6)   The employer is generally entitled to take what he is told by his employee at face value, unless he has good reason to think to the contrary. He does not generally have to make searching inquiries of the employee or seek permission to make further inquiries of his medical advisers (para 29).

(7)   To trigger a duty to take steps, the indications of impending harm to health arising from stress at work must be plain enough for any reasonable employer to realise that he should do something about it (para 31).

(8)   The employer is only in breach of duty if he has failed to take the steps which are reasonable in the circumstances, bearing in mind the magnitude of the risk of harm occurring, the gravity of the harm which may occur, the costs and practicability of preventing it, and the justifications for running the risk (para 32).

(9)   The size and scope of the employer's operation, its resources and the demands it faces are relevant in deciding what is reasonable; these include the interests of other employees and the need to treat them fairly, for example, in any redistribution of duties (para 33).

(10)   An employer can only reasonably be expected to take steps which are likely to do some good: the court is likely to need expert evidence on this (para 34).

(11)   An employer who offers a confidential advice service, with referral to appropriate counselling or treatment services, is unlikely to be found in breach of duty (paras 17 and 33).

(12)   If the only reasonable and effective step would have been to dismiss or demote the employee, the employer will not be in breach of duty in allowing a willing employee to continue in the job (para 34).

(13)   In all cases, therefore, it is necessary to identify the steps which the employer both could and should have taken before finding him in breach of his duty of care (para 33).

(14)   The claimant must show that that breach of duty has caused or materially contributed to the harm suffered. It is not enough to show that occupational stress has caused the harm (para 35).

(15)   Where the harm suffered has more than one cause, the employer should only pay for that proportion of the harm suffered which is attributable to his wrongdoing, unless the harm is truly indivisible. It is for the defendant to raise the question of apportionment (paras 36 and 39).

(16)   The assessment of damages will take account of any pre-existing disorder or vulnerability and of the chance that the claimant would have succumbed to a stress related disorder in any event (para 42).

We will now apply these principles to the facts of the four cases before us. For convenience we are including only a brief summary of the individual cases in the main body of this judgment. They are given more extensive treatment in the appendix.

5.   Mrs Hatton

[44]   Mrs Hatton began teaching in 1976. From 1980 to 1995 she taught French at a comprehensive school in Huyton, Liverpool. In October 1995 she was signed off from work because of depression and debility and never returned. She retired on ill health grounds in August 1996. The defendant school governors, the

employers, appeal against the order of Judge Trigger in the Liverpool County Court on 7 August 2000 awarding her a total of £90,765.83 in damages and interest.

[45] She had two months off work suffering from depression in 1989, following the break-up of her marriage. Her two sons, born in about 1983 and 1988, lived with her. But she continued to enjoy her work and was coping with the workload until September 1992.

[46] Mrs Hatton's workload was no greater or more burdensome than that of any other teacher in a similar school. Nor had she complained to anyone about it. Certain changes had taken place in the school years 1992–1993 and 1993–1994 but their effect had been absorbed by September 1994. In 1992 the school went over to a modular GCSE French course. No other teacher found that this course involved more preparation and marking after the first few weeks. Mrs Hatton did not complain. The head of her department was absent from January 1993 and retired in May 1993 and supply teachers were used for a while. No one knew that this was involving her in much more work outside school. In September 1993 it was decided to use English rather than supply teachers to help out with French. Mrs Hatton was off work for a considerable part of 1993 to 1994 but did not tell anyone at the school that she attributed her absences to overwork. In September 1994 a new head of department was appointed and the use of English teachers stopped. Her work regime this year was entirely normal compared with other French teachers. The only difference in the year from September 1995 was a retiming and reduction by one in her free periods, about which she did complain to the deputy head.

[47] Mrs Hatton's pattern of absence and illness was on the face of it readily attributable to causes other than stress at work. In January 1994 she was off work for a month following an attack in the street. In April 1994 one of her sons had to go into hospital for a considerable period. A deputy head sent her home. She remained away for the rest of the term, certified with depression and debility. She saw a stress counsellor in August 1994 but did not tell the school about this. When she returned in September 1994 she attributed her absence to her son's illness. During the school year 1994–1995 she had no absences due to depression or debility, but she did have a number of absences for minor physical ailments, including 19 days for sinusitis. She was a smoker who had suffered from this before.

[48] Her workload and her pattern of absence taken together could not amount to a sufficiently clear indication that she was likely to suffer from psychiatric injury as a result of stress at work such as to trigger a duty to do more than was in fact done. The school could not reasonably be expected to probe further into the causes of her absence in the summer term 1994 when she herself had attributed it to problems at home which the school knew to be real. Hence the claim must fail at the first threshold of foreseeability.

[49] Even if the breakdown had been foreseeable, the judge would have had to resolve the conflict in the expert evidence as to its causes and what if anything the school might have done to prevent it. The judge was entitled to find that her own perception of stress at work was at least a contributory factor. But he should have had difficulty in concluding that it was the only factor, given the evidence of the

employers' expert witness, Dr Wood. He should also have identified a specific breach of duty which had contributed to the illness: an omission to do something without which it would in all probability not have happened. If there was no breach of duty in not probing further into her account of the summer of 1994, the only possible candidates are a failure to probe further into her pattern of physical illness in 1994 to 1995 or to react to her complaint about the 1995 timetable. It would, however, be difficult to conclude that anything the school could have done by that stage would have made a difference.

[50] This is a classic case where no one can be blamed for the sad events which brought Mrs Hatton's teaching career to an end. It was sought to meet some of the obvious difficulties in her case by the argument that teaching is such a stressful profession that by 1995 all employers should have had in place systems which would overcome the reluctance of people like Mrs Hatton to reveal their difficulties and seek help. We have already explained why we take the view that, although an employer who does have such a system is unlikely to be found in breach of duty, it is not for this court to impose such a duty upon all employers, or even upon all employers in a particular profession.

6. Mr Barber

[51] Mr Barber was also an experienced secondary school teacher. He was appointed head of maths at East Bridgwater Community School in 1984 and remained there until 12 November 1996 when he ceased work on medical advice. He accepted early retirement on 31 March 1997. The defendant local education authority, the employers, appeal against the order of Judge Roach in the Exeter County Court on 8 March 2001 awarding him a total of £101,041.59 in damages and interest.

[52] The school was under particular pressure in the year 1995 to 1996. It was a comprehensive school in a deprived area of Bridgwater. Its roll had more than halved between the mid-1980s and the mid-1990s and resources had fallen accordingly. Restructuring became essential. However, there was comparatively little effect upon the maths department, as opposed to others. In September 1995 Mr Barber, in common with other heads of department, became the 'area of experience co-ordinator' in maths. There was still the same number of maths teachers but the two former deputy heads of his department were given pastoral rather than management roles. To keep his former salary level Mr Barber took on another responsibility, as project manager in charge of publicity and media relations. He was working long hours.

[53] The evidence was that all the area of experience co-ordinators, and the senior management team, were suffering from work overload at this time. In addition to the restructuring and worries over falling rolls, the school was due for an Ofsted inspection in autumn 1996. While everyone was in the same boat, the evidence did not support the suggestion that Mr Barber was more overworked than any of his peers in these difficult circumstances. The judge found that his workload was not so extreme as to put his employers on notice.

[54] Mr Gill, one of the two deputy heads, was in charge of the timetable and curriculum and saw all the co-ordinators periodically. In October 1995 Mr Barber

told him that the loss of his deputies was resulting in more work, and in February 1996 that work overload was affecting both him and the maths department. Mr Gill did not appreciate that Mr Barber was by then finding things too much; he advised Mr Barber to prioritise and delegate more.

[55] Mr Barber had developed depressive symptoms during the autumn 1995 term but told no one at school about these. He felt worse during the spring 1996 term but again told no one at school. He explored the possibility of other jobs or taking early retirement. In May 1996 he had three weeks off work with depression: he was surprised to be told the diagnosis as he had never thought of himself in that way. When he came back he had an informal meeting with the head, Mrs Hayward, and raised his concerns that he was finding things difficult. On 16 July 1996, he saw Mrs Newton, the other deputy head, and told her that he could not cope and that the situation was becoming detrimental to his health. She referred him to Mr Gill, who was more sympathetic. This was very shortly before the end of the summer term. He did not tell either of them about the symptoms of weight loss, lack of sleep and out of body experiences which he described in his evidence.

[56] Mrs Hayward retired unexpectedly at the end of term and Mr Gill became acting headmaster. On return for the autumn term he expressed some concern about Mr Barber and asked a colleague to keep an eye on him. Mr Barber had continued to suffer symptoms of stress over the summer holidays but had not been able to discuss these with his doctor. He first raised them with the doctor in October. In November he lost control in the classroom and was advised to stop work immediately.

[57] This was a classic case in which it is essential to consider at what point the school's duty to take some action was triggered, what that action should have been, and whether it would have done some good. Instead, the judge first considered whether the illness was caused by stress at work and reached the conclusion that it was. No doubt this was because the school had argued that Mr Barber's breakdown was caused by other things, and the judge had to resolve that issue. There was certainly evidence entitling him to hold that stress at work had made a material contribution. But that in itself was not enough to lead to the conclusion that the school was in breach of duty or that its breach caused the harm.

[58] Mr Barber did not think of himself as a candidate for psychiatric illness until it was diagnosed in May 1996. The first the school knew of any possible adverse effects upon his health of the difficulties at work which they were all experiencing was after his return. He simply told Mrs Hayward that he was not coping very well. He made a more explicit reference to his health to Mrs Newton and Mr Gill, but did not explain the symptoms from which he was suffering. This was just before the summer holidays, which are usually a source of relaxation and recuperation for hard-pressed teachers. Indeed he was unable to tell his own doctor about his symptoms until the month before the crisis arose. He told no one at school of any problems during that term.

[59] In those circumstances it is difficult indeed to identify a point at which the school had a duty to take the positive steps identified by the judge. It might have been different if Mr Barber had gone to Mr Gill at the beginning of the autumn

term and told him that things had not improved over the holidays. But it is expecting far too much to expect the school authorities to pick up the fact that the problems were continuing without some such indication. Given the speed with which matters came to a head that term it might be difficult to sustain the judge's finding that temporary help would have averted the crisis. But in our view the evidence, taken at its highest, does not sustain a finding that they were in breach of their duty of care towards him.

7. Mrs Jones

[60] Mrs Jones was employed as an administrative assistant at Trainwell, a local authority training centre, from August 1992 until 20 January 1995 when she went off sick with anxiety and depression. She never returned and was made redundant when the centre closed at the end of 1996. The defendant local authority, the employers, appeal against the order of Judge Nicholl in the Birmingham County Court on 31 October 2000 awarding her a total of £157,541 damages and interest.

[61] Mrs Jones's job was unique, a new post resulting from the consolidation of training activities in one site. The tasks were varied and the deadlines tight. They included submitting monthly claims to the local Training and Enterprise Council on which the whole operation depended. The judge found that she was having to work grossly excessive hours over the 37 per week required by her contract of employment. There was unchallenged evidence that her personnel officer, Mr King, had acknowledged in February 1993 that they knew it was a gamble to expect one person to do the work of two to three.

[62] She complained of overwork to her immediate managers, Mr Papworth and his deputy, from an early stage. She complained to Mr King at head office in February 1993. She also complained to him of unfair treatment and that she had been threatened with non-renewal of her temporary post if she persisted in her complaints of overwork. He said that he would try to get her extra help. Extra help was earmarked for her by Mr Papworth's superior but diverted by Mr Papworth to other tasks. In July 1994, Mrs Jones complained to Mrs York, who had taken over as her personnel officer, in a five page document listing the problems under 'health', 'excessive workload', 'equal opportunities' and 'managerial disagreements'. Once again it was noted that extra help should be provided but none was forthcoming. In November 1994, Mrs Jones invoked the formal grievance procedure, complaining of discrimination in her unsuccessful application for an instructor's job at Trainwell and harassment during her time there which had affected her health. The grievance hearing did not take place until January 1995 when it was adjourned. She went off sick shortly afterwards.

[63] The judge also found that she had been 'harassed' by Mr Papworth. He meant that she had been treated unreasonably in such matters as his reaction to her complaints of overwork, dismissing these with the unfounded suggestion that she had more than enough time to do what was required of her, threatening her with loss of her job if she complained, failing to allocate the extra help provided to her, and completely inappropriate behaviour around the grievance hearing. This was not a case like Mr Barber's where everyone was overworked and under pressure, but one where the job itself made unreasonable demands upon an employee in a comparatively junior grade, and the management response to her complaints was itself unreasonable.

[64] Mrs Jones did not go off work sick during any of this time. She did not even consult her general practitioner until March 1994, when she consulted him about abdominal problems which he noted might be psychosomatic. Thereafter she suffered from headaches which were not eased by multiple analgesics, although he diagnosed migraine rather than psychiatric illness. There was therefore no specific medical event which might have alerted her employers to the risk of the breakdown which occurred in January 1995.

[65] However, the employers did know that excessive demands were being placed upon Mrs Jones. They also knew that she was complaining of unreasonable behaviour by her immediate manager. These were taken sufficiently seriously for extra help to be arranged, not once but twice, but it was not actually provided. She made two written formal complaints, one in July and one in November 1994, that problems at work were causing harm to her health. It was not disputed that they did in fact cause her breakdown in January 1995.

[66] The question, therefore, is not whether they had in fact caused harm to her health before January 1995, but whether it was sufficiently foreseeable that they would do so for it to be a breach of duty for the employers to carry on placing unreasonable demands upon her and not to follow through their own decision that something should be done about it. We have concluded, not without some hesitation, that the evidence before the judge was sufficient to entitle him to reach the conclusion that it was. We are conscious that the employers relied mainly on the evidence of Mr Papworth, which the judge did not find impressive. They did not call either Mr King or Mrs York to explain what they had made of Mrs Jones's complaints, and in particular her complaints in 1994 of the adverse effect that these problems were having on her health. Unlike the other cases before us, this was one such as was envisaged by Lord Slynn of Hadley in *Waters v Comr of Police of the Metropolis* [2000] ICR 1064, 1068C–D, where the employer knew that the employee was being badly treated by another employee and could have done something to prevent it.

[67] Once it is concluded that the combination of the way in which she was being treated and her formal complaints about it made injury to her health foreseeable, it is not difficult to identify what might have been done to prevent the injury which in fact occurred. The judge was entitled to conclude that failure to do this caused her breakdown. There was no challenge to the quantification of damages in this case. We have not therefore been able to consider whether any of the matters discussed earlier in this judgment might have led to any modification of the award. Our conclusion on liability should not be taken as any indication of our view on the appropriate measure of damages in this or any other such case.

8. Mr Bishop

[68] Mr Bishop worked for the defendant company, the employer, from 1979 until February 1997 when he had a mental breakdown and attempted suicide. He never returned to work and was dismissed in 1998. The employer appeals against the order of Judge Kent-Jones in the Leeds County Court on 26 January 2001 awarding him general damages of £7,000 and adjourning his claim for loss of earnings.

[69] The employer was taken over by an American company in 1992 and reorganisation began. New shift patterns were introduced in 1994. Work was reorganised so that employees were expected to do a greater variety of tasks. Mr Bishop was at that time employed on mixer cleaning and graphite blowing. But in 1995 the mixer cleaning tasks were spread among other employees for health and safety reasons. Mr Bishop was employed mainly in receiving and distributing raw materials. Most employees welcomed the new shifts and coped well with the reorganisation. Mr Bishop did not. He was a meticulous worker, set in his ways, who found it hard to adjust and to make the very limited decisions now expected of him.

[70] He complained about this to his manager, Mr Fairhurst, and asked to go back to his old work. His opposite number on the alternating shift also mentioned to Mr Fairhurst, and less formally to the foreman, his concern that Mr Bishop was not coping. Mr Fairhurst explained to Mr Bishop that there was nothing he could do: his old job was no longer available and he could not rearrange the work so as to give Mr Bishop what he wanted. He tried to reassure Mr Bishop that he was doing a good job and had nothing to worry about.

[71] Nevertheless, Mr Bishop did worry. He went to see his general practitioner in November 1996. He was advised to change his job. He did not tell his employers about this. He was away from work between 24 January and 16 February 1997. Some of this time he would have been off shift. For the other times he submitted two sick notes referring to 'neurasthenia'. He returned to work for two days, after which there was a holiday and then the usual four days off. He returned on 24 February and his breakdown took place the following day.

[72] There was nothing unusual, excessive or unreasonable about the demands which were being placed upon Mr Bishop by his work. The sad fact was that he was unable to cope with the changes. His employers knew that he was unhappy and wanted to go back to the old ways, but they were not told of the advice given to him by his doctor. The two sicknotes were not in themselves such clear signs of a risk to his mental health that a reasonable employer should have realised that something should be done.

[73] Even if they had been, there was nothing that the employer could reasonably be expected to do. The job that he wanted was no longer available. The work which was available could not be reorganised to suit one employee. The reality was that the general practitioner's advice was correct: the only solution would have been to dismiss him. The employer could not be in breach of duty for failing to dismiss an employee who wanted to continue and master the job despite the advice given to him by his own doctor.

9.   Conclusion

[74] We therefore allow the employers' appeals in the cases of Mrs Hatton, Mr Barber and Mr Bishop. Not without some hesitation, we dismiss the appeal in the case of Mrs Jones.

APPENDIX

A.   Mrs Hatton

[Paragraphs [75]–[129] set out the judge's findings, evidence not recorded by the judge and expert medical evidence.]

OUR CONCLUSION ON LIABILITY

[130]   We consider that this judgment cannot stand. At the very least the action should be retried in order that findings of fact might be made which properly reflected the evidence and proper reasons given why one side's evidence should be preferred to the other side's. There was, as our analysis has shown, overwhelming evidence which tended to show that except during the two terms following [the head of department's] departure Mrs Hatton was not given any more work than was reasonable for a French teacher of her experience to undertake. The judge did not explain why, despite all this evidence, he was disposed to find that she was subjected to an increased workload.

[131]   It is, however, possible to go one step further. For the reasons set out in paragraphs 48–50 of our main judgment, the judge approached the question of the school's legal duty to Mrs Hatton in the wrong way. We are satisfied that even on Mrs Hatton's own evidence her breakdown in health was not reasonably foreseeable by the school. The judge should also have identified the specific breach of duty which contributed to her illness and explained why anything the school could have done at the time she complained about the 1995 timetable could have made any difference.

DAMAGES

[132]   The issue as to damages arises in this way. There is no dispute about the award of £6,000 for general damages or the award for lost earnings between 31 August 1996 and 1 December 1998. The employers, however, challenge the way in which the judge approached the question of compensating her for loss of earnings, or earning capacity after that date.

[133]   The judge accepted the evidence of [the claimant's expert, a neuropsychologist specialising in dealing with people with brain injuries] that she would have been well enough to seek employment as a teacher again by about June 1998. He said that given the economic problems on Merseyside and the difficulties of obtaining part-time teaching work in private schools in the area, it would be reasonable to expect her to have obtained such employment by December 1998. After that date he deducted from the net salary she would have received at the school a notional net earning capacity which gradually increased from £600 per month to £625 per month by the date of the trial. So far as the future was concerned he applied a multiplier of six to a net loss of £8,760 per annum. In the result, the award was made up as follows:

General damages	£6,000
Past loss of earnings (gross of CRU)	£46,876.14

Future loss of earnings	£53,560
	£106,436.14
CRU	£18,866.31
	£87,569.83
Interest	£3,106
	£90,675.83

[134]   The employers complained that the basis for the monthly figure of £600 was not explained. Moreover Mrs Hatton did not seek to adduce any evidence of her earning capacity. In the absence of such evidence the judge should have made a modest lump sum award for disadvantage on the labour market.

[135]   The employers were not arguing that she should give credit for her ill-health retirement pension of £500 a month. They maintained, however, as an alternative argument, that the evidence suggested that she had a significantly greater earning capacity than that suggested by the judge. She had told the judge that she had checked with the Teachers' Pension Agency as to what she could and could not do, so as to avoid impinging on her pension, and that she had found out that she was not allowed to teach at a school run by a local education authority if she wished to continue to receive her pension. In any event, she said that she did not think she would want to go back into a situation like the one she left before.

[136]   The employers argued that it was not just to have no regard to her pension payment when calculating her losses, while allowing her to take into account the possibility of losing her pension as a reason for limiting her job search. She had said that she was searching for work at an annual salary of £12,000 gross (£9,575 net). This figure should have been taken as the best indicator of her residual earning capacity.

[137]   Mr Atherton showed us how the judge had intervened during his final submissions at the trial to indicate that he was thinking of finding that Mrs Hatton had an earning capacity which he would draw from his knowledge of the world in the absence of evidence. He said that the judge's approach was reasonable, given Mrs Hatton's disadvantage in the labour market due to her age, medical history and lack of transferable skills. He showed us that even Dr Wood had considered that Mrs Hatton would not be able to cope with the pressures of teaching in the public sector. She had not in fact said that she had made no effort to resume public sector teaching because she might lose her pension, and Mr Atherton said that no inference to that effect could fairly be made. Her lack of success in applying for jobs suggested that the salary figures suggested by the employers were unrealistically high.

[138]   If we had upheld this judgment on liability, we would have awarded her a sum of £10,000 in respect of her loss of earning capacity for the period from 1 December 1998 onwards. The idea that she might have been able to go on teaching at any comprehensive school and avoided stress-related illness appears to us to be a little far-fetched, and Mrs Hatton clearly made no attempt to find any public sector teaching, part-time or otherwise, for fear of losing her pension. We consider

that there is considerable force in the employers' contentions, and that justice demands that we should approach the question of compensation for the period in the broad-brush way we have indicated.

B. *Mr Barber*

[Paragraphs [139]–[163] set out the judge's findings, other background evidence and evidence about Mr Barber's health.]

LIABILITY: OUR CONCLUSIONS

[164] Mr Hogarth criticised the judge for failing to link causation with breach of duty. The judge had so structured his judgment that he had concluded that Mr Barber's depressive illness was caused by the stress he suffered at work following the restructuring before he considered the nature of the duty the employers owed him, the circumstances in which they were in breach of that duty, and whether it was reasonably foreseeable to them that Mr Barber would suffer a psychiatric illness as a consequence of that breach.

[165] It appears to us that these criticisms were well-founded. We have set out our reasons for holding that the judge's findings on liability cannot stand in paragraphs 57 to 59 of our main judgment, and we need not repeat them here.

DAMAGES

[166] There is no appeal against the judge's award of £10,000 by way of general damages for a moderately severe psychiatric illness. The judge went on to find that Mr Barber was fit to return to work on 1 April 1998. He expressed the view that there should be no reduction for the possibility of any future psychiatric difficulty in the event that Mr Barber had not suffered his depressive illness in 1996, and had continued to work for the employer. The judge said that Mr Barber had never suffered from mental illness before, and had seldom visited his general practitioner, and that there was nothing in the experts' reports to justify such a finding.

[167] The judge also took the view on the balance of probability that Mr Barber would have continued in his chosen profession until retirement age but for his illness, provided that he had received assistance to alleviate the work overload and the pressures to which he had been subjected during 1996.

[168] The parties had agreed that a multiplier of four from the date of the trial was appropriate by way of a compromise of any dispute there might otherwise have been about Mr Barber's likely retirement age, and the judge computed his award of damages on this basis.

[169] Mr Hogarth submitted that the judge was wrong to approach his assessment of what might happen in the future by making a finding on the balance of probability that Mr Barber would otherwise have continued working until his normal retirement age, and by extrapolating from that assessment a conclusion that this would have happened, making no discount from his award for

the chance that things might not have turned out that way. He relied in this context on the judgment of Otton LJ in *Doyle v Wallace* [1998] PIQR Q146, 148–150, where reference is made to a passage in the speech of Lord Reid in *Davies v Taylor* [1974] AC 207, 213, and to the judgment of Stuart-Smith LJ in *Allied Maples Group Ltd v Simmons & Simmons* [1995] 1 WLR 1602, 1609–1611.

[170] Mr Glancy invited us to approach Mr Barber's case as if it fell into the second of the three classes of case discussed by Stuart-Smith LJ in the *Allied Maples* case, at pp 1610C–1611A. This is the type of case in which the defendant has negligently failed to provide ear-muffs or breathing apparatus or a safety-belt, and a question arises whether the injured employee would have used this equipment if it had been provided. In these circumstances, once it is decided on the balance of probability that the employee would have taken advantage of these facilities if they had been available, the court will find that he would have done so, and makes its further findings on this basis.

[171] This type of case, however, which focuses on what would probably have happened in the past, is entirely different from a case where a court has to make an estimate of what may happen in the future. If there is a chance that an event may occur which would mean that an injured claimant would not have gone on working until retirement age in any event, then a familiar way of taking that chance into account is to reduce the multiplier used for calculating future loss. The first instance decision of Otton J in *Page v Smith* [1993] PIQR Q55, 75–76 provides a good example of this technique at work.

[172] Mr Glancy argued, in the alternative, that an appropriate adjustment to the multiplier had already been made when the multiplier of four was agreed. While we have no doubt that ordinary contingencies were taken into account, like the chance of death or some other kind of serious incapacitating injury or illness befalling Mr Barber before retirement age, when the multiplier was agreed, we can see no evidence of any further discount being made for the chance to which Mr Hogarth referred.

[173] In our judgment the judge was wrong not to reduce the multiplier for future loss to cover the chance that if Mr Barber had continued with a similar teaching job, his health might nevertheless have broken down in the same way. He was a man, after all, who had showed himself on the evidence unable to adopt the alleviating measures that were necessary if he was to manage his not unreasonable workload successfully. There was evidence that he had disliked the changes the school had felt obliged to introduce, and on the hypothesis (which the judge adopted) that he would have opted to soldier on as a teacher until his normal retirement age, we consider that there was a significant chance, which the judge should have taken into account when computing damages, that he would have found it altogether too much for him, to the extent that his health would have been detrimentally affected in the same way.

[174] Given that on this hypothesis we are to imagine that he would have continued to work uninterruptedly from November 1996 onwards, we consider that a annual multiplier of one (not four) would have been more appropriate for computing future loss if proper account were taken of the chance to which we have referred. In the event we have decided to allow the employers' appeal on

liability, so that this part of our decision will only become relevant if another court were to hold that we were wrong on the liability issue.

C.   Mrs Jones

[Paragraphs [175]–[194] and [196]–[199] set out the evidence and the judge's findings.]

[195]   The employer argued that Mrs Jones had taken no time off for depression; her own general practitioner did not diagnose it in August or September 1994; she made no visits to the occupational health department; she made out she was fine when colleagues asked; the employer had no knowledge of her vulnerability; and even her husband did not realise that she was heading for a breakdown.

THE ARGUMENTS ON APPEAL

[200]   The employer takes issue with the judge's finding that Mrs Jones's mental illness was foreseeable. The employer relies upon all the points relied upon before the trial judge, outlined at paragraph 195 above. But the employer also takes issue with his findings of fact as to the hours worked by Mrs Jones and the 'harassment' suffered from Mr Papworth [her line manager].

[201]   As to the volume of work, the judge was well aware of the discrepancies in Mrs Jones's case. He was also well aware of the need to treat her evidence with some caution, because he had rejected her account of the earlier episode in 1991. But he noted that Mrs Jones's present account was consistent with the account she said that she had given to Mr King [her personnel officer] in February 1993. Mr King had acknowledged that it was a gamble to expect one person to do the work of two to three. The judge also noted that no one had done a proper time and motion study of what the job required. Mrs Bell [who had stayed on to train Mrs Jones in the work] thought that it was manageable but she was a high flier. All the other observations were that it was too much for one person. Both Mr King and Mrs York [who took over from Mr King as Mrs Jones's personnel officer] had proposed extra help. Mr Papworth himself had acknowledged that he could see what she meant about the excessive hours. Perhaps the best indication was the chaos which ensued when Mrs Jones left.

[202]   The issue is not exactly how many hours Mrs Jones actually worked. The judge was entitled to find that she regularly worked way beyond the 37 hours for which she was paid. She was a dedicated and ambitious employee who was anxious to show that she could do the work required even if it took more than the allotted hours. The issue is whether the demands placed upon her were reasonable in all the circumstances. It is not necessarily reasonable to expect so much of an administrative assistant whose pay and status are not those of a professional with an open-ended commitment to getting the job done. The judge was amply justified in reaching the conclusion that Mrs Jones was overworked.

[203]   This is allied to the question of harassment. The judge based his findings on Mr Papworth's general and specific shortcomings as a manager. Again, whether those collectively amount to 'harassment' as it is understood in other contexts is not the point. The point is whether the behaviour towards Mrs Jones was reasonable in all the circumstances. An employee in her position should not be placed in a dilemma where she feels unable to complain about her workload because of threats, not only to her future employment, but also to her future employability. The combination of unreasonable demands and an unreasonable reaction to complaints about those demands justifies a finding of unreasonable conduct even if the epithet 'harassment' is not appropriate.

[204]   But that finding does not answer the questions which had to be answered in this case. The judge had first to consider the issue of foreseeability. The employer had some powerful points to make: in particular, there was no sickness absence during the period in question; there was no complaint of injury to health to Mr King in 1993; the complaint of injury to health in July 1994 was unspecific; had it been further investigated, it would have elicited nothing of any value because Mrs Jones's own doctor had not yet been consulted about, let alone detected any work-related illness; and her own husband, who was exceptionally involved and supportive, had not anticipated it. It is also argued that the employer had no knowledge of the earlier episode in 1991; but that is less powerful, because she was also working for the employer at the time, albeit in a different post.

[205]   The judge did not clearly separate the issues of foreseeability, breach of duty and causation as he should have done. It is impermissible to reason that because an employer has behaved unreasonably the risk of psychiatric injury should have been foreseen. Equally it is impermissible to reason that because an injury has resulted from stress at work it has resulted from an employer's breach of duty.

[206]   However, Mr Anderson is right to argue on behalf of Mrs Jones that unreasonable demands are relevant to the question of foreseeability. Placing unreasonable demands upon an employee and then responding in an unreasonable way to the employee's complaints about those demands are among the factors to be taken into account in deciding whether the employer knew or ought to have known that the pressures of the job were causing occupational stress. Mrs York clearly did know that much. This knowledge was coupled with two express warnings from Mrs Jones that this occupational stress was indeed damaging her health. On balance, therefore, and bearing in mind that neither Mr King nor Mrs York gave evidence, the judge was entitled to find that actual damage to her health was foreseeable.

[207]   Once that hurdle is crossed, Mr Anderson is also right to argue that it was easy to identify a relevant breach of duty. Senior management knew that there were complaints of overwork which were likely to have some substance but that line management was making it impossible to make an effective complaint. They actually offered help. But because of line management's attitude that help was never effective. If psychiatric harm was the foreseeable result of doing nothing when there were obvious steps which could have been taken it is easier to conclude that there had been a breach of duty. Although the judge does not in terms address the risk/benefit question he was entitled to conclude that there was a breach of duty when it was the employer's own unreasonable demands which were producing a foreseeable risk of harm to the employee's health.

[208]   Unlike the others before us, this is the sort of case described by Lord Slynn in *Waters v Comr of Police of the Metropolis* [2000] ICR 1064, 1068:

'If an employer knows that acts being done by employees during their employment may cause physical or mental harm to a particular fellow employee and he does nothing to supervise or prevent such acts, when it is in his power to do so, it is clearly arguable that he may be in breach of his duty to that employee. It seems to me that he may also be in breach of that duty if he can foresee that such acts may happen and, if they do, that physical or mental harm may be caused to an individual.'

[209]   The question still arises of whether that breach of duty caused the harm which was suffered. Was the judge entitled to conclude that if something had been done to lighten Mrs Jones's workload and acknowledge the validity of her complaints her eventual breakdown could have been avoided? The underlying vulnerability would still have been there, as would Mrs Jones's basic ambition to become an instructor rather than an administrator. But the judge gave sound reasons for preferring the view of the expert psychologist instructed on behalf of Mrs Jones to that of the expert instructed for the employer, who had not been supplied with all the relevant material.

CONCLUSION

[210]   It must be acknowledged that although the judge gave a long and detailed judgment, it did not address each of the issues in turn in a systematic manner. This was not an easy case and would have benefited from such an approach. Nevertheless, there was evidence before the judge which entitled him to reach the factual conclusions he did, and from those to conclude that the indications of risk to mental health were strong enough for a reasonable employer to think that he should do something about it, not least because senior management *did* think that there was something they should do. That something was to cease placing unreasonable demands upon Mrs Jones. There was also expert evidence from which the judge was entitled to conclude that it was the failure to take those steps which caused, or at least materially contributed to, Mrs Jones's mental illness. There is no challenge to his assessment of the damages resulting. It was for these reasons, which are set out more succinctly in paragraphs 66 and 67 of our main judgment, that we are dismissing the employer's appeal in Mrs Jones's case.

D.   *Mr Bishop*

[Paragraphs [211]–[222] set out the evidence.]

[223]   The most striking feature of Mr Bishop's case was that his employers had no notice that he was likely to suffer a psychiatric illness if he continued in his job. Mr Bishop had concealed from his employers the advice that his doctor had given him the previous November, and two sicknotes referring to neurasthenia are a shallow foundation for the finding the judge made with the benefit of hindsight. Mr Bishop knew that his employers had no other work for him, and that his doctor had advised him to change jobs. He chose to go back to work, as he was entitled to do, but there is in our judgment no evidential basis for a finding that the breakdown in his health was reasonably foreseeable, and in any event there was nothing the employers could have done to continue Mr Bishop's employment, if he could not cope with it, because work of the kind he wanted to do was not now available.

[224]　We have set out in paragraphs 72 and 73 of our main judgment our reasons for allowing this appeal.

APPENDIX 4

MENTAL CAPACITY ACT 2005, PT 1

PERSONS WHO LACK CAPACITY

THE PRINCIPLES

1 The principles

(1) The following principles apply for the purposes of this Act.

(2) A person must be assumed to have capacity unless it is established that he lacks capacity.

(3) A person is not to be treated as unable to make a decision unless all practicable steps to help him to do so have been taken without success.

(4) A person is not to be treated as unable to make a decision merely because he makes an unwise decision.

(5) An act done, or decision made, under this Act for or on behalf of a person who lacks capacity must be done, or made, in his best interests.

(6) Before the act is done, or the decision is made, regard must be had to whether the purpose for which it is needed can be as effectively achieved in a way that is less restrictive of the person's rights and freedom of action.

PRELIMINARY

2 People who lack capacity

(1) For the purposes of this Act, a person lacks capacity in relation to a matter if at the material time he is unable to make a decision for himself in relation to the matter because of an impairment of, or a disturbance in the functioning of, the mind or brain.

(2) It does not matter whether the impairment or disturbance is permanent or temporary.

(3) A lack of capacity cannot be established merely by reference to –

   (a)   a person's age or appearance, or
   (b)   a condition of his, or an aspect of his behaviour, which might lead others to make unjustified assumptions about his capacity.

(4) In proceedings under this Act or any other enactment, any question whether a person lacks capacity within the meaning of this Act must be decided on the balance of probabilities.

(5) No power which a person ('D') may exercise under this Act –

    (a)   in relation to a person who lacks capacity, or

    (b)   where D reasonably thinks that a person lacks capacity,

is exercisable in relation to a person under 16.

(6) Subsection (5) is subject to section 18(3).

3 Inability to make decisions

(1) For the purposes of section 2, a person is unable to make a decision for himself if he is unable –

    (a)   to understand the information relevant to the decision,

    (b)   to retain that information,

    (c)   to use or weigh that information as part of the process of making the decision, or

    (d)   to communicate his decision (whether by talking, using sign language or any other means).

(2) A person is not to be regarded as unable to understand the information relevant to a decision if he is able to understand an explanation of it given to him in a way that is appropriate to his circumstances (using simple language, visual aids or any other means).

(3) The fact that a person is able to retain the information relevant to a decision for a short period only does not prevent him from being regarded as able to make the decision.

(4) The information relevant to a decision includes information about the reasonably foreseeable consequences of –

    (a)   deciding one way or another, or

    (b)   failing to make the decision.

4 Best interests

(1) In determining for the purposes of this Act what is in a person's best interests, the person making the determination must not make it merely on the basis of –

    (a)   the person's age or appearance, or

    (b)   a condition of his, or an aspect of his behaviour, which might lead others to make unjustified assumptions about what might be in his best interests.

(2) The person making the determination must consider all the relevant circumstances and, in particular, take the following steps.

(3) He must consider –

    (a)   whether it is likely that the person will at some time have capacity in relation to the matter in question, and

    (b)   if it appears likely that he will, when that is likely to be.

(4) He must, so far as reasonably practicable, permit and encourage the person to participate, or to improve his ability to participate, as fully as possible in any act done for him and any decision affecting him.

(5) Where the determination relates to life-sustaining treatment he must not, in considering whether the treatment is in the best interests of the person concerned, be motivated by a desire to bring about his death.

(6) He must consider, so far as is reasonably ascertainable –

    (a)   the person's past and present wishes and feelings (and, in particular, any relevant written statement made by him when he had capacity),

    (b)   the beliefs and values that would be likely to influence his decision if he had capacity, and

    (c)   the other factors that he would be likely to consider if he were able to do so.

(7) He must take into account, if it is practicable and appropriate to consult them, the views of –

    (a)   anyone named by the person as someone to be consulted on the matter in question or on matters of that kind,

    (b)   anyone engaged in caring for the person or interested in his welfare,

    (c)   any donee of a lasting power of attorney granted by the person, and

    (d)   any deputy appointed for the person by the court,

as to what would be in the person's best interests and, in particular, as to the matters mentioned in subsection (6).

(8) The duties imposed by subsections (1) to (7) also apply in relation to the exercise of any powers which –

    (a)   are exercisable under a lasting power of attorney, or

    (b)   are exercisable by a person under this Act where he reasonably believes that another person lacks capacity.

(9) In the case of an act done, or a decision made, by a person other than the court, there is sufficient compliance with this section if (having complied with the requirements of subsections (1) to (7)) he reasonably believes that what he does or decides is in the best interests of the person concerned.

(10) 'Life-sustaining treatment' means treatment which in the view of a person providing health care for the person concerned is necessary to sustain life.

(11) 'Relevant circumstances' are those –

    (a)   of which the person making the determination is aware, and

    (b)   which it would be reasonable to regard as relevant.

[4A Restriction on deprivation of liberty]

[(1) This Act does not authorise any person ('D') to deprive any other person ('P') of his liberty.

(2) But that is subject to —

   (a)   the following provisions of this section, and
   (b)   section 4B.

(3) D may deprive P of his liberty if, by doing so, D is giving effect to a relevant decision of the court.

(4) A relevant decision of the court is a decision made by an order under section 16(2)(a) in relation to a matter concerning P's personal welfare.

(5) D may deprive P of his liberty if the deprivation is authorised by Schedule A1 (hospital and care home residents: deprivation of liberty).]

Prospective Amendment—Subsection prospectively inserted by the Mental Health Act 2007, s 50(1), (2).

[4B Deprivation of liberty necessary for life-sustaining treatment etc]

[(1) If the following conditions are met, D is authorised to deprive P of his liberty while a decision as respects any relevant issue is sought from the court.

(2) The first condition is that there is a question about whether D is authorised to deprive P of his liberty under section 4A.

(3) The second condition is that the deprivation of liberty —

   (a)   is wholly or partly for the purpose of—
        (i)   giving P life-sustaining treatment, or
        (ii)   doing any vital act, or

   (b)   consists wholly or partly of—
        (i)   giving P life-sustaining treatment, or
        (ii)   doing any vital act.

(4) The third condition is that the deprivation of liberty is necessary in order to —

   (a)   give the life-sustaining treatment, or
   (b)   do the vital act.

(5) A vital act is any act which the person doing it reasonably believes to be necessary to prevent a serious deterioration in P's condition.]

Prospective Amendment—Section prospectively inserted by the Mental Health Act 2007, s 50(1), (2).

5 Acts in connection with care or treatment

(1) If a person ('D') does an act in connection with the care or treatment of another person ('P'), the act is one to which this section applies if —

(a) before doing the act, D takes reasonable steps to establish whether P lacks capacity in relation to the matter in question, and

(b) when doing the act, D reasonably believes —
    (i) that P lacks capacity in relation to the matter, and
    (ii) that it will be in P's best interests for the act to be done.

(2) D does not incur any liability in relation to the act that he would not have incurred if P —

(a) had had capacity to consent in relation to the matter, and
(b) had consented to D's doing the act.

(3) Nothing in this section excludes a person's civil liability for loss or damage, or his criminal liability, resulting from his negligence in doing the act.

(4) Nothing in this section affects the operation of sections 24 to 26 (advance decisions to refuse treatment).

6 Section 5 acts: limitations

(1) If D does an act that is intended to restrain P, it is not an act to which section 5 applies unless two further conditions are satisfied.

(2) The first condition is that D reasonably believes that it is necessary to do the act in order to prevent harm to P.

(3) The second is that the act is a proportionate response to —

(a) the likelihood of P's suffering harm, and
(b) the seriousness of that harm.

(4) For the purposes of this section D restrains P if he —

(a) uses, or threatens to use, force to secure the doing of an act which P resists, or
(b) restricts P's liberty of movement, whether or not P resists.

(5) But D does more than merely restrain P if he deprives P of his liberty within the meaning of Article 5(1) of the Human Rights Convention (whether or not D is a public authority).

(6) Section 5 does not authorise a person to do an act which conflicts with a decision made, within the scope of his authority and in accordance with this Part, by —

(a) a donee of a lasting power of attorney granted by P, or
(b) a deputy appointed for P by the court.

(7) But nothing in subsection (6) stops a person —

(a) providing life-sustaining treatment, or
(b) doing any act which he reasonably believes to be necessary to prevent a serious deterioration in P's condition,

while a decision as respects any relevant issue is sought from the court

Prospective Amendment—Subsection in italics prospectively repealed by the Mental Health Act 2007, ss 50(1), (4)(a), 55, Sch 11, Pt 10.

7 Payment for necessary goods and services

(1) If necessary goods or services are supplied to a person who lacks capacity to contract for the supply, he must pay a reasonable price for them.

(2) 'Necessary' means suitable to a person's condition in life and to his actual requirements at the time when the goods or services are supplied.

8 Expenditure

(1) If an act to which section 5 applies involves expenditure, it is lawful for D —

    (a)   to pledge P's credit for the purpose of the expenditure, and
    (b)   to apply money in P's possession for meeting the expenditure.

(2) If the expenditure is borne for P by D, it is lawful for D —

    (a)   to reimburse himself out of money in P's possession, or
    (b)   to be otherwise indemnified by P.

(3) Subsections (1) and (2) do not affect any power under which (apart from those subsections) a person—

    (a)   has lawful control of P's money or other property, and
    (b)   has power to spend money for P's benefit

9 Lasting powers of attorney

(1) A lasting power of attorney is a power of attorney under which the donor ('P') confers on the donee (or donees) authority to make decisions about all or any of the following —

    (a)   P's personal welfare or specified matters concerning P's personal welfare, and
    (b)   P's property and affairs or specified matters concerning P's property and affairs,

and which includes authority to make such decisions in circumstances where P no longer has capacity.

(2) A lasting power of attorney is not created unless —

    (a)   section 10 is complied with,
    (b)   an instrument conferring authority of the kind mentioned in subsection (1) is made and registered in accordance with Schedule 1, and
    (c)   at the time when P executes the instrument, P has reached 18 and has capacity to execute it.

(3) An instrument which—

(a) purports to create a lasting power of attorney, but
(b) does not comply with this section, section 10 or Schedule 1,

confers no authority.

(4) The authority conferred by a lasting power of attorney is subject to —

(a) the provisions of this Act and, in particular, sections 1 (the principles) and 4 (best interests), and
(b) any conditions or restrictions specified in the instrument

10 Appointment of donees

(1) A donee of a lasting power of attorney must be —

(a) an individual who has reached 18, or
(b) if the power relates only to P's property and affairs, either such an individual or a trust corporation.

(2) An individual who is bankrupt may not be appointed as donee of a lasting power of attorney in relation to P's property and affairs.

(3) Subsections (4) to (7) apply in relation to an instrument under which two or more persons are to act as donees of a lasting power of attorney.

(4) The instrument may appoint them to act —

(a) jointly,
(b) jointly and severally, or
(c) jointly in respect of some matters and jointly and severally in respect of others.

(5) To the extent to which it does not specify whether they are to act jointly or jointly and severally, the instrument is to be assumed to appoint them to act jointly.

(6) If they are to act jointly, a failure, as respects one of them, to comply with the requirements of subsection (1) or (2) or Part 1 or 2 of Schedule 1 prevents a lasting power of attorney from being created.

(7) If they are to act jointly and severally, a failure, as respects one of them, to comply with the requirements of subsection (1) or (2) or Part 1 or 2 of Schedule 1 —

(a) prevents the appointment taking effect in his case, but
(b) does not prevent a lasting power of attorney from being created in the case of the other or others.

(8) An instrument used to create a lasting power of attorney —

(a) cannot give the donee (or, if more than one, any of them) power to appoint a substitute or successor, but

(b)   may itself appoint a person to replace the donee (or, if more than one, any of them) on the occurrence of an event mentioned in section 13(6)(a) to (d) which has the effect of terminating the donee's appointment.

11 Lasting powers of attorney: restrictions

(1) A lasting power of attorney does not authorise the donee (or, if more than one, any of them) to do an act that is intended to restrain P, unless three conditions are satisfied.

(2) The first condition is that P lacks, or the donee reasonably believes that P lacks, capacity in relation to the matter in question.

(3) The second is that the donee reasonably believes that it is necessary to do the act in order to prevent harm to P.

(4) The third is that the act is a proportionate response to —

(a)   the likelihood of P's suffering harm, and
(b)   the seriousness of that harm.

(5) For the purposes of this section, the donee restrains P if he —

(a)   uses, or threatens to use, force to secure the doing of an act which P resists, or
(b)   restricts P's liberty of movement, whether or not P resists,

or if he authorises another person to do any of those things.

(6) But the donee does more than merely restrain P if he deprives P of his liberty within the meaning of Article 5(1) of the Human Rights Convention.

(7) Where a lasting power of attorney authorises the donee (or, if more than one, any of them) to make decisions about P's personal welfare, the authority —

(a)   does not extend to making such decisions in circumstances other than those where P lacks, or the donee reasonably believes that P lacks, capacity,
(b)   is subject to sections 24 to 26 (advance decisions to refuse treatment), and
(c)   extends to giving or refusing consent to the carrying out or continuation of a treatment by a person providing health care for P.

(8) But subsection (7)(c) —

(a)   does not authorise the giving or refusing of consent to the carrying out or continuation of life-sustaining treatment, unless the instrument contains express provision to that effect, and
(b)   is subject to any conditions or restrictions in the instrument.

Prospective Amendment—Subsection in italics prospectively repealed by the Mental Health Act 2007, ss 50(1), (4)(b), 55, Sch 11, Pt 10.

12 Scope of lasting powers of attorney: gifts

(1) Where a lasting power of attorney confers authority to make decisions about P's property and affairs, it does not authorise a donee (or, if more than one, any of them) to dispose of the donor's property by making gifts except to the extent permitted by subsection (2).

(2) The donee may make gifts —

    (a)   on customary occasions to persons (including himself) who are related to or connected with the donor, or

    (b)   to any charity to whom the donor made or might have been expected to make gifts,

if the value of each such gift is not unreasonable having regard to all the circumstances and, in particular, the size of the donor's estate.

(3) 'Customary occasion' means —

    (a)   the occasion or anniversary of a birth, a marriage or the formation of a civil partnership, or

    (b)   any other occasion on which presents are customarily given within families or among friends or associates.

(4) Subsection (2) is subject to any conditions or restrictions in the instrument.

13 Revocation of lasting powers of attorney etc

(1) This section applies if —

    (a)   P has executed an instrument with a view to creating a lasting power of attorney, or

    (b)   a lasting power of attorney is registered as having been conferred by P,

and in this section references to revoking the power include revoking the instrument.

(2) P may, at any time when he has capacity to do so, revoke the power.

(3) P's bankruptcy revokes the power so far as it relates to P's property and affairs.

(4) But where P is bankrupt merely because an interim bankruptcy restrictions order has effect in respect of him, the power is suspended, so far as it relates to P's property and affairs, for so long as the order has effect.

(5) The occurrence in relation to a donee of an event mentioned in subsection (6) —

    (a)   terminates his appointment, and

    (b)   except in the cases given in subsection (7), revokes the power.

(6) The events are—

    (a)   the disclaimer of the appointment by the donee in accordance with such requirements as may be prescribed for the purposes of this section in regulations made by the Lord Chancellor,

    (b)   subject to subsections (8) and (9), the death or bankruptcy of the donee or, if the donee is a trust corporation, its winding-up or dissolution,

    (c)   subject to subsection (11), the dissolution or annulment of a marriage or civil partnership between the donor and the donee,

    (d)   the lack of capacity of the donee.

(7) The cases are —

    (a)   the donee is replaced under the terms of the instrument,

    (b)   he is one of two or more persons appointed to act as donees jointly and severally in respect of any matter and, after the event, there is at least one remaining donee.

(8) The bankruptcy of a donee does not terminate his appointment, or revoke the power, in so far as his authority relates to P's personal welfare.

(9) Where the donee is bankrupt merely because an interim bankruptcy restrictions order has effect in respect of him, his appointment and the power are suspended, so far as they relate to P's property and affairs, for so long as the order has effect.

(10) Where the donee is one of two or more appointed to act jointly and severally under the power in respect of any matter, the reference in subsection (9) to the suspension of the power is to its suspension in so far as it relates to that donee.

(11) The dissolution or annulment of a marriage or civil partnership does not terminate the appointment of a donee, or revoke the power, if the instrument provided that it was not to do so.

14 Protection of donee and others if no power created or power revoked

(1) Subsections (2) and (3) apply if —

    (a)   an instrument has been registered under Schedule 1 as a lasting power of attorney, but

    (b)   a lasting power of attorney was not created,

whether or not the registration has been cancelled at the time of the act or transaction in question.

(2) A donee who acts in purported exercise of the power does not incur any liability (to P or any other person) because of the non-existence of the power unless at the time of acting he —

    (a)   knows that a lasting power of attorney was not created, or

(b) is aware of circumstances which, if a lasting power of attorney had been created, would have terminated his authority to act as a donee.

(3) Any transaction between the donee and another person is, in favour of that person, as valid as if the power had been in existence, unless at the time of the transaction that person has knowledge of a matter referred to in subsection (2).

(4) If the interest of a purchaser depends on whether a transaction between the donee and the other person was valid by virtue of subsection (3), it is conclusively presumed in favour of the purchaser that the transaction was valid if —

(a) the transaction was completed within 12 months of the date on which the instrument was registered, or

(b) the other person makes a statutory declaration, before or within 3 months after the completion of the purchase, that he had no reason at the time of the transaction to doubt that the donee had authority to dispose of the property which was the subject of the transaction.

(5) In its application to a lasting power of attorney which relates to matters in addition to P's property and affairs, section 5 of the Powers of Attorney Act 1971 (c 27) (protection where power is revoked) has effect as if references to revocation included the cessation of the power in relation to P's property and affairs.

(6) Where two or more donees are appointed under a lasting power of attorney, this section applies as if references to the donee were to all or any of them.

GENERAL POWERS OF THE COURT AND APPOINTMENT OF DEPUTIES

15 Power to make declarations

(1) The court may make declarations as to —

(a) whether a person has or lacks capacity to make a decision specified in the declaration;

(b) whether a person has or lacks capacity to make decisions on such matters as are described in the declaration;

(c) the lawfulness or otherwise of any act done, or yet to be done, in relation to that person.

(2) 'Act' includes an omission and a course of conduct.

16 Powers to make decisions and appoint deputies: general

(1) This section applies if a person ('P') lacks capacity in relation to a matter or matters concerning —

(a) P's personal welfare, or

(b)   P's property and affairs.

(2) The court may—

(a)   by making an order, make the decision or decisions on P's behalf in relation to the matter or matters, or

(b)   appoint a person (a 'deputy') to make decisions on P's behalf in relation to the matter or matters.

(3) The powers of the court under this section are subject to the provisions of this Act and, in particular, to sections 1 (the principles) and 4 (best interests).

(4) When deciding whether it is in P's best interests to appoint a deputy, the court must have regard (in addition to the matters mentioned in section 4) to the principles that —

(a)   a decision by the court is to be preferred to the appointment of a deputy to make a decision, and

(b)   the powers conferred on a deputy should be as limited in scope and duration as is reasonably practicable in the circumstances.

(5) The court may make such further orders or give such directions, and confer on a deputy such powers or impose on him such duties, as it thinks necessary or expedient for giving effect to, or otherwise in connection with, an order or appointment made by it under subsection (2).

(6) Without prejudice to section 4, the court may make the order, give the directions or make the appointment on such terms as it considers are in P's best interests, even though no application is before the court for an order, directions or an appointment on those terms.

(7) An order of the court may be varied or discharged by a subsequent order.

(8) The court may, in particular, revoke the appointment of a deputy or vary the powers conferred on him if it is satisfied that the deputy —

(a)   has behaved, or is behaving, in a way that contravenes the authority conferred on him by the court or is not in P's best interests, or

(b)   proposes to behave in a way that would contravene that authority or would not be in P's best interests.

[16A Section 16 powers: Mental Health Act patients etc]

[(1) If a person is ineligible to be deprived of liberty by this Act, the court may not include in a welfare order provision which authorises the person to be deprived of his liberty.

(2) If—

(a)   a welfare order includes provision which authorises a person to be deprived of his liberty, and

(b)   that person becomes ineligible to be deprived of liberty by this Act,

the provision ceases to have effect for as long as the person remains ineligible.

(3) Nothing in subsection (2) affects the power of the court under section 16(7) to vary or discharge the welfare order.

(4) For the purposes of this section —

(a)   Schedule 1A applies for determining whether or not P is ineligible to be deprived of liberty by this Act;

(b)   'welfare order' means an order under section 16(2)(a).]

Prospective Amendment—Section prospectively inserted by the Mental Health Act 2007, s 50(1), (3).

17 Section 16 powers: personal welfare

(1) The powers under section 16 as respects P's personal welfare extend in particular to —

(a)   deciding where P is to live;

(b)   deciding what contact, if any, P is to have with any specified persons;

(c)   making an order prohibiting a named person from having contact with P;

(d)   giving or refusing consent to the carrying out or continuation of a treatment by a person providing health care for P;

(e)   giving a direction that a person responsible for P's health care allow a different person to take over that responsibility.

(2) Subsection (1) is subject to section 20 (restrictions on deputies).

18 Section 16 powers: property and affairs

(1) The powers under section 16 as respects P's property and affairs extend in particular to —

(a)   the control and management of P's property;

(b)   the sale, exchange, charging, gift or other disposition of P's property;

(c)   the acquisition of property in P's name or on P's behalf;

(d)   the carrying on, on P's behalf, of any profession, trade or business;

(e)   the taking of a decision which will have the effect of dissolving a partnership of which P is a member;

(f)   the carrying out of any contract entered into by P;

(g)   the discharge of P's debts and of any of P's obligations, whether legally enforceable or not;

(h)   the settlement of any of P's property, whether for P's benefit or for the benefit of others;

(i)   the execution for P of a will;

(j)   the exercise of any power (including a power to consent) vested in P whether beneficially or as trustee or otherwise;

(k)   the conduct of legal proceedings in P's name or on P's behalf.

(2) No will may be made under subsection (1)(i) at a time when P has not reached 18.

(3) The powers under section 16 as respects any other matter relating to P's property and affairs may be exercised even though P has not reached 16, if the court considers it likely that P will still lack capacity to make decisions in respect of that matter when he reaches 18.

(4) Schedule 2 supplements the provisions of this section.

(5) Section 16(7) (variation and discharge of court orders) is subject to paragraph 6 of Schedule 2.

(6) Subsection (1) is subject to section 20 (restrictions on deputies).

19 Appointment of deputies

(1) A deputy appointed by the court must be —

(a)   an individual who has reached 18, or

(b)   as respects powers in relation to property and affairs, an individual who has reached 18 or a trust corporation.

(2) The court may appoint an individual by appointing the holder for the time being of a specified office or position.

(3) A person may not be appointed as a deputy without his consent.

(4) The court may appoint two or more deputies to act —

(a)   jointly,

(b)   jointly and severally, or

(c)   jointly in respect of some matters and jointly and severally in respect of others.

(5) When appointing a deputy or deputies, the court may at the same time appoint one or more other persons to succeed the existing deputy or those deputies —

(a)   in such circumstances, or on the happening of such events, as may be specified by the court;

(b)   for such period as may be so specified.

(6) A deputy is to be treated as P's agent in relation to anything done or decided by him within the scope of his appointment and in accordance with this Part.

(7) The deputy is entitled —

(a)   to be reimbursed out of P's property for his reasonable expenses in discharging his functions, and

    (b)   if the court so directs when appointing him, to remuneration out of P's property for discharging them.

(8) The court may confer on a deputy powers to —

    (a)   take possession or control of all or any specified part of P's property;

    (b)   exercise all or any specified powers in respect of it, including such powers of investment as the court may determine.

(9) The court may require a deputy—

    (a)   to give to the Public Guardian such security as the court thinks fit for the due discharge of his functions, and

    (b)   to submit to the Public Guardian such reports at such times or at such intervals as the court may direct.

20 Restrictions on deputies

(1) A deputy does not have power to make a decision on behalf of P in relation to a matter if he knows or has reasonable grounds for believing that P has capacity in relation to the matter.

(2) Nothing in section 16(5) or 17 permits a deputy to be given power —

    (a)   to prohibit a named person from having contact with P;

    (b)   to direct a person responsible for P's health care to allow a different person to take over that responsibility.

(3) A deputy may not be given powers with respect to —

    (a)   the settlement of any of P's property, whether for P's benefit or for the benefit of others,k

    (b)   the execution for P of a will, or

    (c)   the exercise of any power (including a power to consent) vested in P whether beneficially or as trustee or otherwise.

(4) A deputy may not be given power to make a decision on behalf of P which is inconsistent with a decision made, within the scope of his authority and in accordance with this Act, by the donee of a lasting power of attorney granted by P (or, if there is more than one donee, by any of them).

(5) A deputy may not refuse consent to the carrying out or continuation of life-sustaining treatment in relation to P.

(6) The authority conferred on a deputy is subject to the provisions of this Act and, in particular, sections 1 (the principles) and 4 (best interests).

(7) A deputy may not do an act that is intended to restrain P unless four conditions are satisfied.

(8) The first condition is that, in doing the act, the deputy is acting within the scope of an authority expressly conferred on him by the court.

(9) The second is that P lacks, or the deputy reasonably believes that P lacks, capacity in relation to the matter in question.

(10) The third is that the deputy reasonably believes that it is necessary to do the act in order to prevent harm to P.

(11) The fourth is that the act is a proportionate response to —

    (a)   the likelihood of P's suffering harm, and

    (b)   the seriousness of that harm.

(12) For the purposes of this section, a deputy restrains P if he —

    (a)   uses, or threatens to use, force to secure the doing of an act which P resists, or

    (b)   restricts P's liberty of movement, whether or not P resists,

or if he authorises another person to do any of those things.

(13) But a deputy does more than merely restrain P if he deprives P of his liberty within the meaning of Article 5(1) of the Human Rights Convention (whether or not the deputy is a public authority).

<hr>

Amendments—Mental Health Act 2007, s 51.

Prospective Amendments—Words in italics prospectively repealed by the Mental Health Act 2007 ss 55, Sch 11, Pt 10.

21 Transfer of proceedings relating to people under 18

(1) The Lord Chief Justice, with the concurrence of the Lord Chancellor, may by order make provision as to the transfer of proceedings relating to a person under 18, in such circumstances as are specified in the order —

    (a)   from the Court of Protection to a court having jurisdiction under the Children Act 1989 (c 41), or

    (b)   from a court having jurisdiction under that Act to the Court of Protection.

(2) The Lord Chief Justice may nominate any of the following to exercise his functions under this section—

    (a)   the President of the Court of Protection;

    (b)   a judicial office holder (as defined in section 109(4) of the Constitutional Reform Act 2005).

<hr>

Amendments—SI 2006/1016.

[POWERS OF THE COURT IN RELATION TO SCHEDULE A1]

Amendment—Cross heading prospectively inserted by the Mental Health Act 2007, s 50(7), Sch 9, Pt 1, paras 1, 2.

[21A Powers of court in relation to Schedule A1]

[(1) This section applies if either of the following has been given under Schedule A1 —

(a)   a standard authorisation;
(b)   an urgent authorisation.

(2) Where a standard authorisation has been given, the court may determine any question relating to any of the following matters—

(a)   whether the relevant person meets one or more of the qualifying requirements;
(b)   the period during which the standard authorisation is to be in force;
(c)   the purpose for which the standard authorisation is given;
(d)   the conditions subject to which the standard authorisation is given.

(3) If the court determines any question under subsection (2), the court may make an order —

(a)   varying or terminating the standard authorisation, or
(b)   directing the supervisory body to vary or terminate the standard authorisation.

(4) Where an urgent authorisation has been given, the court may determine any question relating to any of the following matters —

(a)   whether the urgent authorisation should have been given;
(b)   the period during which the urgent authorisation is to be in force;
(c)   the purpose for which the urgent authorisation is given.

(5) Where the court determines any question under subsection (4), the court may make an order—

(a)   varying or terminating the urgent authorisation, or
(b)   directing the managing authority of the relevant hospital or care home to vary or terminate the urgent authorisation.

(6) Where the court makes an order under subsection (3) or (5), the court may make an order about a person's liability for any act done in connection with the standard or urgent authorisation before its variation or termination.

(7) An order under subsection (6) may, in particular, exclude a person from liability.]

Amendment—Section prospectively inserted by the Mental Health Act 2007, s 50(7), Sch 9, Pt 1, paras 1, 2.

Powers of the court in relation to lasting powers of attorney

22 Powers of court in relation to validity of lasting powers of attorney

(1) This section and section 23 apply if —

(a)   a person ('P') has executed or purported to execute an instrument with a view to creating a lasting power of attorney, or

(b)   an instrument has been registered as a lasting power of attorney conferred by P.

(2) The court may determine any question relating to —

(a)   whether one or more of the requirements for the creation of a lasting power of attorney have been met;

(b)   whether the power has been revoked or has otherwise come to an end.

(3) Subsection (4) applies if the court is satisfied—

(a)   that fraud or undue pressure was used to induce P —

(i)   to execute an instrument for the purpose of creating a lasting power of attorney, or

(ii)   to create a lasting power of attorney, or

(b) that the donee (or, if more than one, any of them) of a lasting power of attorney —

(i)   has behaved, or is behaving, in a way that contravenes his authority or is not in P's best interests, or

(ii)   proposes to behave in a way that would contravene his authority or would not be in P's best interests.

(4) The court may—

(a)   direct that an instrument purporting to create the lasting power of attorney is not to be registered, or

(b)   if P lacks capacity to do so, revoke the instrument or the lasting power of attorney.

(5) If there is more than one donee, the court may under subsection (4)(b) revoke the instrument or the lasting power of attorney so far as it relates to any of them.

(6) 'Donee' includes an intended donee.

23 Powers of court in relation to operation of lasting powers of attorney

(1) The court may determine any question as to the meaning or effect of a lasting power of attorney or an instrument purporting to create one.

(2) The court may —

(a)   give directions with respect to decisions —
(i) which the donee of a lasting power of attorney has authority to make, and
(ii) which P lacks capacity to make;

(b)   give any consent or authorisation to act which the donee would have to obtain from P if P had capacity to give it.

(3) The court may, if P lacks capacity to do so —

    (a) give directions to the donee with respect to the rendering by him of reports or accounts and the production of records kept by him for that purpose;

    (b) require the donee to supply information or produce documents or things in his possession as donee;

    (c) give directions with respect to the remuneration or expenses of the donee;

    (d) relieve the donee wholly or partly from any liability which he has or may have incurred on account of a breach of his duties as donee.

(4) The court may authorise the making of gifts which are not within section 12(2) (permitted gifts).

(5) Where two or more donees are appointed under a lasting power of attorney, this section applies as if references to the donee were to all or any of them.

ADVANCE DECISIONS TO REFUSE TREATMENT

24 Advance decisions to refuse treatment: general

(1) 'Advance decision' means a decision made by a person ('P'), after he has reached 18 and when he has capacity to do so, that if —

    (a) at a later time and in such circumstances as he may specify, a specified treatment is proposed to be carried out or continued by a person providing health care for him, and

    (b) at that time he lacks capacity to consent to the carrying out or continuation of the treatment,

the specified treatment is not to be carried out or continued.

(2) For the purposes of subsection (1)(a), a decision may be regarded as specifying a treatment or circumstances even though expressed in layman's terms.

(3) P may withdraw or alter an advance decision at any time when he has capacity to do so.

(4) A withdrawal (including a partial withdrawal) need not be in writing.

(5) An alteration of an advance decision need not be in writing (unless section 25(5) applies in relation to the decision resulting from the alteration).

24 Advance decisions to refuse treatment: general

(1) 'Advance decision' means a decision made by a person ('P'), after he has reached 18 and when he has capacity to do so, that if —

(a) at a later time and in such circumstances as he may specify, a specified treatment is proposed to be carried out or continued by a person providing health care for him, and

(b)   at that time he lacks capacity to consent to the carrying out or continuation of the treatment,

the specified treatment is not to be carried out or continued.

(2) For the purposes of subsection (1)(a), a decision may be regarded as specifying a treatment or circumstances even though expressed in layman's terms.

(3) P may withdraw or alter an advance decision at any time when he has capacity to do so.

(4) A withdrawal (including a partial withdrawal) need not be in writing.

(5) An alteration of an advance decision need not be in writing (unless section 25(5) applies in relation to the decision resulting from the alteration).

25 Validity and applicability of advance decisions

(1) An advance decision does not affect the liability which a person may incur for carrying out or continuing a treatment in relation to P unless the decision is at the material time —

(a)   valid, and

(b)   applicable to the treatment.

(2) An advance decision is not valid if P —

(a)   has withdrawn the decision at a time when he had capacity to do so,

(b)   has, under a lasting power of attorney created after the advance decision was made, conferred authority on the donee (or, if more than one, any of them) to give or refuse consent to the treatment to which the advance decision relates, or

(c)   has done anything else clearly inconsistent with the advance decision remaining his fixed decision.

(3) An advance decision is not applicable to the treatment in question if at the material time P has capacity to give or refuse consent to it.

(4) An advance decision is not applicable to the treatment in question if —

(a)   that treatment is not the treatment specified in the advance decision,

(b)   any circumstances specified in the advance decision are absent, or

(c)   there are reasonable grounds for believing that circumstances exist which P did not anticipate at the time of the advance decision and which would have affected his decision had he anticipated them.

(5) An advance decision is not applicable to life-sustaining treatment unless —

    (a)   the decision is verified by a statement by P to the effect that it is to apply to that treatment even if life is at risk, and

    (b)   the decision and statement comply with subsection (6).

(6) A decision or statement complies with this subsection only if —

    (a)   it is in writing,

    (b)   it is signed by P or by another person in P's presence and by P's direction,

    (c)   the signature is made or acknowledged by P in the presence of a witness, and

    (d)   the witness signs it, or acknowledges his signature, in P's presence.

(7) The existence of any lasting power of attorney other than one of a description mentioned in subsection (2)(b) does not prevent the advance decision from being regarded as valid and applicable.

26 Effect of advance decisions

(1) If P has made an advance decision which is —

    (a)   valid, and

    (b)   applicable to a treatment,

the decision has effect as if he had made it, and had had capacity to make it, at the time when the question arises whether the treatment should be carried out or continued.

(2) A person does not incur liability for carrying out or continuing the treatment unless, at the time, he is satisfied that an advance decision exists which is valid and applicable to the treatment.

(3) A person does not incur liability for the consequences of withholding or withdrawing a treatment from P if, at the time, he reasonably believes that an advance decision exists which is valid and applicable to the treatment.

(4) The court may make a declaration as to whether an advance decision —

    (a)   exists;

    (b)   is valid;

    (c)   is applicable to a treatment.

(5) Nothing in an apparent advance decision stops a person —

    (a)   providing life-sustaining treatment, or

    (b)   doing any act he reasonably believes to be necessary to prevent a serious deterioration in P's condition,

while a decision as respects any relevant issue is sought from the court.

27 Family relationships etc

(1) Nothing in this Act permits a decision on any of the following matters to be made on behalf of a person —

(a)   consenting to marriage or a civil partnership,

(b)   consenting to have sexual relations,

(c)   consenting to a decree of divorce being granted on the basis of two years' separation,

(d)   consenting to a dissolution order being made in relation to a civil partnership on the basis of two years' separation,

(e)   consenting to a child's being placed for adoption by an adoption agency,

(f)   consenting to the making of an adoption order,

(g)   discharging parental responsibilities in matters not relating to a child's property,

(h)   giving a consent under the Human Fertilisation and Embryology Act 1990 (c 37).

(2) 'Adoption order' means —

(a)   an adoption order within the meaning of the Adoption and Children Act 2002 (c 38) (including a future adoption order), and

(b)   an order under section 84 of that Act (parental responsibility prior to adoption abroad).

28 Mental Health Act matters

(1) Nothing in this Act authorises anyone –

(a)   to give a patient medical treatment for mental disorder, or

(b)   to consent to a patient's being given medical treatment for mental disorder, if, at the time when it is proposed to treat the patient, his treatment is regulated by Part 4 of the Mental Health Act.

[(1A) Subsection (1) does not apply in relation to any form of treatment to which section 58A of that Act (electro-convulsive therapy, etc) applies if the patient comes within subsection (7) of that section (informal patient under 18 who cannot give consent).

(1B) Section 5 does not apply to an act to which section 64B of the Mental Health Act applies (treatment of community patients not recalled to hospital).]

(2) 'Medical treatment', 'mental disorder' and 'patient' have the same meaning as in that Act.

Prospective amendments—Subsections (1A) and (1B) prospectively inserted: Mental Health Act 2007, s 28 (10), s 35(4). For transitional provisions and savings see MHA 2007, s 53, Sch 10, paras 1, 3.

29 Voting rights

(1) Nothing in this Act permits a decision on voting at an election for any public office, or at a referendum, to be made on behalf of a person.

(2) 'Referendum' has the same meaning as in section 101 of the Political Parties, Elections and Referendums Act 2000 (c 41).

30 Research

(1) Intrusive research carried out on, or in relation to, a person who lacks capacity to consent to it is unlawful unless it is carried out —

    (a)   as part of a research project which is for the time being approved by the appropriate body for the purposes of this Act in accordance with section 31, and

    (b)   in accordance with sections 32 and 33.

(2) Research is intrusive if it is of a kind that would be unlawful if it was carried out —

    (a)   on or in relation to a person who had capacity to consent to it, but

    (b)   without his consent.

(3) A clinical trial which is subject to the provisions of clinical trials regulations is not to be treated as research for the purposes of this section.

(4) 'Appropriate body', in relation to a research project, means the person, committee or other body specified in regulations made by the appropriate authority as the appropriate body in relation to a project of the kind in question.

(5) 'Clinical trials regulations' means —

    (a)   the Medicines for Human Use (Clinical Trials) Regulations 2004 (SI 2004/1031) and any other regulations replacing those regulations or amending them, and

    (b)   any other regulations relating to clinical trials and designated by the Secretary of State as clinical trials regulations for the purposes of this section.

(6) In this section, section 32 and section 34, 'appropriate authority' means —

    (a)   in relation to the carrying out of research in England, the Secretary of State, and

    (b)   in relation to the carrying out of research in Wales, the National Assembly for Wales

31 Requirements for approval

(1) The appropriate body may not approve a research project for the purposes of this Act unless satisfied that the following requirements will

be met in relation to research carried out as part of the project on, or in relation to, a person who lacks capacity to consent to taking part in the project ('P').

(2) The research must be connected with —

    (a)   an impairing condition affecting P, or
    (b)   its treatment.

(3) 'Impairing condition' means a condition which is (or may be) attributable to, or which causes or contributes to (or may cause or contribute to), the impairment of, or disturbance in the functioning of, the mind or brain.

(4) There must be reasonable grounds for believing that research of comparable effectiveness cannot be carried out if the project has to be confined to, or relate only to, persons who have capacity to consent to taking part in it.

(5) The research must —

    (a)   have the potential to benefit P without imposing on P a burden that is disproportionate to the potential benefit to P, or
    (b)   be intended to provide knowledge of the causes or treatment of, or of the care of persons affected by, the same or a similar condition.

(6) If the research falls within paragraph (b) of subsection (5) but not within paragraph (a), there must be reasonable grounds for believing —

    (a)   that the risk to P from taking part in the project is likely to be negligible, and
    (b)   that anything done to, or in relation to, P will not —
        (i)   interfere with P's freedom of action or privacy in a significant way, or
        (ii)   be unduly invasive or restrictive.

(7) There must be reasonable arrangements in place for ensuring that the requirements of sections 32 and 33 will be met.

32 Consulting carers etc

(1) This section applies if a person ('R') —

    (a)   is conducting an approved research project, and
    (b)   wishes to carry out research, as part of the project, on or in relation to a person ('P') who lacks capacity to consent to taking part in the project.

(2) R must take reasonable steps to identify a person who —

    (a)   otherwise than in a professional capacity or for remuneration, is engaged in caring for P or is interested in P's welfare, and
    (b)   is prepared to be consulted by R under this section.

(3) If R is unable to identify such a person he must, in accordance with guidance issued by the appropriate authority, nominate a person who —

    (a)   is prepared to be consulted by R under this section, but

    (b)   has no connection with the project.

(4) R must provide the person identified under subsection (2), or nominated under subsection (3), with information about the project and ask him —

    (a)   for advice as to whether P should take part in the project, and

    (b)   what, in his opinion, P's wishes and feelings about taking part in the project would be likely to be if P had capacity in relation to the matter.

(5) If, at any time, the person consulted advises R that in his opinion P's wishes and feelings would be likely to lead him to decline to take part in the project (or to wish to withdraw from it) if he had capacity in relation to the matter, R must ensure —

    (a)   if P is not already taking part in the project, that he does not take part in it;

    (b)   if P is taking part in the project, that he is withdrawn from it.

(6) But subsection (5)(b) does not require treatment that P has been receiving as part of the project to be discontinued if R has reasonable grounds for believing that there would be a significant risk to P's health if it were discontinued.

(7) The fact that a person is the donee of a lasting power of attorney given by P, or is P's deputy, does not prevent him from being the person consulted under this section.

(8) Subsection (9) applies if treatment is being, or is about to be, provided for P as a matter of urgency and R considers that, having regard to the nature of the research and of the particular circumstances of the case —

    (a)   it is also necessary to take action for the purposes of the research as a matter of urgency, but

    (b)   it is not reasonably practicable to consult under the previous provisions of this section.

(9) R may take the action if —

    (a)   he has the agreement of a registered medical practitioner who is not involved in the organisation or conduct of the research project, or

    (b)   where it is not reasonably practicable in the time available to obtain that agreement, he acts in accordance with a procedure approved by the appropriate body at the time when the research project was approved under section 31.

(10) But R may not continue to act in reliance on subsection (9) if he has reasonable grounds for believing that it is no longer necessary to take the action as a matter of urgency.

33 Additional safeguards

(1) This section applies in relation to a person who is taking part in an approved research project even though he lacks capacity to consent to taking part.

(2) Nothing may be done to, or in relation to, him in the course of the research —

- (a) to which he appears to object (whether by showing signs of resistance or otherwise) except where what is being done is intended to protect him from harm or to reduce or prevent pain or discomfort, or
- (b) which would be contrary to —
  - (i) an advance decision of his which has effect, or
  - (ii) any other form of statement made by him and not subsequently withdrawn,

of which R is aware.

(3) The interests of the person must be assumed to outweigh those of science and society.

(4) If he indicates (in any way) that he wishes to be withdrawn from the project he must be withdrawn without delay.

(5) P must be withdrawn from the project, without delay, if at any time the person conducting the research has reasonable grounds for believing that one or more of the requirements set out in section 31(2) to (7) is no longer met in relation to research being carried out on, or in relation to, P.

(6) But neither subsection (4) nor subsection (5) requires treatment that P has been receiving as part of the project to be discontinued if R has reasonable grounds for believing that there would be a significant risk to P's health if it were discontinued.

34 Loss of capacity during research project

(1) This section applies where a person ('P') —

- (a) has consented to take part in a research project begun before the commencement of section 30, but
- (b) before the conclusion of the project, loses capacity to consent to continue to take part in it.

(2) The appropriate authority may by regulations provide that, despite P's loss of capacity, research of a prescribed kind may be carried out on, or in relation to, P if —

- (a) the project satisfies prescribed requirements,

(b)   any information or material relating to P which is used in the research is of a prescribed description and was obtained before P's loss of capacity, and

(c)   the person conducting the project takes in relation to P such steps as may be prescribed for the purpose of protecting him.

(3) The regulations may, in particular, —

(a)   make provision about when, for the purposes of the regulations, a project is to be treated as having begun;

(b)   include provision similar to any made by section 31, 32 or 33.

INDEPENDENT MENTAL CAPACITY ADVOCATE SERVICE

35 Appointment of independent mental capacity advocates

(1) The appropriate authority must make such arrangements as it considers reasonable to enable persons ('independent mental capacity advocates') to be available to represent and support persons to whom acts or decisions proposed under sections 37, 38 and 39 relate [*or persons who fall within section 39A, 39C or 39D*].

(2) The appropriate authority may make regulations as to the appointment of independent mental capacity advocates.

(3) The regulations may, in particular, provide —

(a)   that a person may act as an independent mental capacity advocate only in such circumstances, or only subject to such conditions, as may be prescribed;

(b)   for the appointment of a person as an independent mental capacity advocate to be subject to approval in accordance with the regulations.

(4) In making arrangements under subsection (1), the appropriate authority must have regard to the principle that a person to whom a proposed act or decision relates should, so far as practicable, be represented and supported by a person who is independent of any person who will be responsible for the act or decision.

(5) The arrangements may include provision for payments to be made to, or in relation to, persons carrying out functions in accordance with the arrangements.

(6) For the purpose of enabling him to carry out his functions, an independent mental capacity advocate—

(a)   may interview in private the person whom he has been instructed to represent, and

(b)   may, at all reasonable times, examine and take copies of —

(i)   any health record,

(ii)   any record of, or held by, a local authority and compiled in connection with a social services function, and

(iii)   any record held by a person registered under Part 2 of the Care Standards Act 2000 (c 14),

which the person holding the record considers may be relevant to the independent mental capacity advocate's investigation.

(7) In this section, section 36 and section 37, 'the appropriate authority' means —

(a)   in relation to the provision of the services of independent mental capacity advocates in England, the Secretary of State, and

(b)   in relation to the provision of the services of independent mental capacity advocates in Wales, the National Assembly for Wales.

Prospective Amendments—Words prospectively inserted by the Mental Health Act 2007, s 50 (7), Sch 9, Pt 1, paras 1, 3.

36 Functions of independent mental capacity advocates

(1) The appropriate authority may make regulations as to the functions of independent mental capacity advocates.

(2) The regulations may, in particular, make provision requiring an advocate to take such steps as may be prescribed for the purpose of —

(a)   providing support to the person whom he has been instructed to represent ('P') so that P may participate as fully as possible in any relevant decision;

(b)   obtaining and evaluating relevant information;

(c)   ascertaining what P's wishes and feelings would be likely to be, and the beliefs and values that would be likely to influence P, if he had capacity;

(d)   ascertaining what alternative courses of action are available in relation to P;

(e)   obtaining a further medical opinion where treatment is proposed and the advocate thinks that one should be obtained.

(3) The regulations may also make provision as to circumstances in which the advocate may challenge, or provide assistance for the purpose of challenging, any relevant decision.

37 Provision of serious medical treatment by NHS body

(1) This section applies if an NHS body —

(a)   is proposing to provide, or secure the provision of, serious medical treatment for a person ('P') who lacks capacity to consent to the treatment, and

(b)   is satisfied that there is no person, other than one engaged in providing care or treatment for P in a professional capacity or for remuneration, whom it would be appropriate to consult in determining what would be in P's best interests.

(2) But this section does not apply if P's treatment is regulated by Part 4 [or 4A] of the Mental Health Act.

(3) Before the treatment is provided, the NHS body must instruct an independent mental capacity advocate to represent P.

(4) If the treatment needs to be provided as a matter of urgency, it may be provided even though the NHS body has not been able to comply with subsection (3).

(5) The NHS body must, in providing or securing the provision of treatment for P, take into account any information given, or submissions made, by the independent mental capacity advocate.

(6) 'Serious medical treatment' means treatment which involves providing, withholding or withdrawing treatment of a kind prescribed by regulations made by the appropriate authority.

(7) 'NHS body' has such meaning as may be prescribed by regulations made for the purposes of this section by —

    (a)   the Secretary of State, in relation to bodies in England, or
    (b)   the National Assembly for Wales, in relation to bodies in Wales.

Prospective Amendments—Words in square brackets prospectively inserted by the Mental Health Act 2007, s 35(4), (6).

38 Provision of accommodation by NHS body

(1) This section applies if an NHS body proposes to make arrangements —

    (a)   for the provision of accommodation in a hospital or care home for a person ('P') who lacks capacity to agree to the arrangements, or
    (b)   for a change in P's accommodation to another hospital or care home,

and is satisfied that there is no person, other than one engaged in providing care or treatment for P in a professional capacity or for remuneration, whom it would be appropriate for it to consult in determining what would be in P's best interests.

(2) But this section does not apply if P is accommodated as a result of an obligation imposed on him under the Mental Health Act.

[(2A) And this section does not apply if —

    (a)   an independent mental capacity advocate must be appointed under section 39A or 39C (whether or not by the NHS body) to represent P, and
    (b)   the hospital or care home in which P is to be accommodated under the arrangements referred to in this section is the relevant hospital or care home under the authorisation referred to in that section.]

(3) Before making the arrangements, the NHS body must instruct an independent mental capacity advocate to represent P unless it is satisfied that —

(a) the accommodation is likely to be provided for a continuous period which is less than the applicable period, or
(b) the arrangements need to be made as a matter of urgency.

(4) If the NHS body —

(a) did not instruct an independent mental capacity advocate to represent P before making the arrangements because it was satisfied that subsection (3)(a) or (b) applied, but
(b) subsequently has reason to believe that the accommodation is likely to be provided for a continuous period —
    (i)   beginning with the day on which accommodation was first provided in accordance with the arrangements, and
    (ii) ending on or after the expiry of the applicable period,

it must instruct an independent mental capacity advocate to represent P.

(5) The NHS body must, in deciding what arrangements to make for P, take into account any information given, or submissions made, by the independent mental capacity advocate.

(6) 'Care home' has the meaning given in section 3 of the Care Standards Act 2000 (c 14).

(7) 'Hospital' means —

(a) a health service hospital as defined by section 275 of the National Health Service Act 2006 or section 206 of the National Health Service (Wales) Act 2006, or
(b) an independent hospital as defined by section 2 of the Care Standards Act 2000.

(8) 'NHS body' has such meaning as may be prescribed by regulations made for the purposes of this section by —

(a) the Secretary of State, in relation to bodies in England, or
(b) the National Assembly for Wales, in relation to bodies in Wales.

(9) 'Applicable period' means —

(a) in relation to accommodation in a hospital, 28 days, and
(b) in relation to accommodation in a care home, 8 weeks.

[(10) For the purposes of subsection (1), a person appointed under Part 10 of Schedule A1 to be P's representative is not, by virtue of that appointment, engaged in providing care or treatment for P in a professional capacity or for remuneration.]

Amendments—Words substituted by the National Health Service (Consequential Provisions) Act 2006, s 2, Sch 1, paras 277, 278.

Prospective Amendments—Subsections prospectively inserted by the Mental Health Act 2007, s 50(7), Sch 9, Pt 1, paras 1, 4(1), (2), (3).

39 Provision of accommodation by local authority

(1) This section applies if a local authority propose to make arrangements —

    (a)   for the provision of residential accommodation for a person ('P') who lacks capacity to agree to the arrangements, or

    (b)   for a change in P's residential accommodation,

and are satisfied that there is no person, other than one engaged in providing care or treatment for P in a professional capacity or for remuneration, whom it would be appropriate for them to consult in determining what would be in P's best interests.

(2) But this section applies only if the accommodation is to be provided in accordance with —

    (a)   section 21 or 29 of the National Assistance Act 1948 (c 29), or

    (b)   section 117 of the Mental Health Act,

as the result of a decision taken by the local authority under section 47 of the National Health Service and Community Care Act 1990 (c 19).

(3) This section does not apply if P is accommodated as a result of an obligation imposed on him under the Mental Health Act.

[(3A) And this section does not apply if —

    (a)   an independent mental capacity advocate must be appointed under section 39A or 39C (whether or not by the local authority) to represent P, and

    (b)   the place in which P is to be accommodated under the arrangements referred to in this section is the relevant hospital or care home under the authorisation referred to in that section.]

(4) Before making the arrangements, the local authority must instruct an independent mental capacity advocate to represent P unless they are satisfied that —

    (a)   the accommodation is likely to be provided for a continuous period of less than 8 weeks, or

    (b)   the arrangements need to be made as a matter of urgency.

(5) If the local authority —

    (a)   did not instruct an independent mental capacity advocate to represent P before making the arrangements because they were satisfied that subsection (4)(a) or (b) applied, but

    (b)   subsequently have reason to believe that the accommodation is likely to be provided for a continuous period that will end 8 weeks or more after the day on which accommodation was first provided in accordance with the arrangements,

they must instruct an independent mental capacity advocate to represent P.

(6) The local authority must, in deciding what arrangements to make for P, take into account any information given, or submissions made, by the independent mental capacity advocate.

[(7) For the purposes of subsection (1), a person appointed under Part 10 of Schedule A1 to be P's representative is not, by virtue of that appointment, engaged in providing care or treatment for P in a professional capacity or for remuneration.]

Prospective Amendments—Subsections prospectively inserted by Mental Health Act 2007, s 50(7), Sch 9, Pt 1, paras 1, 5(1), (2), (3).

[39A Person becomes subject to Schedule A1]

[(1) This section applies if —

  (a)   a person ('P') becomes subject to Schedule A1, and
  (b)   the managing authority of the relevant hospital or care home are satisfied that there is no person, other than one engaged in providing care or treatment for P in a professional capacity or for remuneration, whom it would be appropriate to consult in determining what would be in P's best interests.

(2) The managing authority must notify the supervisory body that this section applies.

(3) The supervisory body must instruct an independent mental capacity advocate to represent P.

(4) Schedule A1 makes provision about the role of an independent mental capacity advocate appointed under this section.

(5) This section is subject to paragraph 161 of Schedule A1.

(6) For the purposes of subsection (1), a person appointed under Part 10 of Schedule A1 to be P's representative is not, by virtue of that appointment, engaged in providing care or treatment for P in a professional capacity or for remuneration.]

Prospective Amendment—Section prospectively inserted by the Mental Health Act 2007, s 50(7), Sch 9, Pt 1, paras 1, 6.

[39B Section 39A: supplementary provision]

[(1) This section applies for the purposes of section 39A.

(2) P becomes subject to Schedule A1 in any of the following cases.

(3) The first case is where an urgent authorisation is given in relation to P under paragraph 76(2) of Schedule A1 (urgent authorisation given before request made for standard authorisation).

(4) The second case is where the following conditions are met.

(5) The first condition is that a request is made under Schedule A1 for a standard authorisation to be given in relation to P ('the requested authorisation').

(6) The second condition is that no urgent authorisation was given under paragraph 76(2) of Schedule A1 before that request was made.

(7) The third condition is that the requested authorisation will not be in force on or before, or immediately after, the expiry of an existing standard authorisation.

(8) The expiry of a standard authorisation is the date when the authorisation is expected to cease to be in force.

(9) The third case is where, under paragraph 69 of Schedule A1, the supervisory body select a person to carry out an assessment of whether or not the relevant person is a detained resident.]

Prospective Amendment—Section prospectively inserted by the Mental Health Act 2007, s 50(7), Sch 9, Pt 1, paras 1, 6.

[39C Person unrepresented whilst subject to Schedule A1]

[(1) This section applies if —

- (a) an authorisation under Schedule A1 is in force in relation to a person ('P'),
- (b) the appointment of a person as P's representative ends in accordance with regulations made under Part 10 of Schedule A1, and
- (c) the managing authority of the relevant hospital or care home are satisfied that there is no person, other than one engaged in providing care or treatment for P in a professional capacity or for remuneration, whom it would be appropriate to consult in determining what would be in P's best interests.

(2) The managing authority must notify the supervisory body that this section applies.

(3) The supervisory body must instruct an independent mental capacity advocate to represent P.

(4) Paragraph 159 of Schedule A1 makes provision about the role of an independent mental capacity advocate appointed under this section.

(5) The appointment of an independent mental capacity advocate under this section ends when a new appointment of a person as P's representative is made in accordance with Part 10 of Schedule A1.

(6) For the purposes of subsection (1), a person appointed under Part 10 of Schedule A1 to be P's representative is not, by virtue of that appointment, engaged in providing care or treatment for P in a professional capacity or for remuneration.]

Prospective Amendment—Section prospectively inserted by the Mental Health Act 2007, s 50(7), Sch 9, Pt 1, paras 1, 6.

[39D Person subject to Schedule A1 without paid representative]

[(1) This section applies if —

  (a)   an authorisation under Schedule A1 is in force in relation to a person ('P'),
  (b)   P has a representative ('R') appointed under Part 10 of Schedule A1, and
  (c)   R is not being paid under regulations under Part 10 of Schedule A1 for acting as P's representative.

(2) The supervisory body must instruct an independent mental capacity advocate to represent P in any of the following cases.

(3) The first case is where P makes a request to the supervisory body to instruct an advocate.

(4) The second case is where R makes a request to the supervisory body to instruct an advocate.

(5) The third case is where the supervisory body have reason to believe one or more of the following—

  (a)   that, without the help of an advocate, P and R would be unable to exercise one or both of the relevant rights;
  (b)   that P and R have each failed to exercise a relevant right when it would have been reasonable to exercise it;
  (c)   that P and R are each unlikely to exercise a relevant right when it would be reasonable to exercise it.

(6) The duty in subsection (2) is subject to section 39E.

(7) If an advocate is appointed under this section, the advocate is, in particular, to take such steps as are practicable to help P and R to understand the following matters —

  (a)   the effect of the authorisation;
  (b)   the purpose of the authorisation;
  (c)   the duration of the authorisation;
  (d)   any conditions to which the authorisation is subject;
  (e)   the reasons why each assessor who carried out an assessment in connection with the request for the authorisation, or in connection with a review of the authorisation, decided that P met the qualifying requirement in question;
  (f)   the relevant rights;
  (g)   how to exercise the relevant rights.

(8) The advocate is, in particular, to take such steps as are practicable to help P or R —

(a) to exercise the right to apply to court, if it appears to the advocate that P or R wishes to exercise that right, or

(b) to exercise the right of review, if it appears to the advocate that P or R wishes to exercise that right.

(9) If the advocate helps P or R to exercise the right of review —

(a) the advocate may make submissions to the supervisory body on the question of whether a qualifying requirement is reviewable;

(b) the advocate may give information, or make submissions, to any assessor carrying out a review assessment.

(10) In this section —

'relevant rights' means —

(a) the right to apply to court, and

(b) the right of review;

'right to apply to court' means the right to make an application to the court to exercise its jurisdiction under section 21A;

'right of review' means the right under Part 8 of Schedule A1 to request a review.]

Prospective Amendment—Section prospectively inserted by the Mental Health Act 2007, s 50(7), Sch 9, Pt 1, paras 1, 6.

[39E Limitation on duty to instruct advocate under section 39D]

[(1) This section applies if an advocate is already representing P in accordance with an instruction under section 39D.

(2) Section 39D(2) does not require another advocate to be instructed, unless the following conditions are met.

(3) The first condition is that the existing advocate was instructed —

(a) because of a request by R, or

(b) because the supervisory body had reason to believe one or more of the things in section 39D(5).

(4) The second condition is that the other advocate would be instructed because of a request by P.]

Prospective Amendments—Section prospectively inserted by Mental Health Act 2007, s 50(7), Sch 9, Pt 1, paras 1, 6.

40 Exceptions

[[(1)] The duty imposed by section *37(3), 38(3) or (4) or 39(4) or (5)* [, 39(4) or (5), 39A(3), 39C(3) or 39D(2)] does not apply where there is —

(a) a person nominated by P (in whatever manner) as a person to be consulted on matters to which that duty relates,

(b) a donee of a lasting power of attorney created by P who is authorised to make decisions in relation to those matters, or

(c)   a deputy appointed by the court for P with power to make decisions in relation to those matters.

[(2) A person appointed under Part 10 of Schedule A1 to be P's representative is not, by virtue of that appointment, a person nominated by P as a person to be consulted in matters to which a duty mentioned in subsection (1) relates.]]

Amendment—Section substituted by Mental Health Act 2007, s 49.

Prospective Amendments—Subsection (1) prospectively numbered as such , words in italics repealed and subsequent words in square brackets substituted; subsection (2) prospectively inserted by the Mental Health Act 2007, s 50(7), Sch 9, Pt 1, paras 1, 7(1), (2), (3), (4).

41 Power to adjust role of independent mental capacity advocate

(1) The appropriate authority may make regulations —

(a)   expanding the role of independent mental capacity advocates in relation to persons who lack capacity, and

(b)   adjusting the obligation to make arrangements imposed by section 35.

(2) The regulations may, in particular —

(a)   prescribe circumstances (different to those set out in sections 37, 38 and 39) in which an independent mental capacity advocate must, or circumstances in which one may, be instructed by a person of a prescribed description to represent a person who lacks capacity, and

(b)   include provision similar to any made by section 37, 38, 39 or 40.

(3) 'Appropriate authority' has the same meaning as in section 35.

MISCELLANEOUS AND SUPPLEMENTARY

42 Codes of practice

(1) The Lord Chancellor must prepare and issue one or more codes of practice —

(a)   for the guidance of persons assessing whether a person has capacity in relation to any matter,

(b)   for the guidance of persons acting in connection with the care or treatment of another person (see section 5),

(c)   for the guidance of donees of lasting powers of attorney,

(d)   for the guidance of deputies appointed by the court,

(e)   for the guidance of persons carrying out research in reliance on any provision made by or under this Act (and otherwise with respect to sections 30 to 34),

(f)   for the guidance of independent mental capacity advocates,

[(fa) for the guidance of persons exercising functions under Schedule A1, (fb) for the guidance of representatives appointed under Part 10 of Schedule A1,]

(g) with respect to the provisions of sections 24 to 26 (advance decisions and apparent advance decisions), and

(h) with respect to such other matters concerned with this Act as he thinks fit.

(2) The Lord Chancellor may from time to time revise a code.

(3) The Lord Chancellor may delegate the preparation or revision of the whole or any part of a code so far as he considers expedient.

(4) It is the duty of a person to have regard to any relevant code if he is acting in relation to a person who lacks capacity and is doing so in one or more of the following ways —

(a) as the donee of a lasting power of attorney,

(b) as a deputy appointed by the court,

(c) as a person carrying out research in reliance on any provision made by or under this Act (see sections 30 to 34),

(d) as an independent mental capacity advocate,

[(da) in the exercise of functions under Schedule A1,

(db) as a representative appointed under Part 10 of Schedule A1,]

(e) in a professional capacity,

(f) for remuneration.

(5) If it appears to a court or tribunal conducting any criminal or civil proceedings that —

(a) a provision of a code, or

(b) a failure to comply with a code,

is relevant to a question arising in the proceedings, the provision or failure must be taken into account in deciding the question.

(6) A code under subsection (1)(d) may contain separate guidance for deputies appointed by virtue of paragraph 1(2) of Schedule 5 (functions of deputy conferred on receiver appointed under the Mental Health Act).

(7) In this section and in section 43, 'code' means a code prepared or revised under this section.

Prospective Amendments—Paras in square brackets prospectively inserted by the Mental Health Act 2007, s 50(7), Sch 9, Pt 1, paras 1, 8(1), (2), (3).

43 Codes of practice: procedure

(1) Before preparing or revising a code, the Lord Chancellor must consult —

(a) the National Assembly for Wales, and

(b) such other persons as he considers appropriate.

(2) The Lord Chancellor may not issue a code unless —

(a)   a draft of the code has been laid by him before both Houses of Parliament, and

(b)   the 40 day period has elapsed without either House resolving not to approve the draft.

(3) The Lord Chancellor must arrange for any code that he has issued to be published in such a way as he considers appropriate for bringing it to the attention of persons likely to be concerned with its provisions.

(4) '40 day period', in relation to the draft of a proposed code, means —

(a)   if the draft is laid before one House on a day later than the day on which it is laid before the other House, the period of 40 days beginning with the later of the two days;

(b)   in any other case, the period of 40 days beginning with the day on which it is laid before each House.

(5) In calculating the period of 40 days, no account is to be taken of any period during which Parliament is dissolved or prorogued or during which both Houses are adjourned for more than 4 days.

44 Ill-treatment or neglect

(1) Subsection (2) applies if a person ('D') —

(a)   has the care of a person ('P') who lacks, or whom D reasonably believes to lack, capacity,

(b)   is the donee of a lasting power of attorney, or an enduring power of attorney (within the meaning of Schedule 4), created by P, or

(c)   is a deputy appointed by the court for P.

(2) D is guilty of an offence if he ill-treats or wilfully neglects P.

(3) A person guilty of an offence under this section is liable —

(a)   on summary conviction, to imprisonment for a term not exceeding 12 months or a fine not exceeding the statutory maximum or both;

(b)   on conviction on indictment, to imprisonment for a term not exceeding 5 years or a fine or both.

****

APPENDIX 5

SELECT BIBIOGRAPHY

- Report of the Butler Committee on Mentally Abnormal Offenders, Cmnd 6244 (1975)

- M J Crawford et al 'Psychosocial interventions following self-harm. Systematic Review of their efficacy in preventing suicide' (2007) *British Journal of Psychiatry* 190: 11–17

- I M Hunt et al 'Suicide within 12 months of mental health service contact in different age and diagnostic groups' (2006) *British Journal of Psychiatry* 188: 135–142

- N S King 'Post-concussion syndrome: clarity among the controversy?' (2003) *British Journal of Psychiatry – Editorial* (Oct)

- *A New Homicide Act for England and Wales?* Law Com No 177 (2005)

- B Mahendra *Adult Psychiatry in Family and Child Law* (Family Law, 2006)

- B Mahendra 'Behaviour, not diagnosis, the key: some misconceptions in the psychiatry of family and child law' [Feb 2008] Fam Law 159

- D J Power et al 'Dangerous Patients and the Public' in *Criminal Law and Forensic Psychiatry* (Barry Rose, 1996)

- M Rinaldi and R Perkins 'Implementing evidence-based supported employment' (2007) *Psychiatric Bulletin* 31: 244–249

- Social Exclusion Unit *Mental Health and Social Exclusion* (Office of the Deputy Prime Minister, 2004)

- N Swinson et al 'National Confidential Inquiry into Suicide and Homicide by People with Mental illness: new directions' (2007) *Psychiatric Bulletin* 31: 161–163

- C L Van Rooyen and B Mahendra *Psychology in Family and Child Law* (Family Law, 2007)

- C D Webster et al 'Violence risk assessment using structured clinical guidelines professionally' (2002) *International Journal of Mental Health* 1: 185–193

INDEX

References are to paragraph numbers.

Alcohol abuse
cultural influences   6.4
definition
   World Health Organisation,
     by   6.2
dementia, causing   2.4
development of tolerance   6.3
effects of   6.3
   alcoholic hepatitis   6.3
   cirrhosis   6.3
   delirium tremens   6.3
   oesophageal ulceration   6.3
   peptic ulceration   6.3
   sexual dysfunction   6.3
   visual hallucinations   6.3
environmental influences   6.4
gentic links   6.4
long term effects   6.6
physical dependence   6.3
prognosis   6.6
recommended "safe limits"   6.2
rehabilitation   1.7
risk factors   6.4
treatment   6.5
   cognitive behavioural therapy   6.5
   detoxification   6.5
   supportive therapy for   1.7

Anorexia nervosa
causes
   childhool trauma   6.17
   family conflict   6.17
   social factors   6.17
meaning   6.16
prognosis   6.18
symptoms   6.16
treatment   6.18
   controlled re-feeding   6.18
   drugs, with   6.18
   family therapy   6.18
   psychological treatment   6.18

Antisocial behaviour
neighbour disputes   15.3
orders   15.2
parental disputes   15.4
types of   15.2

Asperger's syndrome
diagnosis   8.7
symptoms   8.7

Attention deficit hyperactivity disorder
diagnosis   8.6

Autism
childhood
   background   8.6
   education   8.6
   general features   8.6
   genetic influence   8.6
   residential care   8.6
   treatment   8.6
diagnosis   8.6
MMR vaccine and   8.6
risks associated with   8.8
spectrum of disorder   8.8

Bipolar affective disorder
causes   4.5
   alcohol abuse   4.5
   non-psychiatric origins   4.5
   psychological factors   4.5
cognitive behavioural therapy   4.6
electroconvulsive therapy   4.6
genetic basis for   1.5
genetic influences   4.5
prognosis   4.7
risks associated with   4.8
treatment   4.6
   counselling   4.6
   drugs, with   4.6
   psychological treatment   4.6

Bulimia nervosa
meaning   6.16
prognosis   6.18
symptoms   6.16
treatment   6.18
   controlled re-feeding   6.18
   drugs, with   6.18
   family therapy   6.18
   psychological treatment   6.18

Confusional state
age-related risks   2.14
capacity, regain of   2.14
causes   2.8
   age-related risks   2.8
   alcohol withdrawal   2.8
   prescribed drugs, effect of   2.8
difference to dementia   2.7

Confusional state—*continued*
drugs, inducement as 2.14
meaning 2.7
patients with
sensory impairment 2.10
risks associated with 2.10
aggression 2.10
impairment
capacity, of 2.10
memory, of 2.10
temporary 2.10
symptoms 2.7
treatment 2.9

Degenerative brain disorder
Alzheimer's disease 2.4
Creutzfeldt-Jakob disease 2.4
Huntington's disease 2.4
Parkinson's disease 2.4
Pick's disease 2.4
Deliberate self-harm
assessment 10.3
causes 10.3
difference from attempted
suicide 10.3, 10.9
treatment 10.3
Dementia
"confused", meaning 2.2
Alzheimer's disease 2.4
causes 2.4
alcohol abuse 2.4
degenerative brain disorder 2.4
Alzheimer's disease 2.4
Creutzfeldt-Jakob disease 2.4
Huntington's disease 2.4
Parkinson's disease 2.4
Pick's disease 2.4
endocrine disorder 2.4
head injuries 2.4
poisoning 2.4
clinical symptoms 2.3
antisocial behaviour 2.3
disinhibited behaviour 2.3
mood changes 2.3
neurological conditions 2.3
short term memory loss 2.3
terminal symptoms 2.3
incontinence 2.3
loss of speech 2.3
state of infantilisim 2.3
violent behaviour 2.3
confusional state 2.2, 2.7
age-related risks 2.14
capacity, regain of 2.14
causes 2.8
age-related risks 2.8
alcohol withdrawal 2.8
prescribed drugs, effect of 2.8
difference to dementia 2.7
drugs, inducement as 2.14
meaning 2.7
patients with
sensory impairment 2.10

Dementia—*continued*
confusional state—*continued*
risks associated with 2.10
aggression 2.10
impairment
capacity, of 2.10
memory, of 2.10
temporary 2.10
symptoms 2.7
treatment 2.9
effect on capacity 2.14
impact on carers 2.14
meaning 2.2
palliative care 2.5
drug treatment 2.5
risk of developing 2.14
risks associated with 2.6
senile dementia
meaning 2.2
susceptibility to infection 2.14
vascular dementia 2.4
Depressive illness
clinical symptoms 4.2
loss of
attention/concentration 4.2
mood changes 4.2
physiological changes 4.2
psychomotor function,
retardation 4.2
cultural influences 9.5
psychomotor function
retardation, meaning 4.2
risk of developing 4.9
risk of suicide 4.9
Disability discrimination
mental impairment
long term effects 12.6
meaning 12.6
Domestic violence
abused spouse 11.2
alcohol abuse 11.2, 11.8
childhood experiences, effect
on 11.2
children, directly involving
alcohol abuse 11.8
drug abuse 11.8
psychiatric disorders 11.3
risk to 11.3
socio-economic influences 11.3, 11.8
children, indirectly involving
contact disputes 11.4, 11.8
emotional harm to 11.4, 11.8
residence disputes 11.4, 11.8
cultural factors 11.2, 11.8
drug abuse 11.2, 11.8
personality disorders and 11.8
repeated violence, risk of 11.2
sexual
factors causing 11.6, 11.8
victims of, mental state 11.2

Drug abuse
amphetamines 6.10
  effect of 6.10
cannabis 6.8
  components 6.8
  effect of 6.8
  misuse of
    symptoms 6.8
  use of 6.8
    cultural influences 6.8
cocaine 6.11
  effect of 6.11
ecstasy 6.12
generally 6.7
hallucinogenic drugs 6.12
opiate drugs 6.9
  effects of 6.9
  effects on life expectancy 6.9
  overdose 6.9
  physical dependence 6.9
  types of 6.9
  withdrawal, symptoms 6.9
rehabilitation 1.7
treatment 6.13
  counselling 6.13
  detoxification 6.13
  maintanence therapy 6.13
    purpose of 6.13
  supportive therapy for 1.7
untreated, effects of 6.13

Eating disorders
anorexia nervosa 6.16, 6.17, 6.18
bulimia nervosa 6.16, 6.17, 6.18
causes
  childhool trauma 6.17
  family conflict 6.17
  social factors 6.17
classification 6.16
treatment 6.18
  controlled re-feeding 6.18
  drugs, with 6.18
  family therapy 6.18
  psychological treatment 6.18

Employment
employees suffering from
  disability
    protection 12.6
psychiatric disorder and 12.1, 12.2
secondary disability 12.3, 12.4
work-related psychiatric injury 12.5

Functional mental disorder
environmental factors affecting 2.1

Head injuries
affect on patient 2.11
frontal lobe syndrome 2.11
post-concussional state 2.12
  personality change 2.12
  post-traumatic epilepsy 2.12
  rehabilitation 2.14

Head injuries—*continued*
  post-concussional state—*continued*
    risks associated with 2.13
    symptoms 2.12
    treatment 2.12
  psychiatric classification of 2.11

Learning disabilities
causes 8.2, 8.8
definition 8.1
genetic disorders 8.2
IQ test and 8.1
lack of capacity 8.5
management 8.3
  assessment of need 8.3
  community support 8.3
  provision of care 8.3
people with
  supportive therapy for 1.7
prognosis
  appropriate support 8.4
  improvement of functioning 8.4
risks associated with 8.8
varying levels of 8.1
vulnerability 8.5

Mania
clinical symptoms 4.3
  speech disorder 4.3, 4.9
risk of developing 4.9
risk of violence 4.9
treatment 4.6

Mental disorder
behaviour and 1.3, 1.8
  circumstances affecting 1.8
behavioural disorder 1.3
childbirth, following 9.2, 9.3, 9.4
  risks associated with 9.9
cultural influences 9.5, 9.9
delusion
  meaning 1.4
diagnosis 1.6
  value of 1.6
distinction between normal,
  abnormal and
  pathological 1.4
environmental factors, effect on 1.5
forensic psychiatry 10.7
functional
  meaning 2.1
genetic basis for 1.5
learning disabilities
  pathological state,
    classification as 1.4
maladaptive behaviour 1.8
meaning 1.1
organic
  meaning 2.1
origins 1.5
pathology, diagnosis 1.4
personality disorders 1.3

Mental disorder—*continued*
prisoners with
risk factors influencing
reoffending 10.7
psychiatric classification of 1.4
treatment 1.7
drugs, with 1.7
psychological treatment 1.7
supportive therapy 1.7
types of 1.3
violent behaviour
affective disorders and 10.5
alcohol, effect on 10.5
personality disorders and 10.5
prescription drugs 10.5
psychopathy 10.5
psychotic violence 10.5
risks associated with 10.9
systematic disorders and 10.5
unassociated with 10.6, 10.9
Mental illness
comparison to mental disorder 1.3
disability discrimination 12.6
symptoms affecting 1.3
Mentally disordered person
capacity
change in diagnosis 14.7
code of practice
Mental Capacity Act 2005
under 14.2
meaning 14.2
Mental Capacity Act 2005
under 14.2
witness, as 14.5
civil capacity
lack of
factors influences 14.3
meaning 14.3
medical treatment, consent
to 14.3
criminal proceedings
defence of suggestibility 14.6
testamentary capacity 14.4
Mood disorders
types of 4.1
Munchausen's syndrome
by proxy 9.8
risks associated with 9.8
symptoms
risks associated with 9.9

Neuroses
meaning 5.1
Neurotic disorder
acute stress disorder
symptoms 5.12
treatment 5.12
adjustment disorder
symptoms 5.12
treatment 5.12

Neurotic disorder—*continued*
anxiety
causes 5.7
environmental factors 5.7
genetic factors 5.7
chronic anxiety states
prognosis 5.9
effect on family life 5.10
generalied anxiety state 5.4
symptoms 5.4
meaning 5.3
panic attacks
phobic disorders 5.6
common types of 5.6
meaning 5.6
symptoms 5.5
prognosis 5.9
risks associated with 5.10
treatment 5.8
cognitive behavioural
therapy 5.8
drugs with 5.8
graded exposure 5.8
psychological treament 5.8
social care 5.8
classification 5.3
cultural influences 9.5
effects of 5.15
hysteria
conversion symptoms 5.13
dissociative symptoms 5.13
treatment 5.13
meaning 5.1
minor depressive illness 5.2
cognitive behavioural therapy 5.2
symptoms 5.2
obsessive-compulsive disorder 5.11
antidepressants for 5.11
behaviour therapy 5.11
symptoms 5.11
treatment 5.11
post-traumatic stress disorder 13.1
alcohol abuse and 5.12
clinical features 13.2
concurrent psychiatric
disorder 13.3
drug abuse and 5.12
exaggerated responses 13.4
factors causing 13.2
malingering, meaning 13.6, 13.7
meaning 5.12
personality, significance of 13.2,
13.7
pre-existing psychiatric
disorder 13.3
secondary disability, factors
influencing 13.5, 13.7
severity of event 13.2
symptoms 5.12
treatment 5.12
cognitive behavioural
therapy 5.12
counselling 5.12

Neurotic disorder—*continued*
  post-traumatic stress
      disorder—*continued*
      treatment—*continued*
        debriefing exercises   5.12
        eye movement
          desensitisation and
          reprocessing   5.12
        when occurring   5.12
    risk of developing   5.15
    somatoform disorders
      chronic fatigue syndrome   5.14
      cognitive behavioural
        therapy   5.14
      dysmorphic disorder   5.14
      hypochondriasis   5.14
      prognosis   5.14
      symptoms   5.14
      treatment   5.14
    stress reactions
      prognosis   5.12

Organic mental disorder
  acute disorder   2.1
  cerebral, origins of   2.1
  chronic disorder   2.1
  classification of   2.1
  meaning   2.1
  psychiatric consequences of head
    injuries   2.1

Paranoid disorders
  association with alcohol/drug
    abuse   3.9
  cause of   3.9
  paraphrenia   3.9
  risks associated with   3.10
  treatment with drugs   3.11
Parental alienation syndrome
  false allegations of abuse   11.5
  meaning   11.5
Parental disputes
  contact and   15.4
  residence and   15.4
Pathological gambling
  dependence   6.14
  risks associated with   6.14
  treatment   6.14
Personality disorders
  abnormal behaviour patterns   7.2
  anxious   7.3
  causes   7.5, 7.9
  classification of   7.3
  dependent   7.3
  development in childhood   7.5
  diagnosis   7.2
  emotionally unstable
    borderline   7.3
    impulsive   7.3
  environmental influences   7.5
  general features   7.2
  genetic influences   7.5

Personality disorders—*continued*
  meaning   7.1
  mental illness and   7.2
  Munchausen's syndrome
    risks associated with   9.8, 9.9
  obsessive-compulsive   7.3
  paranoid   7.3
  prognosis   7.7
  psychosocial treatment   7.6, 7.7
  relationships, effect on   7.5
  risks associated with   7.8, 7.9
  schizoid   7.3
  social environment   7.5
  treatment   7.6
  types of   1.3
Post-traumatic stress disorder
  alcohol abuse and   5.12
  clinical features   13.2
  concurrent psychiatric
    disorder   13.3
  drug abuse and   5.12
  exaggerated responses   13.4
  factors causing   13.2
  malingering, meaning   13.6, 13.7
  meaning   5.12
  personality, significance of   13.2,
       13.7
  pre-existing psychiatric
    disorder   13.3
  secondary disability, factors
    influencing   13.5, 13.7
  severity of event   13.2
  symptoms   5.12
  treatment   5.12
    cognitive behavioural
      therapy   5.12
    counselling   5.12
    debriefing exercises   5.12
    eye movement desensitisation
      and reprocessing   5.12
  when occurring   5.12
Psychiatric disorder
  behaviour and   1.2
  childbirth, following   9.2, 9.3, 9.4
    risks associated with   9.9
  cultural influences   9.5
    catatonic schizophrenia   9.5
  De Clerambault's syndrome   9.7
  delusional state
    cultural influences   9.5
  diagnosis   1.6
    value of   1.6
  employment, effect on   12.1, 12.2
  environmental factors, effect on   1.5
  erotomania   9.7
  functional
    meaning   2.1
  genetic basis for   1.5
  meaning   1.1
  morbid jealousy   9.6
    risks associated with   9.9
  Munchausen's syndrome
    symptoms   9.9

Psychiatric disorder—*continued*
organic
  meaning 2.1
origins 1.2
Othello syndrome 9.6
post-partum
  depressive illness 9.3
    clinical diagnosis 9.3
    risks associated with 9.3
    treatment 9.3
  meaning 9.2
  psychosis 9.4
    clinical diagnosis 9.4
    treatment 9.4
stalking 9.7
treatment 1.7
  drugs, with 1.7
  psychological treatment 1.7
  supportive therapy 1.7
types of 1.3
Psychopathy
classification of 7.4
diagnosis 7.4
meaning 7.4
substance misuse, association
  with 7.4
symptoms 7.4
Psychoses
bipolar affective disorder 4.4, 4.5,
    4.6, 4.7, 4.8
depressive illness 4.2, 4.9
mania 4.3, 4.9
types of 4.1
Psychoses disorder
morbid jealousy 9.6
risks associated with 9.9
Psychotic disorders
features 3.1
paranoid disorders 3.9, 3.10
schizophrenia 3.1, 3.2, 3.3, 3.4, 3.5,
    3.6, 3.7, 3.8, 3.11
types of 3.1

Schizophrenia
alcohol abuse 3.11
  effect on condition 3.7
casuses
  cognitive changes 3.3
catatonic
  cultural influences causing 9.5
clinical symptoms 3.3
  auditory hallucinations 3.3
  delusions 3.3

Schizophrenia—*continued*
clinical symptoms—*continued*
  depression 3.3
  diagnosis 3.3
  self-neglect 3.3
  speech disorder 3.3
demographic trends 3.4
drug abuse 3.11
  effect on condition 3.7
environmental influences 3.4, 3.5
genetic basis for 1.5
genetic risk 3.4, 3.11
meaning 3.2
prognosis 3.7
risks associated with 3.8
social support, effect of 3.7
treatment 3.6
  drugs, with 3.6, 3.11
  in-patient treatment 3.6
  rehabilitation 3.11
Sexual violence
absence of mental illness 10.8, 10.9
children, against
  emotional effect on child 11.7
  factors for prognosis 11.7
  mental disorder and 11.7
  risk assessment 11.7
domestic
  factors causing 11.6, 11.8
factors affecting 10.8
risk assessment of 10.8
substance abuse and 10.8
Substance abuse
meaning 6.1
Substance misuse
cultural influences 6.19
effect of 6.19
physical and behavioural changes
  related to 6.15
risks associated with 6.15
social influences 6.19
Suicidal behaviour
age groups 10.2
diagnostic groups 10.2
examination of mental state 10.2
intent 10.2
  definition by Law
    Commission 10.2
psychiatric patients by 10.2
risk factors 10.2, 10.9

Unipolar depressive order
risks associated with 4.5